Frege's Logic

Frege's Logic

Danielle Macbeth

Harvard University Press

Cambridge, Massachusetts, and London, England | 2005

Library of Congress Cataloging-in-Publication Data

Macbeth, Danielle
    Frege's Logic / Danielle Macbeth.
       p.   cm.
    Includes bibliographical references and index.
    ISBN 0–674–01707–2 (alk. paper)
     1. Frege, Gottlob, 1848–1925.   2. Logic, Symbolic and mathematical
  I. Title.
    B3245.F24M36   2005
    160′.92—dc22   2004060673

Contents

Preface

Although this is a book about Frege's logic, it is not a work of logic in any standard sense. No theorems are proved, and few technical results are discussed. My aim is rather to develop a novel reading of Frege's logical language *Begriffsschrift* and to defend that reading textually as a reading of Frege's writings. I want to show that Frege's logical language, though it can of course be read as a language of quantificational logic, can also be read very differently, indeed, as a radically different *kind* of logical language from that we inherit from Peano, Russell, and Wittgenstein. The task is threefold: to provide a logical justification for all aspects of Frege's peculiar notation, to motivate and explain the developments in Frege's views over the course of his intellectual life, and to explicate his most developed, critically reflective conception of his *Begriffsschrift,* his formula language of pure thought.

Frege's logical language, as it is to be read here, is something essentially new; it takes substantial intellectual work to understand it, even on its own terms. Indeed, Frege himself, on our account, came fully to understand the exact nature of his logic only many years after its first presentation in 1879. As a result of this difficulty, no adequate defense of the reading as the definitive reading of Frege's texts can be provided here; only the ground is laid for a thoroughgoing critique of other readings and for a systematic exploration of the fundamental philosophical significance of the logic here outlined. Certainly there are in the early writings (and, in regard to some aspects of Frege's views, even in the writings of the early 1890s) texts that also support this or that quantificational reading. For example, in the 1879 *Begriffsschrift* Frege seems clearly to think that an adequate specification of everything necessary for a correct inference can be given in terms of truth conditions; his early conception of meaning seems to be essentially that of the quantificational logician. That conception is superseded in the mature logic in response to fundamental problems with the early view. So it is with various other aspects of Frege's views. Already in 1879 Frege had developed the logical notation he needed for his logicist program. Only much later did he come to a fully adequate understanding of the way that notation functions as a notation of a properly logical language. It is Frege's late, hard-won understanding of his *Begriffsschrift* logic that is the object and goal of this study.

At the heart of Frege's conception of logic is his notion of logical generality. Chapter 1 sets out both the general strategy pursued in understanding it and some of the textual motivation Frege provides for that strategy. In Chapter 2 the nature of Frege's logical language as we read it, the *kind* of language it is, is illustrated by analogy with a novel way of reading the formula language of arithmetic, one that is achieved by way of a thoroughgoing transformation of the way that notation is normally read; and an account is developed of what Frege calls "genuine hypotheticals," that is, *Begriffsschrift* generalized conditional judgments expressed using Latin italic letters. Chapter 3 explores the evolution in Frege's thinking between 1879 and 1906 regarding the nature of functions, the expressive role of the concavity and German letters, and the contents of the laws of logic. These developments in turn prepare the way for the discussion in Chapter 4 of Frege's *Sinn/Bedeutung* distinction. An answer to the vexed question of how to understand Frege's notion of *Sinn* is sketched, and again the formula language of arithmetic provides the model. The last chapter turns to consideration of Basic Law V, why on our account Frege thought his logicist program required it, why exactly it fails, and why logic, at least Frege's logic as it is understood here, can get along perfectly well without it.

The conception of a properly logical language that emerges is, interestingly enough, profoundly Kantian in at least two fundamental respects. First, much as Kant in his Transcendental Logic takes the minimum unit of cognitive awareness to be items situated within the whole of nature as it is unified under the categories of relation (substance, causality, and community), so Frege, in his fully developed logic as it is understood here, takes the minimum unit of cognitive significance to be the judgment as situated within the whole of a language. Though on his early view the content of a sentence is taken to be given by truth conditions that are in principle intelligible for a sentence taken in isolation, Frege's best wisdom, as encapsulated in his distinction between the *Sinn* and the *Bedeutung* of an expression, is that the thoughts expressed by sentences are constitutively related one to another in the language taken as a whole. Fregean thoughts, on our view, are inferentially articulated structures through which truth-values, the *Bedeutungen* of sentences, are designated, where these structures are fixed in turn by the rules of the language that govern judgment and inference in that language. Because Frege understands judgments to be advances from thoughts to truth-values and thinks that inferences can be made only on the basis of thoughts that are acknowledged to be true, it follows that neither inference nor judgment can be understood independently of the other in Frege's logic. As the point might be put, Frege's developed conception of meaning is neither strictly representationalist (as it is in most standard semantic theories) nor merely inferentialist (as it is in Brandom's alternative account); instead, it incorporates in a quite unprecedented way elements of both. Here we hear an echo of a second Kantian theme. Cognition, Kant thinks, constitutively involves both intuition through which an object is given and a concept through which it is thought. Similarly, on Frege's account, judgment and inference—that is, the striving for truth—constitutively involve both an intentional word-world relation of designation to a *Bedeutung* and an inferentially articulated sense that contains a mode of presentation of that *Bedeutung*. Of course, the analogy is not exact; there are many deep and important differences between Frege and Kant, and thinking through those differences would certainly illuminate the logic here understood as Frege's. That, however, is a study that can be undertaken only after the logic itself is clarified. Our first task, the task of this study, is to learn to read *Begriffsschrift*, and by extension Frege's writings about that logical language, in a new way.

I have incurred many debts over the years this work has been in progress. Tom Ricketts and Sanford Shieh wrote very helpful comments to an invited lecture on *Begriffsschrift* that I gave at a meeting of the American Philosophical Association in December 1997. I hope that here they will find responses to their objections that are more satisfactory than those I was able to formulate at the time. Tom, Michael Kremer, Mark Lance, John MacFarlane, and Joan Weiner generously commented on parts of early drafts; Wolfgang Kienzler provided me with helpful comments on various aspects of a more recent draft; and two anonymous readers wrote extensive and very helpful criticisms of the penultimate draft. My most profound intellectual debt is to my teachers John McDowell and Robert Brandom; almost every aspect of the account developed here bears the mark of their influence. I also owe a special debt of gratitude to Bob for his encouragement and support. The National Endowment for the Humanities generously provided me a fellowship (No. FB-33981–97) in support of the project through the winter term and summer of 1997, and Haverford College generously extended that leave, with support, through the fall of 1997. I also gratefully acknowledge the encouragement of my colleagues in the Philosophy Department at Haverford College and the excellent research assistance of James Gulick. My thanks, finally, go to John Hawthorn and to Alexander Hawthorn. Without their patience and good humor, this intellectual adventure could not have been so deeply satisfying.

Frege's Logic

Introduction

The first prerequisite for learning anything is utterly lacking—I mean, the knowledge that we do not know.
—*GRUNDLAGEN*, 1884

Frege's logic is universally regarded as a notational variant of standard quantificational logic. The question whether it actually is such a logic is never raised, the grounds for doubt never explored. Why, for instance, is *Begriffsschrift* written in two dimensions with all logical signs, save for identity, presented in an array on the left? Why does Frege use both Latin italic and German letters in the expression of generality? Why does he demand that the premises of an inference be acknowledged to be true? Why does he not recognize the existential quantifier? Most puzzling of all, why does he think that the notion of *Sinn* (as it is understood after 1890) is a properly logical notion, and that a sentence can express a sense even in the case in which it fails to have a truth-value?[1] None of these familiar features of Frege's system of logic would come naturally, even as mistakes, in a quantificational logic. They are not logically motivated and, in many cases, are quite inexplicable. Yet Frege himself seems never to have had even the slightest misgivings about them. Could it be that Frege's logic is something hitherto unknown to us? My aim is to suggest that it is.

In *Begriffsschrift*, instead of writing a multiply embedded conditional such as, say, '~P ⊃ (Q ⊃ R)' in a linear array, one writes it thus:

thereby achieving, according to Frege, "a clear articulation of the sentence by writing the individual clauses—e.g. consequent and antecedents—one beneath the other, and to the left of these, by means of combination of strokes, I exhibit the logical relation which binds the whole together" (*CP* 236). But even granting that Frege's two-dimensional notation is especially perspicuous in just this way, it is in another way much less perspicuous than a linear notation of quantificational logic. In any standard notation the truth conditions of a sentence are manifest; a good notation of that logic is, as Quine once put it, "designed with no other thought than to facilitate the tracing of truth conditions."[2] *Begriffsschrift* seems not to have been so designed. For although we can read a *Begriffsschrift* sentence such as

as saying that if not-R then if Q then P, that is, as saying the same as '~R ⊃ (Q ⊃ P)', we can also read it differently, for instance, as saying that if not-R and Q, then P (that is, as saying the same as '(~R & Q) ⊃ P'). Various different, equally acceptable paths through a sentence written in Frege's two-dimensional notation are possible, and only relative to this or that path can truth conditions be formulated.[3] Truth conditions are easily formulated for any *Begriffsschrift* sentence, but the sentence does not itself trace truth conditions; one must read it in some one way, choose some one path among the many equally acceptable paths, in order to recover truth conditions from it. Whereas the guiding idea of the linear notation of quantificational logic is that meaning is to be understood directly in terms of truth (and, perhaps, satisfaction), the guiding idea of Frege's two-dimensional notation seems almost to be that the content of a sentence must, for the purposes of judgment and inference, be variously analyzable, that only relative to an analysis can truth conditions be formulated for a sentence.[4]

We know that Frege faced considerable difficulties in finding publishers for his writings, difficulties that were compounded by the practical problems his two-dimensional script posed for the printer. As he was also made to see, his strange notation furthermore presented a serious obstacle for his readers.[5] Yet he unequivocally rejected Peano's linear notation as logically defective for his purposes. As he concludes the 1896 essay "On Mr. Peano's Conceptual Notation and My Own," "the Peano notation is unquestionably more convenient for the typesetter, and in many cases takes up less room than mine, but . . . these advantages seem to me, due to the inferior perspicuity and logical defectiveness [of that notation], to have been paid for too dearly—at any rate for the purposes I want to pursue" (*CP* 248). Was Frege unaccountably blind to the virtues of Peano's linear notation, or perhaps uncharacteristically stubborn in his adherence to his own notation? Or is it rather the case, as he himself claims, that for his purposes only a two-dimensional notation can combine "uninterrupted rigor of demonstration and maximal logical precision, together with perspicuity and brevity" (*CP* 237)? If so, his purposes are not those of the quantificational logician.

Two other features of Frege's logical notation provide further grounds for calling the standard reading into doubt. First, it includes a sign, the judgment stroke, to distinguish those judgeable contents that are acknowledged to be true from those that are not. Such a sign is needed in logic, Frege argues, because inferences can be drawn only from premises acknowledged to be true.[6] "In presenting an inference, one must utter the premises with assertoric force, for the truth of the premises is essential to the correctness of the inference. If in representing an inference in my conceptual notation one were to leave out the judgment strokes before the premised propositions, something essential would be missing . . . What is essential to an inference must be counted as part of logic" (*PMC* 79). A judgment stroke is not, however, essential to an inference in a standard quantificational logic. In our logics the truth of the premises is irrelevant to the correctness of an inference; what matters is only whether the conclusion is true on the assumption that the premises are true. Yet Frege persisted in his "error" of defending the inclusion of a judgment stroke in his logic even after Wittgenstein had pointed out that the judgment stroke has no place in logic, at least in logic as Wittgenstein understands it.[7] Again we must ask, was Frege unaccountably blind to the point, or is his conception of logic different from the conception we inherit from Russell and Wittgenstein?

Frege's use of two different sorts of letters in the expression of generality, German letters with the concavity and Latin italic letters without it, raises the same question.[8] Again there seems to be no logical justification for Frege's conventions, and again Frege persists in his "error" even after it has been pointed out to him. As he tells Jourdain, he could have used Latin italic letters in all cases, as Russell and Peano do, but to do so, he says, would be "at the cost of perspicuity of formulae" (*PMC* 189 n. 52). In a quantificational logic just the opposite would seem to be true: using different sorts of letters for free and bound variables would mask the fact that it is just those free variables that are bound if a quantifier is attached. Was Frege simply confused? Or is it rather the case that the distinction he aims to mark by using one sort of letter without the concavity and another with it is a different distinction from that between a free and a bound variable?

The fact that Frege uses different sorts of letters with and without the concavity suggests that his concavity with German letter should not be read as a variable-binding universal quantifier. That it should not be so read is further indicated by the fact that Frege nowhere gives even the slightest indication that his "universal quantifier" (the concavity with German letter) and his "existential quantifier" (the concavity flanked by negation strokes) are interdefinable. There is no simple sign in Frege's logic for the existential quantifier, and it seems never even to occur to him that he could treat the existential quantifier as the primitive sign for generality and then define the universal quantifier in terms of it. This is generally treated as a minor omission—for instance, by Dummett and by Kneale and Kneale[9]—but if it is, it is an odd one. Frege more than once remarks that the conditional stroke and the conjunction stroke are interdefinable (*BGS* §7; *PW* 200), and in the late essay "Compound Thoughts" he spells out in tedious detail six possible binary sentence connectives, any one of which could be treated as primitive in logic (see *CP* 390–406). Frege clearly seems to think that knowing which choices are governed by a fact of logic and which choices are not so governed is itself a logical matter. Had he thought that there were two logically admissible quantifiers usable for the expression of generality, and that the choice of one as primitive was not governed by any fact of logic, he would have said so. Yet he did not.

Frege's second great logical innovation—as he thought of it—after the development of his notation and the system of logic presented in *Begriffsschrift* was the introduction in the early 1890s of the distinction between the *Sinn* and the *Bedeutung* of an expression.[10] This distinction, too, is deeply problematic on the assumption that Frege's logic is a quantificational logic. First, it seems not to be a logical distinction at all. Given the quantificational conception of meaning directly in terms of truth, Frege's notion of *Sinn* (however exactly it is to be understood—another problem) cannot be a logical notion; so, it is often argued, Frege's introduction of the distinction between sense and meaning in the early 1890s is really the discovery of a theory of sense conceived as a theory of the cognitive aspect of language use aimed at supplementing the properly logical, semantic theory presented already in *Begriffsschrift*. As Evans puts it,

Frege's theory of Meaning [*Bedeutung*] for the fragment of language he was concerned with after 1890 corresponds exactly to the theory that was implicit in the earlier works, the *Begriffsschrift* and the *Grundlagen*. The analysis of singular sentences, and the analysis of quantified sentences based upon the analysis of singular sentences, did not alter with the discovery of sense; rather, Frege saw more clearly what kind of analysis he had provided, and saw the need for something more. In later works, Frege was grafting on to this enduring theory his new conception of sense.[11]

On this reading, which originates with Dummett, "it was not . . . qua logician, but qua philosopher, that Frege pushed his inquiries further . . . He wanted to give a general account of the workings of language."[12] But this does not seem to be Frege's view. Frege describes the discovery of his distinction between sense and meaning as a properly logical advance, as "a thoroughgoing development of my logical views" (GG 6). According to Frege, his mature understanding of *Sinn* and *Bedeutung* is essential to an adequate understanding of how his *Begriffsschrift* notation functions.

That Frege should take the introduction of the *Sinn/Bedeutung* distinction to be a logical advance is puzzling enough on the quantificational reading. That he should conclude in light of that distinction that a sentence can express a thought although it designates no truth-value is so utterly incomprehensible that it can seem more reasonable to deny—despite the textual evidence—that Frege ever thought such a thing.[13] The problem, quite simply, is that because on the quantificational conception of sentential meaning the content of a sentence is given by what is the case if it is true, by its truth conditions, the idea that a sentence might express a thought yet fail to have a truth-value is completely, and obviously, incoherent. What a sentence of quantificational logic expresses is given by its truth conditions; if they are satisfied then the sentence is true, and if they are not satisfied then the sentence is false. It is, then, manifestly contradictory to claim, as Frege does, that a sentence might be fully contentful, express a thought, yet fail to have either the truth-value True or the truth-value False. On the quantificational reading, that idea really is, as Evans puts it, "the great fault-line in Frege's mature philosophy of language": "What can it mean on Frege's, or on anyone's, principles, for there to be a perfectly determinate thought which simply has no truth-value?"[14] "Where thoughts, or beliefs, are concerned, surely failing to have the value True *just is* having the value False."[15] One might, however, equally well reason contrapositively: because, as Frege claims after 1890, a sentence (on his understanding of it) can express a thought despite failing to have a truth-value, his conception of meaning is not that of the quantificational logician.

Certainly Frege's notation can be read as a notation of quantificational logic, and any one of his "mistakes" taken alone might be excusable, albeit oddly inexplicable. But Frege makes too many mistakes on the quantificational reading, mistakes that seem to be completely arbitrary and often manifest. Is it really credible that Frege would have made such mistakes, and so many of them? If we think this, perhaps it is only because we can see no alternative.

But, it will be objected, Russell did, after all, learn quantificational logic from Frege. Certainly that is what one is told. The historical evidence suggests otherwise.

In July 1900 Russell attended the first World Congress of Philosophy in Paris and was there introduced to Peano, who told him of his new mathematical logic. That meeting, Russell says in his autobiography, "was a turning point in my intellectual life."[16] Once back in England Russell quickly mastered Peano's system of logic, and by the end of September he had extended it to a complete logic of relations. Russell was euphoric.

> My sensations resembled those one has after climbing a mountain in a mist, when, on reaching the summit, the mist suddenly clears, and the country becomes visible for forty miles in every direction. For years I had been endeavoring to analyze the fundamental notions of mathematics, such as order and cardinal number. Suddenly, in the space of a few weeks, I discovered what appeared to be definitive answers to the problems which had baffled me for years. And in the course of discovering these answers, I was introducing a new mathematical technique, by which regions formerly abandoned to the vaguenesses of philosophers were conquered for the precision of exact formulae. Intellectually, the month of September 1900 was the highest point of my life.[17]

Russell may have had a copy of *Grundgesetze* in the fall of 1900, for, as he writes to Jourdain in 1910, he recalls having "first got *Grundgesetze* late in 1900."[18] But, as he goes on, "I could not understand Frege's use of Greek, German, and Latin letters, and I put him away for nearly two years, by which time I had discovered for myself most of what he had to say, and was therefore able to understand him."

Russell did not learn quantificational logic from Frege. But he did learn a logic of relations from Peirce; he knew Peirce's work while he was developing the polyadic predicate calculus, and in particular, he knew that Peirce had developed a complete logic of relations already in 1883 based on Boole's logical algebra.[19] But Peirce's logic of relations is, as Russell notes, "difficult and complicated to so great a degree that it is possible to doubt its utility."[20] What Russell took to be the fundamental insight of Peano's logic, the insight that distinguished it as a properly modern logic, lay in its drawing a logical distinction between singular terms such as 'Socrates' and general terms such as 'man', and thereby treating sentences containing them (for example, 'Socrates is mortal' and 'all men are mortal') as different in logical form.[21] It was just this, Russell thought, that was "the first serious advance in real logic since the time of the Greeks."[22] His own extension of the insight to the logic of relations was, as he describes it, a merely technical development.[23] It was Peano's discovery, not Frege's, that enabled Russell "to simplify the logic of relations [as developed by Peirce] enormously by making use of Peano's notation," and thereby to discover "what appeared to be definitive answers to the problems which had baffled [Russell] for years."[24]

By the summer of 1901 the intellectual honeymoon was over. Russell had discovered the contradiction in his logic and, try as he might, he could not discover what had gone wrong, the source of the error. It was at that point that Russell seems to have begun to study Frege's writings, thinking, perhaps, that Frege's system of logic in *Grundgesetze* might hold the key to a solution to the paradox. Peano had said in his 1895 review of *Grundgesetze* that the work was marred by an unnecessary subtlety; perhaps its subtlety was just what was needed to resolve the contradiction.[25] What Russell discovered, of course, was, first, that Frege's notation could—though with difficulty[26]—be read as a notation of Russell's own logic, and also that the contradiction was derivable in Frege's system as well. We have been reading Frege's notation as a notation of quantificational logic ever since.

The full polyadic predicate calculus was Russell's contribution, an extension of Peano's logic following Peirce's work on the logic of relations. Only later, after he had developed quantificational logic, did Russell read that logic back into Frege's astonishingly ill conceived notation. Russell simply assumed that Frege had independently developed essentially the logic that Russell had developed, and in the heady early days of the discovery of quantificational logic that assumption would have been quite natural. We have no such excuse. Is the logic that Frege first developed in 1879 and, by his own account, brought to maturity with the introduction of the distinction of *Sinn* and *Bedeutung* in the early 1890s a quantificational logic? The question has not been asked. Yet it must be asked. For the simple fact of the matter is, we do not know.

1

The Starting Point

> Arithmetic . . . was the starting point of the train of thought which led me to my "conceptual notation."
>
> —*BEGRIFFSSCHRIFT*, 1879

Frege developed his *Begriffsschrift,* or concept-script, as a special-purpose instrument to further his logicist program of demonstrating that the truths of arithmetic are derivable by appeal only to the laws of logic and definitions. Arithmetic was the starting point. As is announced in the subtitle of *Begriffsschrift*—a formula language of pure thought modeled upon the formula language of arithmetic—arithmetic was also the model for *Begriffsschrift.* It provided both a general model of how a conceptual notation ought to function and a model for the use of letters in the expression of laws.[1] Frege's mature conception of a concept is essentially that of an arithmetical function: "a concept is a function whose value is always a truth-value" (*CP* 146), and his understanding of the way concepts are derived from judgments is modeled on the way different concepts can be derived from identities such as '$2^4 = 16$' in the formula language of arithmetic (see *PW* 16–17). Even Frege's mature understanding of his logical language in terms of the notions of *Sinn* and *Bedeutung* is essentially an extension of his discovery, in *Grundlagen,* of the meaning of an arithmetical identity such as '$1 + 1 + 1 = 3$'.[2] The formula language of arithmetic informs *Begriffsschrift,* Frege's formula language of pure thought, at every level and at every stage in its development.[3] To understand how it does—and thereby how we might understand Frege's use of letters, his conception of a concept, his notion of analysis, and his *Sinn/Bedeutung* distinction—we need to understand his starting point, the science of arithmetic as it posed for him the problem that *Begriffsschrift* was to solve. That starting point will provide in turn the starting point for the reading to be pursued here.

1.1 The Fundamental Idea of Frege's Conceptual Notation

In an essay written in 1896 that compares his own notation to Peano's, Frege says that "the fundamental idea of my conceptual notation" is to

8

"limit to the bare minimum the number of modes of inference, and set these up as rules of this new language" (*CP* 236). The point is first made in "Boole's Logical Calculus and the Concept-script," written shortly after *Begriffsschrift* (that is, in 1880 or 1881): "I sought as far as possible to translate into formulae everything that could also be expressed verbally as a rule of inference, so as not to make use of the same thing in different forms. Because modes of inference must be expressed verbally, I only used a single one by giving as formulae what could otherwise have also been introduced as modes of inference" (*PW* 37). In order to keep to the bare minimum the modes of inference employed, all rules of inference—save for *modus ponens,* which is required if anything at all is to be inferred[4]—are to be expressed in *Begriffsschrift* as formulae. This is the fundamental idea of Frege's notation. It is motivated, we will see, by the project of logicism as Frege conceives it.

The primary value of mathematical knowledge, Frege thinks, lies not in what is known but in how it is known, "not so much its subject-matter as the degree to which it is intellectually perspicuous and affords insight into its logical relations" (*PW* 157). That is why "it is in the nature of mathematics to prefer proof, where proof is possible" (*GL* §2), and in the nature of mathematics to achieve its full and adequate expression only in what Frege calls a "system," that is, a complete and adequate axiomatization. In the Introduction to *Grundgesetze*—the subtitle of which is "Exposition of the System"—Frege outlines what such a system, that is, a complete and adequate axiomatization, involves:

> It cannot be demanded that everything should be proved, because that is impossible; but we can require that all propositions used without proof be expressly declared as such, so that we can see distinctly what the whole structure rests upon. After that we must try to diminish the number of those primitive laws as far as possible, by proving everything that can be proved. Furthermore, I demand—and in this I go beyond Euclid—that all methods of inference employed be specified in advance; otherwise we cannot be certain of satisfying the first requirement. (*GG* 2)

To have such a system for arithmetic, one that consists of the fewest possible axioms, definitions of all nonprimitive terms, and an exhaustive list of rules of permissible inference, would be to have, "though in embryonic form" (*BGS* §13), "as in a kernel" (*PW* 205), the whole content of that science. Because "the essence of explanation lies precisely in the fact that a wide, possibly unsurveyable, manifold is governed by one or a few sentences" (*PW* 36), such an axiomatization is the goal of arithmetic, as of any science. "Our only concern is to generate the whole of mathematics from this kernel" (*PW* 205).

But not every science can be founded on logic alone. The empirical sciences, for instance, cannot be so grounded. Nor can geometry, for, as Frege argues, the truths of geometry do not govern thinking concerning all that is but only "all that is spatially intuitable, whether actual or product of our fancy" (*GL* §14). Geometry, like the natural sciences, has its own special axioms, axioms that can be negated without contradiction. It follows that geometry cannot be grounded in logic alone. The truths of arithmetic, by contrast, "govern . . . the widest domain of all; for to [arithmetic] belongs not only the actual, not only the intuitable, but everything thinkable": "try denying any one of them [the fundamental propositions of the science of number], and complete confusion ensues. Even to think at all seems no longer possible" (*GL* §14). The "extensive applicability of mathematical doctrines" (*CP* 112) is prima facie grounds for thinking that arithmetic is merely a more highly developed logic. The task of Frege's logicism is to prove that it is by showing, first, "that there is no such thing as a peculiarly arithmetical mode of inference that cannot be reduced to the general inference-modes of logic" (*CP* 113), and second, that the fundamental concepts of arithmetic, its "building blocks," are "reducible to logic by means of definitions" (*CP* 114).[5]

The aim of Frege's logicism is to develop a system for arithmetic, a complete and adequate axiomatization of the whole content of that science revealing its ultimate grounding in pure logic. Knowing that is not sufficient, however. We need also to understand the precise nature of the defects this system is to overcome. In particular, we need to see that whereas Russell understands logicism as the project of rendering proofs deductively gap-free by including as axioms all the truths on which those proofs depend, for Frege the defect of existing proofs seems to be not deductive but instead expressive.

The goal for Russell and for Frege is the same: rigorous, explicitly gap-free proofs. And both Frege and Russell take Euclid's proofs in *The Elements* to provide a paradigm of the sort of defects they aim in their respective logics to overcome. It is clear that for Russell, the problem is that Euclid's proofs are not strictly deductive, not logically valid, because they require the use of postulates conceived as rules of construction that cannot be formulated as axioms without the resources of the full polyadic predicate calculus.[6] Lacking those resources, Euclid could not include among his axioms, for instance, that given any two points there is a line connecting them or that between any two points there is a third. In Euclid's system, the line that connects two given points, or the point that lies between two other given points, must be constructed according to the rules laid out in the postulates. This treatment of postulates as practical rather than theoretical propositions is explicit already in Kant; postulates, Kant thinks, "contain nothing save the synthesis through which we first give ourselves an object and generate its concept—for instance, with a given line, to describe a circle on a plane from a given point."[7] "The whole point" of Kant's appeal to pure intuition in accounting for our knowledge of the truths of arithmetic and geometry, on this view, "is to enable us *to avoid* rules of existential instantiation by actually constructing the desired instances: we do not derive our 'new individuals' from existential premises but construct them from previously given individuals via Skolem functions."[8] If that is right, then Kant's conception of arithmetic as synthetic a priori rather than analytic (that is, grounded in logic alone) is an artifact of his limited logical resources. Russell makes the point in a well-known passage in *The Principles of Mathematics* (§4):

> There was, until very lately, a special difficulty in the principles of mathematics. It seemed plain that mathematics consists of deductions, and yet the orthodox accounts of deduction were largely or wholly inapplicable to existing mathematics . . . In this fact lay the strength of the Kantian view, which asserted that mathematical reasoning is not strictly formal, but always uses intuitions, i.e. the *a priori* knowledge of space and time. Thanks to the progress of Symbolic Logic, especially as treated by Professor Peano, this part of the Kantian philosophy is now capable of final and irrevocable refutation.

Russell takes Euclid's proofs to be deductively invalid on the grounds that Euclid's postulates are rules of construction or practical propositions in Kant's sense. Frege takes a very different view. First, postulates have for him the same logical status as axioms: "a postulate is a truth as is an axiom, its only peculiarity being that it asserts the existence of something with certain properties" (*PW* 207). For, Frege argues, "the truth of a theorem cannot really depend on something we do, when it holds quite independently of us. So the content of our postulate is essentially this, that given any two points there is a straight line connecting them . . . There is no real need to distinguish axioms and postulates. A postulate can be regarded as a special case of an axiom" (*PW* 207). Whereas Kant had argued that because the truth of the theorems of geometry does depend on something we do, namely, our constructions of points and lines in pure intuition, these truths cannot hold "quite independently of us," Frege argues contrapositively that such truths do hold quite independently of us and so cannot depend on something we do. Euclid's postulates, like his axioms, are objectively valid laws, Frege thinks, albeit laws of a special science.

Frege's criticism of Euclid's proofs is not that they are not, and without the resources of the full polyadic predicate calculus cannot be, deductively valid on the grounds that those proofs employ postulates conceived as rules of construction. Frege does not think of postulates as rules of construction; according to him, Euclid's postulates have the status of axioms. Frege's complaint is rather that Euclid, conscientious and rigorous though he is, "often makes tacit use of presuppositions which he specifies neither in his axioms and postulates nor in the premises of the particular theorem [being proved]" (*CN* 85). He does not meet the systematic demand that all modes of inference employed in a proof be specified in advance. For example,

> in the proof of the nineteenth theorem of the first book of *The Elements* (in every triangle, the largest angle lies opposite the largest side), he tacitly uses the statements:
>
> (1) If a line segment is not larger than a second one, the former is equal to or smaller than the latter.
>
> (2) If an angle is the same size as a second one, the former is not larger than the latter.
>
> (3) If an angle is smaller than a second one, the former is not larger than the latter. (*CN* 85)

These are not laws of logic; they are not laws that govern formally valid inferences. They are, rather, materially valid rules that govern the correct use of the (first-level) relations *larger than, equal to,* and *smaller than* as they apply to angles and line segments. Nevertheless, Frege suggests, they are valid rules of inference; "they are used just like those laws [of thought] themselves" (*CN* 85). They are used, that is, to legitimate inferences. But if that is right, then Euclid's proofs are not enthymematic, deductively gappy, as Russell thought; they are instead expressively gappy. Euclid should have explicitly stated in advance (if only in natural language, as Frege does in the passage just quoted) all the inference rules, whether formal or material, that he employs in his proofs. Because he does not, his system does not meet the demand "that all propositions used without proof [which include 'all methods of inference employed'] be expressly declared as such, so that we can see distinctly what the whole structure rests upon" (*GG* 2). Euclid's failing, as Frege understands it, does not lie in the poverty of his logical resources but instead in his not fully realizing the ideal of a system.

In "Logic in Mathematics," Frege's lecture notes for 1914, the same point is made again: "Euclid had an inkling of this idea of a *system;* but he failed to realize it"; and, as Frege immediately goes on, "it almost seems as if at the present time we were further from this goal [of a system] than ever . . . the idea of a system seems almost to have been lost" (*PW* 205). Here again, the problem is not, Frege thinks, that the proofs that are standardly given by mathematicians are invalid, deductively gappy, but that the rules of inference employed in those proofs are not explicitly stated in advance. Because they are not, standard mathematical proofs employ modes of inference whose source, whether in logic alone or in intuition, is unclear. The point is made again in *Grundlagen:*

> The mathematician rests content if every transition to a fresh judgment is self-evidently correct, without enquiring into the nature of this self-evidence, whether it is logical or intuitive . . . Often . . . the correctness of such a transition is immediately self-evident to us, without our ever becoming conscious of the subordinate steps condensed within it; whereupon, since it does not obviously conform to any of the recognized types of logical inference, we are prepared to accept its self-evidence as forthwith intuitive, and the conclusion itself as a synthetic truth—and this even when obviously it holds good of much more than merely what can be intuited.
>
> On these lines what is synthetic and based on intuition cannot be sharply separated from what is analytic. (*GL* §90)

Frege's demand that "every jump must be barred from our deductions" (*GL* §91) is not set by the thought that existing proofs are invalid. It is set by the fact that the rules of inference that govern proofs are not explicitly stated in advance and so are not self-evidently logical, that is, formally valid rules of inference. The task of logicism, as Frege conceives it, is to "not let through anything that was not explicitly presupposed" (*PMC* 100), "to exclude with certainty any tacit presupposition in the foundations of mathematics" (*PMC* 73), "to exclude with certainty anything derived from other sources of knowledge (intuition, sensible experience)"

(*PMC* 57). What is needed, according to Frege, is "a chain of deductions with no link missing, such that no step in it is taken which does not conform to some one of a small number of principles of inference recognized as purely logical" (*GL* §90). Given the universal applicability of the truths of arithmetic, it is reasonable to conjecture that "there is no such thing as a peculiarly arithmetical mode of inference that cannot be reduced to the general inference modes of logic"; the task of Frege's logicism is to "[bring] this nature to light wherever it cannot be recognized immediately, which is quite frequently the case in the writings of mathematicians" (*CP* 113). The "chief purpose" of Frege's *Begriffsschrift* is in this way to "expose each presupposition which tends to creep in unnoticed, so that its source can be investigated" (*BGS* 104).

Because proofs in Euclid's geometry and standard mathematical practice employ rules of inference that are not stated in advance, those proofs, although (usually) valid, each step licensed by a valid rule of inference, are not perspicuously gap-free. They do not satisfy the demands of a system. Because they do not, it cannot be determined whether the rules of inference that govern the reasoning involved are one and all formal, that is, strictly logical laws, or whether some are instead material rules of inference such as the rule that if an angle is the same size as a second one then the former is not larger than the latter. If logicism is true, there are no distinctively arithmetical modes of reasoning. The first task of logicism, then, is to show that the modes of inference commonly employed in arithmetic, mathematical induction, for instance, are reducible to strictly logical modes: "all modes of inference that appear to be peculiar to arithmetic [are to be based] on the general laws of logic" (*CP* 114). The laws that govern those modes of inference are to be translated into formulae and derived from strictly logical laws expressed as formulae. *Begriffsschrift* Parts II and III begin the project. The theorems that are proven are translations of rules of inference into formulae. They express laws that license inferences. That is why, once they have been proven, "the restriction to a single rule of inference . . . [can] be dropped . . . by converting what was expressed as a judgment in a formula into a rule of inference" (*PW* 29). Theorem 53 of *Begriffsschrift*,

for instance, can be converted into the rule that "in any judgment you may replace one symbol by another, if you add as a condition the equation between the two" (*PW* 29). That theorem, in other words, expresses as a formula the rule that licenses inferences such as this:

$$\vdash 5 + 4 > 7$$

$$\vdash \begin{array}{l} \rule{0pt}{0pt} 9 > 7 \\ 5 + 4 = 9 \end{array}$$

and the same is true of the other theorems Frege proves in Parts II and III of *Begriffsschrift*. The generalities proven in Parts II and III of *Begriffsschrift* express inference licenses translated into formulae.

In "Logic in Mathematics" the point is made again. Modes of inference are "subject to laws," and the task of logicism (at least as Frege understands logicism) is to show that the laws that govern inferences in mathematics are one and all derived laws of logic.

> *Are there perhaps modes of inference peculiar to mathematics which, for that very reason, do not belong to logic?* Here one may point to the inference by mathematical induction from n to $n + 1$. Well, even a mode of inference peculiar to arithmetic must be subject to a law and this law, if it is not logical in nature, will belong to mathematics, and can be ranked with the theorems or axioms of this science. For instance, mathematical induction rests on the law that can be expressed as follows:
>
> If the number 1 has the property Φ and if it holds generally for every positive whole number n that if it has the property Φ then $n + 1$ has the property Φ, then every positive whole number has the property Φ . . .
>
> So likewise in other cases one can reduce a mode of inference that is peculiar to mathematics to a general law, if not to a law of logic, then one of mathematics. And from this law one can then draw consequences in accordance with general logical laws. (*PW* 203–204)

The task of logicism, as Frege understands it, is to discover the laws that govern the (valid) inferences in arithmetic so that those laws can be either shown to be derived laws of logic or set up as axioms and derived theorems of the (in that case, special) science of arithmetic.

In order to demonstrate that arithmetic is derived logic, Frege needs to show that all modes of inference employed in arithmetical proofs are strictly logical and that all basic concepts of arithmetic are definable by appeal only to logical notions. At first, he says, he tried to formulate his definitions and proofs in natural language. As he soon discovered, however, "despite all the unwieldiness of the expressions, the more complex the relations became, the less precision—which my purpose required—could be obtained" (*BGS* 104). It was "the logical imperfections of our languages" (*CP* 235) that led him to devise his *Begriffsschrift* or concept-script, the formula language of pure thought. What Frege does not say in the earliest (1879) discussion of *Begriffsschrift* is what exactly these logical imperfections are or how his notation is to overcome them. Only after Frege had been made to realize that the aim of his concept-script, and thus the script itself, had been radically misunderstood did he characterize the defects of natural language that his *Begriffsschrift* was to overcome.

To one interested in perspicuously gap-free chains of reasoning, natural language has a variety of defects. It is, for instance, often ambiguous, using a single word to signify two different things and even, in some cases, using a single word for what are logically different kinds of things. In natural language "the same word may designate a concept and a single object which falls under that concept" (*CN* 84). It also can be very difficult to state logically complex thoughts in natural language, especially those that require multiply embedded signs of generality in their expression. Natural language uses "something" and "it" for the expression of generality, "but if we were restricted to 'something' and 'it', we would only be able to deal with the very simplest cases" (*PW* 260). These deficiencies are nevertheless not, for Frege, the most critical ones. The greatest defect of natural language for his purposes, the one he comes back to again and again, lies in the vast array of inferential moves it permits: "if we try to list all the laws governing the inferences which occur when arguments are constructed in the usual way, we find an almost unsurveyable multitude which apparently has no precise limits" (*CP* 235); "in [ordinary] language, logical relations are almost always only hinted at—left to guessing, not actually expressed" (*CN* 85). An argument conducted in natural language may be perfectly valid, each step legitimated by a (valid) rule of inference, but as long as it is left open what exactly the legitimating rules are, one cannot tell with any certainty whether the argument is valid: "a strictly defined group of modes of inference is simply not present in [ordinary] language, so that on the basis of linguistic form we cannot distinguish between a 'gapless' advance {*lückenloser Fortgang*} [in the argument] and an omission of connecting links" (*CN* 85). Nor, for the same reason, can one tell of a valid argument conducted in natural language on what its validity depends, whether only on strictly logical forms of inference or also on inference forms that belong to some special science. Showing that the truths of arithmetic are derivable on the basis of the laws of logic alone requires "fixed guidelines, along which the deductions are to run; and in verbal language these are not provided" (*CP* 235). It is "the excessive variety of logical forms that have been developed in our language" (*GL* §91) that is, for Frege, the greatest defect of natural language for his purposes.

Much as a few simple elements underlie a wide range of chemical compounds and a few words a multiplicity of sentences so, Frege thinks, a few primitive modes of inference underlie the vast array of inference forms employed in natural language reasoning. The inferences of natural language "have to be resolved into their simple components" (*CP* 235), "split . . . into the logically simple steps of which [they are] composed" (*GG* §0). Only in this way can it be determined whether the fundamental principles on which arithmetic rests are one and all logical. Overcoming the logical defects of natural language for the purposes of Frege's logicism required devising a language within which to express modes of inference—more exactly, the laws that govern those modes of inference—as formulae so that their source, whether in logic or in intuition, could be investigated.

1.2 Generality and the Expression of Laws

The purpose of Frege's *Begriffsschrift* notation is to enable the expression of laws governing inference as formulae in order to show that the laws that govern inferences in arithmetic are derived laws of logic. The goal is a system, a complete and adequate axiomatization of arithmetic; everything on which an arithmetical proof depends is to be stated in advance, either as an axiom or a definition (in *Begriffsschrift*) or as a rule of inference (in natural language). Standard laws governing arithmetical inferences are to be translated as formulae and proved on the basis of the laws of logic, the formal rules that govern inference. In *Begriffsschrift* such laws, both those that govern inferences in arithmetic and those that govern inferences in logic, are expressed as generalized conditionals.

Laws, Frege thinks, are discoverable, objective truths that are nonetheless very different from merely factual truths. As Frege himself puts the point in a late manuscript, "the distinction between law and particular fact cuts very deep. It is what creates the fundamental difference between the activity of the physicist and of the historian. The former seeks to establish laws; history tries to establish particular facts" (*PW* 258). In this regard, the laws of logic are no different from the laws of any other science; logic, like any science, seeks to discover the laws that govern its domain and to systematize those laws in an axiomatic system that reveals "how some are contained in others" (*BGS* §13). What distinguishes the laws of logic from the laws of other sciences is that they do not, as the laws of the special sciences do, govern merely one domain among others. The laws of logic govern the domain of truth itself.

For a time, Frege thought of this difference in terms of the difference between descriptive and prescriptive laws: "if we call them [the laws of logic] laws of thought, or better, laws of judgment, we must not forget we are concerned here with laws which, like the principles of morals or the laws of the state, prescribe how we are to act, and do not, like the laws of nature, define the actual course of events" (*PW* 145). But already in 1897 when this passage was written, Frege also thought that "we could, with equal justice, think of the laws of geometry and the laws of physics as laws of thought or laws of judgment"; even these laws can be conceived "as prescriptions to which our judgments must conform in a different domain if they are to remain in agreement with truth" (*PW* 145–146). Laws of the special sciences, of geometry or of physics, say, describe what is and must be in their respective domains and thereby prescribe how we ought to think about the objects proper to those domains. As Frege came to think, the laws of logic can and should be conceived in just the same way:

> The word 'law' is used in two senses. When we speak of moral or civil laws we mean prescriptions, which ought to be obeyed but with which actual occurrences are not always in conformity. Laws of nature are general features of what happens in nature, and occurrences in nature are always in accordance with them. It is rather in this sense that I speak of laws of truth. Here of course it is not a matter of what happens but of what is. From the laws of truth there follow prescriptions about asserting, thinking, judging, inferring. (*CP* 351)

Logic, on Frege's considered view, does not contrast with, say, psychology in virtue of being a normative science whose aim is to discover what ought to be but perhaps is not. Any science that aims to discover laws rather than facts (for example, the facts of natural history) is normative in a sense: insofar as it discovers laws governing what is, it also sets out prescriptions governing our thoughts, judgments, and inferences regarding what is. The difference between logic and psychology lies rather in the fact that whereas psychology discovers the (empirical) laws of how we actually do think (thereby prescribing how we ought to think about how people actually do think), logic discovers the laws of judgment itself. In so doing, it prescribes laws that govern "the way in which one ought to think if one is to think at all" (*GG* 12), laws that hold "with the utmost generality for all thinking, whatever its subject-matter" (*PW* 128).

Laws, Frege thinks, are fundamentally different from facts. They are not prescriptions, but prescriptions follow from them. Such laws are expressed in *Begriffsschrift* as generalized conditionals, that is, in sentences that on the standard reading of Frege's notation could equally well be written using the universal quantifier and the horseshoe. This reading is called into question by three related and recurring themes in Frege's writings: that the conditional stroke is justified as the primitive sign for a logical relation in *Begriffsschrift* by its role in the formation of generalized conditionals; that generalized conditionals and only generalized conditionals, with one significant exception, are correctly rendered in natural language using 'if . . . then'; and that causal laws are expressed in *Begriffsschrift* as generalized conditionals. All three themes are sounded already in the early essay "On the Aim of the 'Conceptual Notation'":

> If we wish to relate two judgable contents [*beurtheilbare Inhalt*],[9] *A* and *B*, to each other, we must consider the following cases:
>
> (1) *A* and *B*
> (2) *A* and not *B*
> (3) not *A* and *B*
> (4) not *A* and not *B*.
> Now I understand by

$$\begin{array}{c} \rule{2cm}{0.4pt} \\[-8pt] \llcorner \end{array} \begin{array}{l} A \\ B \end{array}$$

the negation of the third case. This stipulation may appear very artificial at first. It is not clear at first why I single out this third case in particular and express its negation by a special symbol. The reason, however, will be immediately evident from an example:

$$\vdash\!\!\!\!\begin{array}{l} x^2 = 4 \\ x + 2 = 4 \end{array}$$

denies the case that x^2 is not equal to 4 while nonetheless $x + 2$ is equal to 4. We can translate it: if $x + 2 = 4$, then $x^2 = 4$. This translation reveals the importance of the relation embedded in our symbol. Indeed, the hypothetical judgment is the form of all laws of nature and of all causal connections in general. To be sure, a rendering by means of "if" is not appropriate in all cases of linguistic usage, but only if an indeterminate constituent—like *x* here—confers generality on the whole. Were we to replace x by 2, then one would not appropriately translate

$$\vdash \begin{array}{l} 2^2 = 4 \\ 2 + 2 = 4 \end{array}$$

by "If $2 + 2 = 4$, then $2^2 = 4$". (CN 95)

Frege claims, first, that the meaning assigned to the conditional stroke, although apparently artificial, is justified by its role in generalized conditionals, and indeed that this is "immediately evident" in the example cited. He furthermore suggests that such a sentence, that is, a generalized conditional, and only such a sentence, is appropriately translated into natural language using 'if . . . then'. Again the significance of the point is supposed to be manifest and to require no further explanation. Frege's third point is that "the hypothetical judgment," by which Frege clearly seems to mean a judgment such as

$$\vdash \begin{array}{l} x^2 = 4 \\ x + 2 = 4, \end{array}$$

as it contrasts with the judgment

$$\vdash \begin{array}{l} 2^2 = 4 \\ 2 + 2 = 4, \end{array}$$

"is the form of all laws of nature and of all causal connections in general." What Frege suggests, in sum, is that the conditional stroke is correctly treated as a primitive symbol in logic in virtue of its role, in conjunction with letters lending generality of content, in the expression of laws, a role that is signaled in natural language by the use of 'if . . . then'.

According to Frege, the "first problem" for the logician is "the perspicuous representation of logical relations by means of written signs" (PW 14). But logics can differ in the logical relations they take to be primitive. In Frege's logic, by contrast with, say, Boole's, it is the relation that is signified by the conditional stroke that is primary: "the precisely defined hypothetical relation between contents of possible judgment has a similar significance for the foundation of my concept-script to that which identity of extensions has for Boolean logic" (PW 16).[10] Frege does not think, however, that a mere conditional, that is, something of the form

$$\begin{array}{l} A \\ B, \end{array}$$

is a "genuine hypothetical." As he puts the point, "of course this alone [the denial of the case 'not *A* and *B*'] doesn't yet give us a genuine hypothetical judgment: that arises only when *A* and *B* have in common an indefinite component which makes the situation described general" (*PW* 52). Although not invariably, Frege most often means by a hypothetical judgment a generalized conditional; it is a generalized conditional and not a mere conditional that is, he thinks, "what is known in the terminology of logic as a hypothetical judgment" (*CP* 244). The meaning of the conditional stroke, Frege's primitive sign for a logical relation, is justified by its role in the formation of such genuine hypothetical judgments: "the outstanding importance of this judgment [a genuine hypothetical or generalized conditional] has persuaded me to give the sign

precisely the meaning of the denial of the case 'not *A* and *B*'" (*PW* 52). Frege emphasizes just this point in *Grundgesetze* by introducing the conditional stroke last, even after the sign for the definite article; in *Grundgesetze* the conditional stroke is self-consciously introduced "in order to enable us to designate the subordination of a concept under a concept, and other important relations" (*GG* §12). Such relations are expressed in *Begriffsschrift* using the conditional in conjunction with signs lending generality of content, that is, in what Frege describes as genuine hypotheticals. The point is made one last time in the 1906 "Introduction to Logic." The relation designated by the conditional stroke "looks strange at first sight," and it does so, Frege suggests, because "people probably feel the lack of an inner connection between the thoughts: we find it hard to accept that it is only the truth or falsity of the thoughts that is to be taken into account, that their content doesn't come into it at all" (*PW* 186–187). As becomes clear in the discussion of generality that follows, the logical importance of this relation lies in the general thoughts that are expressible using it, thoughts that are expressed in natural language using 'if . . . then' (*PW* 189), thoughts that relate concepts one to another (*PW* 191).

Frege's conditional stroke, although in itself somewhat unintuitive as a sign for the primitive logical relation, is justified, according to Frege, by its role in the formation of genuine (that is, generalized) hypotheticals, which express the subordination of one concept to another. The importance of such judgments is signaled, in turn, in the "On the Aim" passage by the appropriateness of using 'if . . . then' in translating such sentences. The claim is reiterated in other writings both early and late. Although it is appropriate to translate, say,

$$\vdash \begin{array}{l} x = 7 \\ x + 3 = 10 \end{array}$$

as 'if $x + 3 = 10$, then $x = 7$', in the case of the judgment

$$\vdash \begin{array}{l} 2 = 7 \\ 2 + 3 = 10 \end{array}$$

"the rendering 'if' would jar with normal usage" (*PW* 11 n). In the 1906 "Introduction to Logic" we read that "there is something unnatural about the form of words 'if 3 is greater than 2, then 3 squared is greater than 2'," but in the context of a generalized conditional "the construction with 'if' seems most idiomatic" (*PW* 189).

There is one exception. In *Begriffsschrift* §5 Frege discusses three especially interesting sorts of cases in which a conditional sentence (one that is not generalized) is to be affirmed. The first case is that in which the consequent "must be affirmed," as, for example, in the case in which it is the content that three times seven equals twenty-one. The second is that in which the antecedent "is to be denied," as, for example, if it is the content that perpetual motion is possible. In both sorts of cases, Frege notes, the content (and so also the truth-value) of the other sentence in the conditional is "immaterial," and there need be no "causal connection" between the two sentences. It is the third sort of case that provides the exception to the rule that generalized conditionals and only generalized conditionals are correctly translated using 'if . . . then'. In this sort of case,

we can make the judgment

$$\vdash \begin{array}{l} A \\ B \end{array}$$

without knowing whether A and B are to be affirmed or denied. For example, let B stand for the circumstance that the moon is in quadrature [with the sun], and A the circumstance that it appears as a semicircle. In this case we can translate

$$\vdash \begin{array}{l} A \\ B \end{array}$$

with the aid of the conjunction "if": "If the moon is in quadrature [with the sun], it appears as a semicircle." (*BGS* §5)

The reason the translation using 'if' is appropriate in this case, even though the sentence is not general, is that this sentence is an instance of a causal law, which is "something general": "the causal connection implicit in the word 'if', however, is not expressed by our symbols [that is, by the conditional, horizontal, and judgment strokes], although a judgment of this kind can be made only on the basis of such a connection; for this connection is something general" (*BGS* §5). In the case in which there is a causal connection between antecedent and consequent, the conditional can be affirmed even though the truth-values of antecedent and consequent are unknown. In this case the conditional is correctly translated using 'if . . . then' despite the fact that "the causal connection implicit in the word 'if'"—which is "something general"—is not expressed in such a conditional.

A second example appears in "A Brief Survey of My Logical Doctrines" (1906). Frege gives as an example of a conditional in which both antecedent and consequent are sentences the sentence 'If $(17^2 \cdot 19)/2^{11}$ is greater than 2, then $((17^2 \cdot 19)/2^{11})^2$ is greater than 2'. This sentence, he suggests, does not sound strange, even though the sentence 'if 3 is greater than 2, then 3^2 is greater than 2' does "sound strange, a little absurd even" (*PW* 200). The essential difference between the two cases, Frege explains, is that in the case of the sentence 'if 3 is greater than 2, then 3^2 is greater than 2', "one sees at once which of the four cases holds," namely, that in which both antecedent and consequent are true, "whereas in the first example one does not" (*PW* 200).[11] In the case of the sentence 'if $(17^2 \cdot 19)/2^{11}$ is greater than 2, then $((17^2 \cdot 19)/2^{11})^2$ is greater than 2', one knows that the conditional is true not by virtue of knowing either that the antecedent is false or that the consequent is true but because it is an instance of the general law that if a number is greater than two then its square is greater than two. One makes the judgment not on the basis of the truth-values of the component sentences but on the basis of an "inner" connection between the thoughts expressed. Because one does, the sentence is appropriately translated using 'if . . . then'.

In "On the Aim" Frege claims that "the hypothetical judgment [that is, a generalized conditional] is the form of all laws of nature and of all causal connections in general" (*CN* 95). In *Begriffsschrift* §5 he suggests that "the causal connection [is] implicit in the word 'if'" and is "something general." In §12 of *Begriffsschrift* we are told that a *Begriffsschrift* generalized conditional "is how causal connections are expressed." As we have also seen, both generalized conditionals of arithmetic and particular instances of such generalities in cases in which the truth-values of antecedent and consequent are not evident are appropriately rendered using 'if' as well. Together these passages indicate that Frege employs the notion of a causal connection not in the narrow sense of a physical cause but in the broad sense of any lawful or internal connection. In this usage one may cite as the cause of something that which constitutes the ground of its truth and thereby a sufficient reason for holding it to be true. A number's being greater than two, for instance, is a sufficient reason to judge that its square is greater than two; hence we can say that there is a causal connection, in the broad sense, between something's being greater than two and its square's being greater than two. It is in this sense of cause that the connective 'if . . . then' of natural language implies a causal connection, and it is this notion of a causal connection as an internal relation among thoughts that is, for Frege, something general. Frege's *Begriffsschrift* notation seems to have been self-consciously designed to express just such "inner relationships" (*CN* 87).

Laws governing modes of arithmetical inference are expressed in *Begriffsschrift* as generalized conditionals, that is, as genuine hypotheticals. The conditional stroke is justified by its role in the expression of such laws as generalized conditionals, and the "outstanding importance" of sentences of this logical form is signaled by their being translated in natural language using 'if . . . then', a translation that reveals an internal or lawful connection. Indeed, for Frege (as for Kant), generality is the essence of lawfulness: "generality . . . is what the word 'law' indicates" (*CP* 289); "it is by means of . . . indefiniteness that the sense acquires the generality expected of a law" (*CP* 171). The point is made again in the opening remarks of the late, unfinished essay "Logical Generality" intended as the fourth part of Frege's *Logischen Untersuchungen:*

> I published an article in this journal on compound thoughts, in which some space was devoted to hypothetical compound thoughts. It is natural to look for a way of making a transition from these to what in physics, in mathematics and in logic are called *laws*. We surely very often express a law in the form of a hypothetical compound sentence composed of one or more antecedents and a consequent. Yet, right at the outset there is an obstacle in our path. The hypothetical compound thoughts I discussed do not count as laws, since they lack the generality that distinguishes laws from particular facts, such as, for instance, those we are accustomed to encounter in history. (*PW* 258)

Laws, Frege seems to think, are inherently general; only sentences that are logically general in form "count" as laws.

Surprisingly, Frege seems also to think that generality is sufficient for the expression of a law, more exactly, that any *Begriffsschrift* generalized conditional has the status or character of a law. The point is suggested already in the just-quoted passage from "Logical Generality" in Frege's remark that "hypothetical compound thoughts [that is, mere conditionals] . . . do not count as laws, since they lack the generality that distinguishes laws from particular facts" (*PW* 258). That Frege thinks that any generalized conditional of *Begriffsschrift* counts as a law is further indicated by a remark made in a letter to Husserl written in the fall of 1906: "In a hypothetical construction we have as a rule improper propositions of such a kind that neither the antecedent by itself nor the consequent by itself expresses a thought, but only the whole propositional complex . . . In mathematics, such component parts are often letters (If $a > 1$, then $a^2 > 1$). The whole proposition thereby acquires the character of a law, namely generality of content" (*PMC* 68–69). Whereas a mere conditional such as, say, 'if $3 > 1$, then $3^2 > 1$' does not have "the character of a law" but is, as one might say, merely truth-functional—that is, it is true just if either '$3 > 1$' is false or '$3^2 > 1$' is true—replacing the two occurrences of the numeral '3' by indicating letters lending generality of content yields, Frege writes, something with "the character of a law." Not only are laws expressed in *Begriffsschrift* as generalized conditionals, but all *Begriffsschrift* generalized conditionals, it seems, have the status of laws. As we will soon see, the idea is not as silly as it might at first appear.

1.3 Understanding Logical Generality: Two Strategies

The distinction between a law and a merely accidental regularity is not a distinction of quantificational logic. Whether it is a law that Fs must be G or whether it is merely a contingent matter of fact that all the Fs there are (and there may be none) are G, the relevant generality is to be expressed as '$(\forall x)(Fx \supset Gx)$'. In effect, quantificational logic treats lawful generalities as if they were contingent generalities; the "extra" content of a lawful generality—that things not only are a certain way but must be that way—is not expressed. The first step in developing the converse strategy to be pursued here is to assimilate merely accidental generalities to laws conceived as necessary truths. We might, for instance, take the sentence '$Fx \rightarrow Gx$' of some imagined logic (not, as we will see, Frege's logic as it is read here) to express a law, something to the effect that anything that falls under the concept F must also fall under the concept G. The negation of this sentence, then, expresses a possibility, that it is possible for something to fall under the concept F without also falling under the concept G. So conceived, the negated sentence does not say that there is in fact a thing that is F and not G; it says only that there could be such an object, that there is no law to the effect that Fs must be G. The extra content that is expressed in a negated universally quantified conditional of quantificational logic—that not only could there be an F that was not G but also that there actually is such an F—is not expressed in our imagined logic. Neither the distinction between a lawful or necessary generality and a contingent one nor that between a mere possibility and an existence claim is a distinction of our imagined logic.

The strategy is obviously flawed, and a simple example shows why. Suppose that it is true, merely as a matter of fact, that all the apples in a certain bag at a particular time are red. That truth would be expressed in our imagined logic as a law or necessary truth to the effect that any apple in that bag at that time must be red: '$Ax \rightarrow Rx$'. But now one could argue that were a particular Granny Smith apple to have been in the bag at the relevant time, it would have been red. That conclusion, however, is false. Had the Granny Smith apple been in the bag then, what would have been false is not that the Granny Smith apple was green (then) but that all the apples in the bag were red (then). As this example reminds us, laws, that is, necessary truths, are inferentially stronger than statements of fact; they support counterfactual reasoning. Because they do, the strategy of assimilating merely accidental generalities to such necessary truths would seem to be mistaken in principle. But it is not, and to understand why, we need only recall one of the many anomalous features of Frege's logic when it is read as a quantificational logic, namely, the fact that it includes a judgment stroke on the grounds that inferences can be drawn only from premises acknowledged to be true. If, in Frege's logic as Frege understands it, "we can draw no conclusion from something false" (*PW* 244), one cannot argue from the "law" '$Ax \rightarrow Rx$' and the falsehood that this Granny Smith apple is in the bag (at the relevant time) to the conclusion that this Granny Smith apple is red. One has, in this case (in which one of one's premises is false), only a true conditional, a conditional whose consequent is true *if* its antecedents are true. "We can go on drawing consequences without knowing whether some sentence Γ is true or false [indeed, while knowing it is false, as in indirect proof]. But . . . the condition 'If Γ holds' is retained throughout. We can only detach it when we have seen that it is fulfilled" (*PW* 245). What the generality '$Ax \rightarrow Rx$' of our imagined logic grounds, then, is only the claim that if this Granny Smith apple is in the bag then it is red, and that is true because the antecedent is false. The antecedent cannot be detached. As long as Frege's stipulation that conclusions can be drawn only from premises that are acknowledged to be true is adhered to, the fact that a merely contingent generality is expressed in our imagined logic as a law generates no difficulties for counterfactual reasoning.

We have proposed to assimilate contingent generalities to lawful generalities and thus also existence claims to statements of possibility. What 'Ax → Rx' says, in our imagined logic, is that As must be R; what its negation says is that it is possible for an A not to be R. This cannot be right as a reading of *Begriffsschrift* generalities, for, as Frege says, the *Begriffsschrift* expression

$$\vdash\!\!\!\!-\!\!\!\curvearrowleft\!\!\alpha\!\!-\!\!\varPhi(\alpha)$$

"stands for the judgment that the function is a fact whatever we may take as its argument" (*BGS* §11). *Begriffsschrift* generalities cannot, then, be understood in terms of necessity in the manner just outlined, that is, as general truths about what is and must be the case. We need another way.

Suppose that it is true that all Fs are G, whether necessarily, as a matter of law, or merely by accident. Obviously, then, if it is given that the object o is F, one can legitimately infer that o is G. The argument form

All F is G.
o is F.
Therefore, o is G.

is valid. Nevertheless, it could be argued, the argument form has a fundamentally different character in the case in which 'all F is G' is a law from the character it has in the case in which 'all F is G' is instead a contingent, accidental truth. Sextus Empiricus takes just this view in *Outlines of Scepticism*, arguing that, depending on the status of the generality, the inference either is circular or has a redundant premise. His example is the generality 'everything human is an animal', and we are to assume, first, that the generality 'everything human is an animal' is true merely by coincidence, in virtue of the fact that, as it happens, each and every human is also an animal. In that case, Sextus claims, the inference

Everything human is an animal.
Socrates is human.
Therefore, Socrates is an animal.

is circular because the fact that Socrates is an animal "is actually confirmatory of the universal proposition in virtue of the inductive mode."[12] Because in the case of this merely contingent or matter-of-factual generality, Sextus argues, one cannot establish that everything human is an animal without first establishing that Socrates, one of the humans, is an animal, the first premise presupposes already the conclusion; the argument is circular.

If, on the other hand, we assume that the generality is lawful, that is, that "being an animal follows being human . . . then at the same time it is said that Socrates is human, it may be concluded that he is an animal . . . and the proposition 'Everything human is an animal' is redundant."[13] In the case in which there is a lawful connection between being human and being an animal, Sextus claims, the argument is valid even without the proposition 'everything human is an animal'. 'Socrates is human; therefore, Socrates is an animal' is not, that is, enthymematic on his view of this case; it is valid just as it stands—though not formally valid. Clearly, then, Sextus does not understand the law as it figures in this case as a kind of necessary truth, for were it such a truth, one could not validly infer that Socrates is an animal solely on the basis of the claim that Socrates is human. What Sextus seems to think instead is that the law serves as a kind of inference license, as a kind of rule, that it functions (as the point might be put) not as a claim *from which* one reasons but instead as a principle or rule *according to which* one reasons.[14] Because what such a principle or rule licenses just is one's concluding that Socrates, say, is an animal given that he is human, it would be inconsistent with its status as such a license were one to require its inclusion among the premises. That is just Sextus's point. One can include the license among one's premises (in order, perhaps, to make as explicit as possible the modes of inference employed in the proof), but one need not; and if one does, one is not transforming an invalid argument into a valid argument.[15]

Whether or not Sextus is right to think that in the case in which the generality is merely contingent the argument is inherently circular, his analysis clearly points to two very different conceptions of the logical structure of the argument. On the first conception, the thought expressed by the sentence 'everything human is an animal' is understood as something from which to reason; it is a fact (assuming that it is true) and as such can supply a premise for an argument. Quite simply, if it is true that everything human is an animal then it is also true that the human Socrates is an animal. In the second case, the thought expressed by that same sentence is understood not as a claim, whether necessary or contingent, but as an inference license, as something according to which one reasons. It is a rule (assuming that it is valid), and as such it justifies one's drawing the conclusion that Socrates is an animal from the premise that Socrates is human. In that case, as Sextus argues, the general sentence need not be included among the premises. The argument is perfectly valid—though not formally valid—without it.

Suppose now that despite this intuitive difference between the two sorts of inference, the difference between the two sorts of generalities they involve is to be taken to concern not the contents expressed but instead the sort of justification that is involved in grounding their truth. Clearly there are two options: take the first case, that of a contingent generality, as one's paradigm, formulate a plausible account for that case, and then treat the second, lawful case the same way; or take the second, lawful case to be paradigmatic, give a plausible account of that case, and then treat the accidental cases similarly.

According to the first strategy, which begins with the case of contingent generalities, the task is to articulate an understanding of a sentence of the form 'all A is B', where the truth of the sentence is merely a matter of contingent historical fact. What in that case should we say that 'all A is B' means? The most plausible answer is simply this: what is the case if it is true. That is, much as it is natural to understand the sentence 'Socrates is snub-nosed' in terms of its truth conditions, in terms of the circumstance that obtains if it is true, so it is natural to understand a contingent generality such as, say, 'all Greek philosophers are snub-nosed' in terms of its truth conditions, what is the case if it is true, namely, that everything that is a Greek philosopher is also snub-nosed. That, of course, is not true, but it could have been true, and what the generality says on this account is simply what is the case on the assumption that it is true.

Extending the account to the case of lawful generalities is straightforward. Because any law (whether conceived as a necessary truth or as a rule of inference) entails a corresponding fact, it is the corresponding fact that we express in our language. Suppose, for instance, that it is a law that humans are mortal (that is, as Sextus would think of it, that being mortal follows being human). It follows that each and every human is mortal. What the relevant sentence of our language says is what is the case if that is true, namely, that everything that falls under the concept *human* falls also under the concept *mortal*. The law is thereby reduced to a fact about objects that fall under the relevant concepts. The guiding idea of the strategy—that for the purposes of logic a lawful generality can be treated as a generality that is true just in case things are a certain way—is grounded in an insight: whether it is accidentally true or whether it is a law that all As are B, the facts remain the same.

The second strategy begins with the lawful case, and here the most natural account, following Sextus, is not in terms of the truth conditions of claims (whether necessary or contingent) but instead in terms of the authority of rules to license judgments on the basis of other judgments. What is wanted is a form of expression that is to be understood not as a statement of a (necessary) truth but as a statement of an inference license, of something according to which to reason. We could, for instance, introduce the form

$$\begin{array}{c} F(x) \\ G(x) \end{array}$$

with the stipulation that it means not that anything that is G is or must be F but instead that being F follows being G, that is, that it is permitted to judge that o is F, for some object o, if it is known to be true that o is G. The sentence so conceived does not say that everything that falls under the concept G falls or must fall also under the concept F; it does not say how things are concerning any objects at all. What it expresses is a rule, an inference license, something according to which to reason. Of course, if it is a valid inference license, one that ought to govern one's reasoning, then it follows that '$(\forall x)(Gx \supset Fx)$' is true, that is, that what this sentence of quantificational logic says is what is so; and contrariwise, if something is found that is G but not also F, then that is enough to show that the inference license is not valid and should not be adopted as a rule according to which to reason. Nevertheless, what the rule says is only something to the effect that certain sorts of judgments are justifiable on the basis of relevant premises.

Now we extend the account to the case of accidental generalities. Suppose that it has been established as a matter of contingent empirical fact that all the Gs there are are F. Our strategy demands that we express this claim as an inference license to the effect that one is permitted to infer from the acknowledged fact that o is G (for some object o) that it is F. Because inferences from premises whose truth is not explicitly acknowledged are never permissible (at least on Frege's view, which we follow here), treating the claim as an inference license is unproblematic. In counterfactual cases, the best one will be able to do is to infer, for some object o that is not in fact G, that if o is G then it is F. Because the antecedent is false in that case, the conditional is true. This strategy, too, is grounded in an insight. Whether it is accidentally true or instead a law that all As are B, the inference potential of the sentence is the same: in either case it is permissible, given that one knows that an object o is A, to infer that o is B. (Notice that this reading suggests why Frege writes such sentences as he does. On this reading, what is "first" is not the antecedent, the condition, but instead the conditioned, the consequent, that is, the claim that one is entitled to make given that the condition is satisfied. The horizontal takes one straight to that claim; the conditional stroke attached below it shows, pictorially, that this claim nonetheless rests on a condition, that the conditioned claim can, literally, stand on its own only if that condition is met. It also indicates why Frege would write the letters in the alphabetical order he does in his examples, that is, "backwards" or top to bottom rather than, as we would find most natural, bottom to top.)

According to Sextus, an argument of the form 'all A is B; o is A; therefore o is B' can be conceived in either of two fundamentally different ways depending on whether one conceives the first premise as a factual claim from which to reason or instead as a rule of inference according to which to reason. As we have also seen, these two conceptions motivate in turn two very different strategies for understanding logical generality on the assumption that no distinction is to be marked in one's logical language between lawful and merely accidental generalities. According to the first strategy, the meaning of a generalized conditional is understood directly in terms of truth (and, perhaps, satisfaction); its meaning is given by what is the case if it is true. According to the second strategy, the meaning of a generalized conditional is understood in terms of the notion of a rule that licenses inferences—in which case the logical problem that would otherwise arise in the case of counterfactual reasoning involving a merely accidental generality is to be blocked by adherence to Frege's stipulation that inferences may be drawn only from premises (correctly) acknowledged to be true. Both strategies, it has been suggested, are founded on insights, the first on the insight that whether it is a law or merely accidental that As are B, the facts remain the same, and the second on the insight that whether it is a law or merely accidentally true that As are B, it is legitimate to infer, given some object o that is A, that o is B. According to the reading pursued here, it is the second strategy that Frege adopts. On this reading, a *Begriffsschrift* generality of the form

is to be understood in terms of the notion of an inference license, as the expression of a rule according to which to reason rather than as a claim regarding what is, or must be, the case.

On this reading, a generality such as 'all A is B' is to be conceived logically as an inference license, both in the case in which it is merely a contingent or accidental matter of fact that all As are B and in the case in which there is a properly lawful connection between being A and being B. Just as is the case in a standard quantificational logic, no distinction is to be marked in the language between lawful and accidental generalities; in either case, to say that a generalized conditional in the language is (or is not) necessary, or apodictic, is only to indicate one's grounds for acknowledging it as true. One acknowledges a "rule" (that is, a *Begriffsschrift* generalized conditional on our reading) such as that, say, being red follows being an apple in the relevant basket at the relevant time on the basis of "an appeal to facts, that is, to truths which cannot be proved and are not general, since they contain assertions about particular objects" (*GL* §3), facts such as that this apple (which is in the basket) is red, and that one is, and so on. Other rules, for instance, the rule of the transitivity of subordination, are provable from the basic laws of logic and for this reason may be called necessary, or apodictic, or analytic. Calling such a rule necessary (or apodictic or analytic), to contrast it with the former sort of rule, is in this way to say something not about the content of the rule but instead about the basis on which it is to be acknowledged. We know that Frege rejected Kant's modal distinctions on the grounds that they are logically without significance. Reading Frege's *Begriffsschrift* generalized conditionals as rules that license inferences, rather than as universally quantified claims, is perfectly consistent with such a view.

We have seen that Frege claims in his elucidation of a *Begriffsschrift* judgment whose content is a generality (expressed using the concavity notation) that it "stands for the judgment that the function is a fact whatever we may take as its argument" (*BGS* §11). This, we noted, is incompatible with treating *Begriffsschrift* generalized conditionals as necessary truths. It is not incompatible, as we have just seen, with treating such sentences as the expression of rules governing inferences. That it is a fact that all As are B is indeed necessary and sufficient for expressing that fact as a rule licensing inferences, that is, as a *Begriffsschrift* generalized conditional as it is read here. Nevertheless, it can seem surprising for our reading that Frege would elucidate generalities of *Begriffsschrift* in just this way. To understand why Frege's elucidation of generality takes the form it does requires some account (however preliminary) of the purpose Frege's elucidations are to serve.[16]

An especially striking feature of Frege's elucidations in *Begriffsschrift* is that they are elucidations of judgments, that is, of sentences to which the judgment stroke has been attached. This suggests that Frege's elucidations concern acts of acknowledging the truth of various contents, not merely those contents themselves; it suggests that they are not so much clarifications of the contents expressed (for in that case no purpose would be served by the presence of the judgment stroke) as clarifications of the judgeability conditions of judgments of various forms in *Begriffsschrift*. If that is right then Frege's *Begriffsschrift* elucidations serve to set out the necessary and sufficient conditions for acknowledging the truth of *Begriffsschrift* sentences of various forms where such a judgment is not the conclusion of an inference but a judgment made solely on the basis of the content itself. It is the correctness of attaching the judgment stroke in various cases that is at issue in Frege's elucidations; and such elucidations are needed, in Frege's system of logic, because the axioms of that system must be acknowledged to be true before any inferences can be drawn on the basis of them. In *Grundgesetze*, after Frege has distinguished *Sinn* from *Bedeutung*, that same end is achieved by setting out the necessary and sufficient conditions under which *Begriffsschrift* sentences of various forms designate the True. Because the truth of a thought is necessary and sufficient for correctly acknowledging its truth, judgeability conditions immediately follow.

On this reading of Frege's elucidations of his primitive signs, the purpose of those elucidations is to clarify the judgeability conditions of the contents expressed by sentences containing those signs. This reading is suggested by the fact that in *Begriffsschrift* Frege's elucidations are invariably of sentential signs to which the judgment stroke has been attached. It is further reinforced by the fact that in his elucidation of logically general sentences of *Begriffsschrift* Frege does not employ his Latin italic letters—which are the principal vehicle for the expression of generality in *Begriffsschrift* (as will be argued in section 2.3) and are correctly used in conjunction with the judgment stroke—but instead the concavity notation. Frege's use of the concavity notation in his elucidation suggests that the elucidation is intended to clarify the correctness of a judgment, that is, the correctness of attaching the judgment stroke in the case in which the content is logically general, and it does so because only in this form (that is, expressed using the concavity) can the generality be "posed in a question" (*PW* 8). Only a generality expressed using the concavity notation can be negated; only a generality so expressed has in this way an "opposite." It follows that only a generality so expressed yields a content of pos-

sible judgment, that is, something that can be acknowledged, or its negation acknowledged, to be true. The *Begriffsschrift* sentence

$$—\!\curvearrowright^{\alpha}\!\!\begin{array}{l}— F(\alpha) \\ \llcorner\!\!- G(\alpha),\end{array}$$

expresses a content of possible judgment; the *Begriffsschrift* sentence

$$—\!\!\begin{array}{l}— F(x) \\ \llcorner\!\!- G(x)\end{array}$$

does not. Indeed, in Frege's logical language, Latin italic letters never appear except in sentences to which the judgment stroke has already been attached.[17] As we will see in section 2.3, one can directly infer a generality
expressed using Latin italic letters in Frege's logic, but it is only inferentially that generalities so expressed can be acknowledged. If Frege's elucidation is of the correctness of acknowledging the truth of a *Begriffsschrift*
generality directly (that is, not as the conclusion of an inference), that elucidation must employ the concavity notation for generality rather than a
Latin italic letter even though, in this case, the judgment stroke is attached. The elucidation tells us that a *Begriffsschrift* generality ought to be
acknowledged as true (on its own merits, not as the conclusion of an inference) just in case the function is a fact whatever is taken as argument. That
is exactly right, whichever of the two strategies outlined earlier one pursues.

According to Frege's elucidation, the necessary and sufficient condition for correctly acknowledging (on its own merits) the truth of a
Begriffsschrift generalized conditional such as

$$—\!\curvearrowright^{\alpha}\!\!\begin{array}{l}— F(\alpha) \\ \llcorner\!\!- G(\alpha)\end{array}$$

is that the function

$$—\!\!\begin{array}{l}— F\xi \\ \llcorner\!\!- G\xi\end{array}$$

yields the value True no matter what object is taken as argument. The
judgment that results provides in turn the basis for the inference license
that is expressed, on our reading, by

$$\vdash\!\!\begin{array}{l}— F(x) \\ \llcorner\!\!- G(x)\end{array}$$

as justified by the law that

It by no means follows that the meaning of that second conditional expressed using Frege's Latin italic letters is fixed by Frege's elucidation of the judgeability conditions of the first *Begriffsschrift* generality, the one expressed using the concavity notation. If, as has been suggested here, what a *Begriffsschrift* generality written using Frege's Latin italic letters expresses is not properly speaking a fact but instead a rule, a principle according to which to reason, then its meaning can be adequately revealed only in inference. That the function is a fact whatever one may take as its argument is necessary and sufficient for judging (on its own merits) that a *Begriffsschrift* generalized conditional is true, and it follows, on our account, that the relevant inference license is valid. Frege's elucidation of a *Begriffsschrift* generality, then, understood as setting out the necessary and sufficient conditions for a correct judgment regarding a *Begriffsschrift* generality, is perfectly consistent with taking *Begriffsschrift* generalized conditionals involving Latin italic letters to express laws conceived as inference licenses. Indeed, as we read it, Frege's elucidation of generality in *Begriffsschrift* could take no other form than the one Frege gives it.

1.4 Our Starting Point

Frege says that arithmetic was his starting point. It seemed to him probable that arithmetic was grounded in logic alone, that all its concepts and modes of inference were strictly logical; his aim was definitively to show that this is so. But to do that he needed a better means of expression than that provided by natural language. In particular, he needed a notation for the expression of the laws that govern the inferences that are actually drawn in arithmetic so that those laws might be proven as theorems on the basis of the laws of logic alone. To that end, he devised a notation that enables the expression of rules of inference as claims, that is, as generalized conditionals (expressed using his Latin italic letters) or, as he also thought of them, as genuine hypotheticals. Unlike a universally quantified conditional of a standard logic, which expresses a fact, a *Begriffsschrift* generalized conditional (expressed using Latin italic letters) expresses a law that governs inferences, and in the first instance, a law that governs inferences in arithmetic, for instance, the law of mathematical induction. It is just this idea, that genuine hypotheticals of *Begriffsschrift* express not claims from which to reason but rules on the basis of which to reason, that provides our starting point. Instead of beginning with the quantificational conception of generality as an account of what Frege means by logical generality, and understanding Frege's conception of lawfulness on that basis, we begin with Frege's conception of a law as that to which a mode of inference is subject, and on that basis develop an account of his conception of logical generality and thereby of his logic.[18] Our starting point is Frege's conception of a law as that which governs a mode of inference. Our first task is to understand *Begriffsschrift* generalized conditionals expressed using Frege's Latin italic letters as formulations of such inference licenses.

2

Logical Generality

It's a question of grasping the property of thoughts that I call logical generality. Of course for this we have to reckon upon a meeting of minds between ourselves and others, and here we may be disappointed.

—"LOGICAL GENERALITY," C. 1923

Frege developed his *Begriffsschrift* in order to show that there are no peculiarly arithmetical modes of inference, no laws of arithmetic that are not derivable from the laws of logic and definitions. Principles of inference that appear to be peculiar to arithmetic are to be translated into formulae in his concept-script and proved on the basis of logic alone. Because these formulae have the logical form of generalized conditionals, what is needed, first and foremost, is an account of such sentences, both of the logical significance of Frege's two-dimensional conditional stroke and of the peculiar logical role his indicating letters play in lending generality of content to conditionals.[1] We begin with some general considerations regarding the kind of language *Begriffsschrift* is on our account.

2.1 Reading *Begriffsschrift*

In a written natural language such as English or German, a sentence is most immediately a record of speech that enables one capable of reading the language to reproduce the relevant sequence of phonemes; it is, in the first instance, "a direction for forming a spoken sentence in a language whose sequences of sounds serve as signs for expressing a sense" (*PW* 260). But although at first the connection between the written word (say, 'Socrates') and that which it signifies (the individual man Socrates) is mediated by the relevant sounds, "once this connection is established, we may also regard the written or printed sentence as an immediate expression of a thought, and so as a sentence in the strict sense of the word" (*PW* 260). We can learn, that is, to read a sentence of ordinary written language in a new way, to read it as a sentence of a fundamentally different kind of language. Instead of reading a sentence of English as "a direction for forming a spoken sentence," we learn to read it as itself "an immediate expression of a thought." Because the meaning of the language as it is conceived in this second way is carried by the written signs themselves, such a language is "written for the eye" not merely in the trivial sense that it is written but also in the more interesting sense that the meanings of sentences are now seen, as it were, rather than heard.

Ordinary written natural language can be read as a language for the eye; it can come to *be* such a language. But written natural language was not formed as such a language. "It simply reproduces the verbal speech," and because it does, "there is only an imperfect correspondence between the way the words are concatenated and the structure of the concepts" (*PW* 12–13). "Speech [and thus also verbal language that reproduces it] often only indicates by inessential marks or by imagery what a concept-script should spell out in full" (*PW* 13). A concept-script, by contrast with verbal language, is explicitly designed in such a way that "it directly expresses the facts without the intervention of speech" (*CN* 88). Thus, whereas in English one would write, for instance, 'Romeo loves Juliet', in a more perspicuous notation one might write simply 'Lrj', understood as (that is, to be read as) a presentation of two individuals, Romeo and Juliet, in a relation of loving, the former to the latter. Such a notation is logically more perspicuous than written English in two ways. First, it is not mediated by spoken English; one cannot read 'Lrj' as one can read written English, as a direction for forming a spoken sentence. The letter 'r' stands for Romeo not by way of the sound the letter makes when it is spoken but directly. It is a simple sign to be understood as representative of Romeo, and similarly for 'j' and 'L'. The sentential sign 'Lrj' is also more perspicuous than written English insofar as it does not, as written English does, mark one object name as the subject. In English, one distinguishes between 'Romeo loves Juliet' and 'Juliet is loved by Romeo': Romeo is the grammatical subject of the first sentence, and Juliet is the grammatical subject of the second. In standard logical notations, as in *Begriffsschrift*, such a distinction is not marked. 'Lrj' expresses the content that is common to the sentences 'Romeo loves Juliet' and 'Juliet is loved by Romeo'. Because, as Frege notes in *Begriffsschrift* §3, only this common content is significant for the correctness of inference, it is this common content that is expressed in a properly logical language.

It is a fundamental insight of modern logic that, for the purposes of logic, a sentence such as 'Romeo loves Juliet' is not about the grammatical subject Romeo, saying of him that he loves Juliet. Nevertheless, as standardly conceived, such a sentence, more perspicuously rendered 'Lrj', does have a logical subject. What it is about, logically, is the ordered pair ⟨Romeo, Juliet⟩; what it says about the people so ordered is that the two-place predicate *loves* applies to them. If it is possible also to conceive the sentence differently, as, say, about Juliet that she is loved by Romeo—if, that is, it is possible also to take 'j' as marking the argument place for the function Lrξ—this is essentially derivative, grounded in the independently meaningful signs 'L', 'r', and 'j'.[2] Indeed, it can seem obvious that sentences should be taken to have such antecedently intelligible parts out of which they are constructed; only so, it would seem, can an adequate account be given of our ability to understand novel sentences. We begin, for instance, with simple names and simple n-ary predicates, assigning to each a semantic value: objects are assigned to the simple names, properties defined over objects are assigned to one-place predicates, binary relations defined over ordered pairs of objects are assigned to two-place predicates, and so on. Simple sentences are formed by appropriately combining those simple parts, and the truth conditions of the sentences, the contents expressed, are determined by the semantic values assigned to their proper parts. Because the meaning expressed by sentences so constructed is determined by the arrangement and meanings of their constituent parts, we explain our ability to grasp the meanings of novel sentences in terms of our grasp of the meanings of their constituent parts and of the ways those parts are correctly combined.

Clearly there is something like this in Frege. Curiously enough, however, Frege does not so much as mention the compositionality of language, the fact that the content expressed by a sentence is a function of the contents expressed by its proper parts, until after the introduction of the technical notions of *Sinn* and *Bedeutung* in the early 1890s. (Nor, for the same reason, will it be mentioned again here until discussion of the distinction between sense and meaning in Chapter 4.) What is emphasized in all his writings, early and late, is, as Frege puts it in the 1914 "Notes for Ludwig Darmstaedter," "I do not begin with concepts and put them together to form a thought or judgment; I come by the parts of a thought by analyzing the thought" (*PW* 253). According to Frege, one of the most important and fundamental insights codified in his logical language is that the subject/predicate distinction is to be replaced by the distinction between argument and function (*BGS* 107), where argument and function are given only relative to an analysis (*BGS* §9). "In this," he claims in *Begriffsschrift* §3, "I strictly follow the example of the formula language of mathematics, in which, also, one can distinguish subject and predicate only by doing violence."

The point is developed for the case of the sentence '$2^4 = 16$' of the formula language of arithmetic in the long Boole essay written shortly after *Begriffsschrift*:

If . . . you imagine the 2 in the content of possible judgment

$$2^4 = 16$$

to be replaced by something else, by (-2) or by 3 say, which may be indicated by putting an x in place of the 2:

$$x^4 = 16,$$

the content of possible judgment is thus split into a constant and a variable part. The former, regarded in its own right but holding a place open for the latter, gives the concept '4th root of 16'.

We may now express

$$2^4 = 16$$

by the sentence '2 is a fourth root of 16' or 'the individual 2 falls under the concept "4th root of 16"' or 'belongs to the class of 4th roots of 16'. But we may also just as well say '4 is a logarithm of 16 to the base 2'. Here the 4 is being treated as replaceable and so we get the concept 'logarithm of 16 to the base 2':

$$2^x = 16.$$

The x indicates here the place to be occupied by the sign for the individual falling under the concept. (*PW* 16–17)

A sentence of the formula language of arithmetic such as '$2^4 = 16$' can be carved up in various ways into function and argument to yield a sentence that ascribes a concept to a number. On one analysis, it says that two is a fourth root of sixteen, on another that four is a logarithm of sixteen to the base two, and so on. But what, we may ask, does the sentence say independent of any such analysis? The answer, we think, is obvious: '$2^4 = 16$' says that two to the fourth power equals sixteen. We read it, that is, in essentially the way we would read the corresponding sentence of natural language. What we need to see is that much as we learn to read sentences of

English in a new way, not as directions for forming spoken sentences but as immediate expressions of thoughts, so we can learn to read sentences of the formula language of arithmetic differently, as sentences of a fundamentally different *kind* of language. This point is critical to the reading aimed at here and thus will be developed with some care.

Imagine, to begin with, someone who has learned to count objects and on that basis a procedure for finding sums: when given a problem of the form $n + m$, the student represents n objects (say, as strokes on a page) and adds units (strokes) m times. Multiplication is easily mastered. Given a problem of the form '$n \times m$', one simply adds n to n $m - 1$ times. The problem of taking (say) a fourth power of n is conceived as the problem of finding the solution to '$n \times n \times n \times n$', and so on. In each case the student knows what to do, what procedure to follow, to find the answer. Now we provide our student with a sign for equality and teach the student to say what hitherto could only be shown, namely, that the sum of n and m is l, or, in the newly acquired notation, '$n + m = l$', and similarly for multiplication and exponentiation. A sentence like '$2^4 = 16$', then, has for the student a fixed logical form: '$f(x,y) = z$', where 'f' indicates the procedure to be followed for arguments x and y, and z is the result of following that procedure for those numbers as arguments. The sentence '$2^4 = 16$' says that two to the fourth power equals sixteen.

Suppose now that we try to teach our student the inverse operations, subtraction, division, roots, and logarithms. As is indicated by the fact that, by contrast with addition, multiplication, and exponentiation, these operations are not closed under the positive whole numbers, such operations involve something essentially new. One way to think about what it is that is new is this. We have sentences such as '$+(2,3) = 5$' that are understood to have the logical form of identities. Such a sentence is built up, first, out of a pair of numbers to which a function is applied, and the result of applying that function to those numbers is then identified with another number, in this case, five: $+(2,3) = 5$. This sentence says of the sum of two and three that it is equal to five. Suppose now that we tried to explain subtraction by saying that what is wanted in that case is the function one gets by taking as arguments not the '2' and the '3' in '$+(2,3) = 5$', but instead the '2' and the '5', leaving the '3' position to be where the value goes. As long as the sentence '$+(2,3) = 5$' is understood by way of its constructional history, as built up in the manner just described, this new function (so called) that one is to get by taking the '2' and the '5' to mark the argument places has a radically different status from that of the addition function. Because the sentence is conceived as built up out of two numbers applied to a function to yield a number that is then identified with another number, our "subtraction function" cannot be recognized as a function, properly speaking, at all. Our so-called function is not really a function but at best a convenient form of words. It is only *as if* we could form such a function.

But of course subtraction is a proper function. What is distinctive of it, and of the other inverse operations, is that to see that it is requires seeing the sentence '+(2,3) = 5' not as having inherently the form of an identity but instead as presenting, by means of familiar arithmetical symbols, an arithmetical relation among three numbers, one that can be carved up in various ways into function and argument. To understand subtraction, that is, one learns to see the sentence '+(2,3) = 5' in a radically new way. One learns to *read* it differently, not as the result of a stepwise process (first take two and three and apply the plus function to them, then take the result and set it equal to five), but simply as exhibiting an arithmetical relationship between two, three, and five, one that can be analyzed in a variety of ways. To see that subtraction and addition are both functions in exactly the same sense is to see that any two of the numerals in '+(2,3) = 5' can be treated as marking the argument places, leaving the one that remains to mark the value of the function for those arguments. Independent of an analysis, the sentence so conceived does not ascribe identity to two numbers or any other predicate (or relation) to any subject (or subjects). The sentence does not say anything in that sense at all. It merely exhibits three numbers in a certain arithmetical relation. Such a language, unlike the language of arithmetic on our first reading of it, is essentially a written language, one that can exploit the two-dimensional writing surface for the sake of perspicuity.

The critical feature of a sentence such as '$2^4 = 16$' in the formula language of arithmetic as it is now being conceived is that it merely presents three numbers in an arithmetical relation and is variously analyzable. A different example of the sort of symbolic notation we have in mind here is this. We know that given a categorical judgment of the form 'No M is N', one can infer that no N is M. If the one sentence is true, then the other is as well. Nonetheless, the two sentences are different (on any standard reading of them); an (immediate) inference is required to get from the one to the other. In a Venn diagram, the content that is common to both sentences is exhibited as follows:

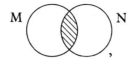

where this diagram is not to be read from left to right (or right to left) but simply taken in as a whole. It does not say that no M is N, nor does it say that no N is M. Instead, it simply presents M and N in the logical relation of mutual exclusion. Similarly, we have suggested, we can learn to read a sentence of the formula language of arithmetic such as '$2^4 = 16$' not from left to right (or right to left), but simply as a presentation of the numbers two, four, and sixteen in a certain arithmetical relation, one that can be read, analyzed into function and argument, in a variety of ways. No doubt we could not come so to read the formula language of arithmetic without having first developed and learned to read it as we ordinarily do (any more than we could come to read written English as an immediate expression of a thought before developing and learning to read it as a direction for forming a spoken sentence, or could learn to subtract before learning to count and to add); but that is a historical and psychological point, not a logical one.

Two fundamentally different, but also fundamentally related, ways one can read the arithmetical sentence '$2^4 = 16$' have been outlined. On the first way of reading, the sentence says of two taken to the fourth power that it is equal to sixteen. If, on this reading, the sentence can also be analyzed as saying of, say, four that it is a logarithm of sixteen to the base two, it says this only in some other, essentially derivative way. The second way to read the sentence, achieved through a thoroughgoing transformation of the first way of reading, is to take it merely to exhibit, by means of familiar features of the symbolism, an arithmetical relation among three numbers, merely to show, much as a Venn diagram does, how things stand if it is true. Only relative to an analysis that identifies some number(s) as argument(s) and the remainder as the function is the sentence so read correctly described as saying something about something. Independent of an analysis, the sentence has no subject and no predicate, no function and no argument; it merely exhibits three numbers in an arithmetical relation.

In essentially the same way we can learn to read the sentence 'Lrj' differently, not as saying of Romeo and Juliet that the former loves the latter but as only showing Romeo, Juliet, and the relation of loving in a certain relation. So conceived, the sentence presents not Romeo and Juliet in the first-level relation of loving but instead, all three—Romeo, Juliet, and loving—in the second-level logical relation of subsumption. The sentence so read does not say that these three entities stand in this relation; independent of an analysis it does not say anything at all. It only shows how things stand if it is true. In order to recover truth conditions from it, we must analyze it into function and argument. If we take 'r' and 'j' to mark the argument places and L$\xi\zeta$ as the (two-place) function, it is read as saying of Romeo and Juliet that the former loves the latter; if we take 'r' alone to mark the argument place, it is read as saying of Romeo that he loves Juliet, that is, that Romeo falls under the concept *loving Juliet;* if we take 'j' to mark the argument place, it is read as saying of Juliet that she is loved by Romeo; if we take 'Lξj' to mark the argument place, it is read as saying of the property *loving Juliet* that it is a property of Romeo, that is, that the property *loving Juliet* falls under the second-level concept *property of Romeo;* and so on. In each case the analysis yields truth conditions, an account of what is the case if the sentence is true and an ascription of the relevant concept to the subject identified as argument. Independent of any analysis, the sentence only shows what is the case if it is true. In that case no predicate is ascribed. In the language so conceived, as in the formula language of arithmetic as we have learned to conceive it, "one can distinguish subject and predicate only by doing violence" (*BGS* §3), only, that is, by carving the sentence up into function and argument.[3]

On the standard reading of a simple sentence of *Begriffsschrift* such as '——Lrj', the sentence has a fixed logical form; it is an ascription of a relation, loving, to an ordered pair of objects: ⟨Romeo, Juliet⟩. What the sentence means, the thought it expresses, is what is the case if it is true, that Romeo loves Juliet. But given such a reading, we can also learn to read the sentence differently, not as an ascription of a relation to a pair of objects but instead as merely exhibiting two objects and a relation in a certain higher-level logical relation. On this latter reading the sentence does not as such present truth conditions, though they are easily formulated relative to an analysis. Instead, it merely exhibits a content that, for the purposes of judgment and inference, can be variously analyzed into function and argument. According to the interpretation pursued here, Frege reads *Begriffsschrift,* and by extension sentences of natural language, in just this way.

In the 1879 logic Frege claims that a *Begriffsschrift* sentence presents "*a mere combination of ideas {blosse Vorstellungsverbindung}*" (*BGS* §2). This early formulation is corrected in the "Seventeen Key Sentences on Logic":

"in the case of thinking it is not really ideas [*Vorstellung*] that are connected but things, properties, concepts, relations" (*PW* 174). According to Frege's considered usage *"Vorstellung"* refers to an idea "in the subjective sense"; "objective ideas" just are concepts and objects (*GL* §27 n. 1 to p. 37). Because already in *Begriffsschrift* Frege thinks of symbols as "usually only representative of their contents—so that each combination [of symbols usually] expresses only a relation between their contents" (*BGS* §8), a sentence of *Begriffsschrift* is to be understood as a combination of things, properties, concepts, and relations, not (say) Romeo and Juliet in the relation of loving but instead Romeo, Juliet, and loving in a certain higher-order relation. A further indication that this is Frege's view, even in the early logic, is the fact that he sees no difference in principle between taking an object name to mark the argument place and taking a concept word to do so. Just as we can analyze the *Begriffsschrift* sentence '——Fo' into the function Fξ for argument o, so we can analyze it into the (second-level) function ϕ(o) for argument Fξ (*BGS* §10). In *Grundgesetze* §22 Frege explicitly says that what is designated by the *Begriffsschrift* sign '——ϕ(ξ)' "is the relation of an object to a concept under which it falls"; that is, it is a sign for the relation of subsumption, a second-level function that takes objects and concepts as arguments to yield truth-values as values. Much as the signs '+' and '=' of the formula language of arithmetic enable, on our reading, the exhibition of arithmetical relations among numbers in an arithmetical identity such as '2 + 3 = 5', so Frege's primitive signs (as here understood) enable the exhibition of logical relations among objects and (first-level) concepts in sentences of the form '——Fo'. On this reading, just as Frege says, "the thought itself does not yet determine what is to be regarded as the subject. If we say 'the subject of this judgment' we do not designate anything definite unless at the same time we indicate a definite kind of analysis" (*PW* 107). As we will see, Frege's two-dimensional conditional stroke preserves just this feature of the notation for the case of logically complex sentences. A *Begriffsschrift* conditional presents sentences in a logical relation; and just as the simple sentence '——Lrj' can, a *Begriffsschrift* conditional can be analyzed in various ways.

2.2 The Logical Justification for a Two-Dimensional Notation

Frege's *Begriffsschrift* notation was designed to enable the expression of "everything necessary for a correct inference" (*BGS* §3), where this expressive project requires in turn, Frege thinks, "the perspicuous representation of logical relations by means of written signs" (*PW* 14), "symbols for the logical relations" (*CN* 89). Because, as Frege also holds, "a simple sequential ordering in no way corresponds to the diversity of logical relations through which thoughts are interconnected," his two-dimensional notation is designed to "facilitate the apprehension of that to which we wish to direct our attention" (*CN* 87). Frege's conditional stroke is his sign for the primitive logical relation, and it is that stroke that gives his logical language its peculiar two-dimensional character. We need, then, to understand that sign in a way that reveals its logical justification.

On the standard reading, Frege's conditional stroke functions in his logic as the horseshoe does in our logic. We know that the *Begriffsschrift* conditional

designates the True just in case either B is false or A is true (*BGS* §5; *GG* §12); so, we assume (following Russell), it expresses precisely the thought that is expressed by 'B ⊃ A'. Frege's discussion in *Begriffsschrift* §5 of *Begriffsschrift* sentences that contain a series of conditions reinforces the reading:

it is easy to see that

$$\begin{array}{l} \text{———} \rule{0.5cm}{0.4pt}\; A \\ \qquad \rule{0.5cm}{0.4pt}\; B \\ \qquad\qquad \rule{0.5cm}{0.4pt}\; \Gamma \end{array}$$

denies the case in which *A* is denied and *B* and *Γ* are affirmed. We must think of this as constructed from

$$\begin{array}{l} \text{———} \rule{0.5cm}{0.4pt}\; A \\ \qquad \rule{0.5cm}{0.4pt}\; B \end{array}$$

and *Γ* in the same way as

$$\begin{array}{l} \text{———} \rule{0.5cm}{0.4pt}\; A \\ \qquad \rule{0.5cm}{0.4pt}\; B \end{array}$$

is constructed from *A* and *B*. (*BGS* §5)

If we must think of

as so constructed (as codifying its constructional history in this way), then we must think of

as forming a single unit relative to the condition Γ, and therefore the whole as of the form 'if Γ, then if B then A', that is, as expressing just what is expressed by '$\Gamma \supset (B \supset A)$'. Adding a further condition, for instance Δ, as in

would be to express what is expressed in standard notation as '$\Delta \supset (\Gamma \supset (B \supset A))$'. Were this the right way to read *Begriffsschrift* conditionals, the only logical justification for Frege's two-dimensional notation would be that it enables us to dispense with brackets.[4]

As it is usually understood, and as Frege seems to understand it in the early logic, a *Begriffsschrift* sentence with multiple conditions has a fixed logical structure. It is to be read according to some such rule as this: beginning at the top left, follow the horizontal until you come to a conditional stroke; say 'if' followed by whatever is to the right of that conditional stroke, then say 'then' and continue. (The rule applies recursively in the case of a condition that is itself a conditional.) Given that the sentence does have this structure, there is no compelling logical justification for a two-dimensional representation of it. In the mature logic Frege self-consciously reads such sentences differently, as similar to "tabular lists" in which "the two-dimensional expanse is utilized to achieve perspicuity"; his own notation, he claims, achieves perspicuity "in much the same way" (*CP* 236). That is, Frege comes explicitly to see what had been implicit in his inferential practice from the beginning: that *Begriffsschrift* conditionals can be read in various ways, just as a table can. Much as the formula language of arithmetic, as we have learned to read it, is a different kind of language from that it is generally taken to be, so Frege comes to suggest, his logical language is a different kind of language from that he originally took it to be.

In a tabular list, for instance, a truth-table for some binary connective in a three-valued logic, the values of a logically compound sentence are set out for all possible combinations of values of its components. We define the connective '*' of some imagined logic, for example, as follows.

*	[1]	[2]	[3]
[1]	1	2	3
[2]	1	3	3
[3]	2	1	3

Such a table sets out clearly and unambiguously the value of any sentence of the form 'a*b' given values for 'a' and 'b', and it does so by way of a two-dimensional array, a "tabular list." But of course all the information contained in the table could also be presented in a linear array. Reading down the columns, left to right, the information on the table could be codified, assuming a suitable convention for reading sentences of this form, as: 1 1 2 . 2 3 1 . 3 3 3. Reading instead by rows, top to bottom, yields: 1 2 3 / 1 3 3 / 2 1 3, again, given suitable conventions for interpreting the sentence. Alternatively, entries could be listed by their values, and so on. Each such path through the table codifies the information contained in the table in a sequential ordering. As we might think of it, each represents the way the table shows up from some one essentially linear perspective. Because it does, each linear presentation of the information contained in the table highlights some relationships while it obscures others. One linear presentation makes it easy to see what the values are for the cases in which the value of the first sentence in the compound is, say, 2 but harder to discover what the values are in the cases in which the value of the second sentence is 2. In another it is easiest to see what the values of the component sentences must be to yield a certain value, and so on. In this way, each linear array suits some purposes at the expense of others. Because all such purposes are equally well served by the table itself, what is expressed in a single two-dimensional table is expressed in one dimension only by an equivalence class of lists. It should be noted, finally, that given one linear representation of the information provided in the table, it would be nontrivial in the absence of the table itself to show that just the same information was contained in another linear ordering. *Begriffsschrift* conditional sentences, as they are to be read here, are essentially similar to such a table.

We saw earlier that what would be expressed in quantificational logic as '(R ⊃ (Q ⊃ P))', is expressed in *Begriffsschrift* instead as

But whereas in the early logic Frege thinks of this latter sentence in terms of its stepwise construction out of R and the conditional formed from P and Q, in the mature logic he suggests that the resultant sentence merely presents (more exactly, should be read as merely presenting) P, Q, and R in a logical relation, one that can be read in various ways.

In

$$\text{``}\quad\begin{array}{l}\Theta\text{''}\\ \Delta\\ \Lambda\end{array}$$

we may call "——Θ" the *main component* and "——Δ" and "——Λ" *subcomponents;* however, we may also regard

$$\text{``}\quad\begin{array}{l}\Theta\text{''}\\ \Delta\end{array}$$

as the *main component* and "——Λ" alone as *subcomponent.* (*GG* §12)

If we take '——Θ' as the main component and '——Δ' and '——Λ' as subcomponents, this sentence could be read as the conditional 'if Δ and Λ, then Θ'; if we take '——Λ' alone as subcomponent, it reads instead as 'if Λ, then if Δ then Θ'. Like our truth-table for the connective *, this *Begriffsschrift* sentence is essentially two-dimensional; corresponding to it are a variety of provably equivalent serially ordered linear structures.

Sentences that are provably equivalent, such as, for instance, 'if Δ and Λ, then Θ' and 'if Δ, then if Λ then Θ', express one and the same thought according to Frege. As he explains in a letter to Husserl,

if *both* the assumption that the content of *A* is false and that of *B* true *and* the assumption that the content of *A* is true and that of *B* false lead to a logical contradiction, and if this can be established without knowing whether the content of *A* or *B* is true or false, and without requiring other than purely logical laws for this purpose, then nothing can belong to the content of *A* as far as it is capable of being judged true or false, which does not also belong to the content of *B*. (*PMC* 70)

Because this content that is common to such equipollent propositions "alone is of concern to logic," "all that would be needed [in an adequate logic] would be a single standard proposition for each system of equipollent propositions" (*PMC* 67). Frege's two-dimensional notation provides just such a standard proposition for the case of conditionals with more than one condition. By contrast with sentences in our standard linear notation, each of which has one and only one main connective (where that connective is, of course, the connective to which rules of inference may be applied), sentences in *Begriffsschrift* have a main connective only relative to an analysis. The sentence

for instance, can be read in four different ways as follows. If, in this sentence, '——S' is treated as the subcomponent and

as the main component, whose main component in turn is

then the result would be most naturally expressed in quantificational logic as 'S ⊃ (R ⊃ (Q ⊃ P))'. In the sentence so read the "main connective" is between the last (that is, lowest) condition S and everything to the right of it; because what is to the right is also logically complex, it is to be read in turn as having its "main connective" between the lowest condition R and the conditional P if Q. So read, the sentence is conceived just as Frege suggests in *Begriffsschrift* it should, as progressively built up out of P to which Q is added as a condition, then R as a condition on the resulting conditional, then S on that conditional in turn. But, as Frege comes explicitly to see, we can also learn to read it differently. Taking '——S' as subcomponent and

as main component (as in the first case), but now taking the main component of this component to be '——P', leaving '——Q' and '——R' as subcomponents, yields instead 'S ⊃ ((R & Q) ⊃ P)'.[5] That is, we take the main component to have its main connection between the two conditions, Q and R, and the conditioned P. A third path through our sentence results from taking both '——S' and '——R' as subcomponents and

as the main component, in which case the result might be expressed in a linear notation as '(S & R) ⊃ (Q ⊃ P)'. If, finally, all of '——S', '——R', and '——Q' are treated as subcomponents with '——P' as the main component, we get '(S & R & Q) ⊃ P'. In this case the main connective is the "first" (that is, rightmost) horizontal; S, R, and Q are all conceived as conditions on the truth of P. Each of 'S ⊃ (R ⊃ (Q ⊃ P))', 'S ⊃ ((R & Q) ⊃ P)', '(S & R) ⊃ (Q ⊃ P)', and '(S & R & Q) ⊃ P' (or their natural language equivalents) represents in this way one path through Frege's two-dimensional structure, one perspective it is possible to take on it. The equivalence of these four formulae, though it must be proven in standard (one-dimensional) notation, is a given of Frege's two-dimensional notation. Just as our truth-table corresponded to an equivalence class of linear presentations of the information it contained, so Frege's one formula corresponds to an equivalence class of formulae in standard one-dimensional notation. The only case in which the two notations are comparable is the limit case of a simple conditional; only in that case is there a one-to-one correspondence between the *Begriffsschrift* conditional and the conditional as it is usually written.

In a linear notation, on the standard reading of it, there is always a main connective; one is to understand a sentence such as 'P ⊃ (Q ⊃ R)' as a conditional whose antecedent is 'P' and whose consequent is 'Q ⊃ R'. The sentence says that either 'P' is false or 'Q ⊃ R' is true. The same thought expressed in Frege's notation, namely, does not, on our reading, say that either 'P' is false or 'Q ⊃ R' is true. Instead, it exhibits a logically complex relationship among the three sentences P, Q, and R, one that can be analyzed as saying that 'P' is false or 'if Q then R' true but can as easily be analyzed in other ways as well. As we can think of it, the array of horizontals and conditional strokes on the left in this expression constitutes a complex sentence connective, one that functions as a single unit, much as (on our second reading of the notation of arithmetic) '+' and '=' function as a single unit in the presentation of an arithmetical relation among three numbers in (say) '2 + 3 = 5'. Frege's conditional stroke, by contrast with the horseshoe, can thus be used to form *n*-adic sentence connectives of any degree of complexity one likes. The *Begriffsschrift* sentence

exhibits a logical relationship among sentences, and the sentence

similarly, exhibits a logical relationship among sentences.

Once we have learned to read Frege's notation in this way, it is easy to see, in Frege's notation, that interchanging subcomponents is permissible. Changing the order of subcomponents does need to be justified, which is why interchange of subcomponents is given as a rule in *Grundgesetze* and is proved as a theorem in *Begriffsschrift*; but in Frege's notation one such rule can cover all cases of this form of embedding. In our standard notations, by contrast, having proved that, say, '(P & Q) ⊃ R' is equivalent to '(Q & P) ⊃ R' will not save one the trouble of having also to prove that, say, 'P ⊃ ((Q & R) ⊃ S)' is equivalent to 'Q ⊃ ((R & P) ⊃ S)'. Indeed, these look, in standard notation, to be quite different sorts of cases. Where Frege has one rule and a two-dimensional notation to fix the equivalence of the four linear sentences discussed earlier, as well as all twenty variants with 'Q', 'R', and 'S' in different orders, a standard linear notation brings with it the demand that one prove, for each pair of the twenty-four sentences involved, that they are equivalent. Just by being set in a two-dimensional space as it is, Frege's conditional stroke combines in this way "logical perfection with the utmost brevity" (*CP* 236), "maximal logical precision, together with perspicuity and brevity" (*CP* 237).

The rule of contraposition in Frege's logic reinforces the point. Depending on how one carves up the judgment

into main component and subcomponents, an application of contraposition yields

(or any variant that switches '——P' and another subcomponent), or

(or the variant that switches instead

and '——S'), or

All these cases involve the application of a single rule to the original sentence variously conceived. But a sentence in our standard linear notation, as normally read, cannot be variously conceived.[6] There are no alternative perspectives to be taken on it. A logically compound sentence in standard notation has one, and only one, main connective, and each embedded sentence in turn has, at most, one main connective. As a result, the natural deduction proof of the equivalence of, say, 'P ⊃ (Q ⊃ (R ⊃ S))' and 'P ⊃ (~(R ⊃ S) ⊃ ~Q)' is quite different from the proof of the equivalence of, say, 'P ⊃ (Q ⊃ (R ⊃ S))' and 'P ⊃ (~S ⊃ (R ⊃ ~Q))'. The former "looks like" a case of contraposition; the latter does not. In the setting of our standard notation, these look to be completely different sorts of cases. In the setting of Frege's notation, it is easy to see that they are both the result of applying a single rule to a single formula.

A multiply conditioned conditional sentence of *Begriffsschrift* corresponds to an equivalence class of formulae in a standard linear notation. But as the rules of interchange of subcomponents and of contraposition reveal, even in Frege's own logical language it is possible to express one and the same thought in different ways. Frege seems to be making just this point in "A Brief Survey of My Logical Doctrines," in which he sets out a condition on two sentences being equipollent that is different from that set out in the letter to Husserl considered earlier: "two sentences *A* and *B* can stand in such a relation that anyone who recognizes the content of *A* as true must thereby also recognize the content of *B* as true and, conversely, that anyone who accepts the content of *B* must straight away accept that of *A*. (Equipollence) . . . I assume there is nothing in the content of either of the two equipollent sentences *A* and *B* that would have to be immediately accepted as true by anyone who grasped it properly" (*PW* 197). Here Frege claims that equipollence is a matter not of provable equivalence (as he suggests in the letter to Husserl) but instead of self-evident equivalence. The reason he does is that this passage occurs in the context of a discussion of his own "logical doctrines" and so presupposes his own logical language. Frege is not here talking about the logical equivalence of two sentences in, say, English or German, as he was in the letter to Husserl; he is not talking about sentences that are provably equivalent, requiring nothing other than "purely logical laws" to establish that if one is true then the other is also. Frege is talking about his own logical language; and in such a language, he claims, the equipollence of two sentences, the fact that they express one and the same thought, is manifest to anyone who understands what they express.[7]

By the criterion of equipollence set out in "A Brief Survey of My Logical Doctrines," the three sentences

express the same thought and differ only in form. Given what the conditional and negation strokes mean in *Begriffsschrift*, one could not be said to grasp the thoughts expressed by any of these sentences without recognizing that if any one is true then the others are as well. That would seem to be why, according to Frege, transitions that take one from any one of these sentences to any other are not inferences, properly speaking, at all; such transitions are not acts of reason that take one from one thought to another, but only transitions from a thought in one form to that thought in another form. As Frege puts the point in "Compound Thoughts," we can see that 'B and A' has the same sense as 'A and B' "without proof" (*CP* 393); (speaking now of 'not [A and B]' and 'not [B and A]') "this interchange should no more be regarded as a theorem here than for compounds of the first kind [that is, 'A and B' and 'B and A'], for there is no difference in sense between these expressions" (*CP* 394). In all such cases "this divergence of expressive symbol and expressed thought is an inevitable consequence of the difference between spatio-temporal phenomena and the world of thoughts" (*CP* 393). Transitions that take one from a thought in one form to that same thought in another form do need to be justified in a properly rigorous system, but they are not inferences, properly speaking, any more than the move from '2 + 3 = 5' to '5 = 2 + 3' is a calculation. Much as a proper calculation—for instance, that involved in going from '2 + 3 = 7 − 2' to '2 + 3 = 5'—requires other identities (in our example, that 7 − 2 = 5), so inferences proper require other premises.

It is easy to read Frege's conditional stroke as a notational variant of the horseshoe of standard logic and to take his elucidation of that *Begriffsschrift* sign as a truth-functional specification of its meaning. But, we have seen, the conditional stroke need not be read as a notational variant of the horseshoe; it can instead be read as something essentially two-dimensional, like a "tabular list." If, as was suggested in section 1.3, Frege's elucidations are to be read as setting out the judgeability conditions of sentences of various forms, as setting out the necessary and sufficient conditions for correctly acknowledging the truth of the contents they express, then Frege's elucidations of the conditional stroke can be read as setting out not the meaning of that sign but only the necessary and sufficient conditions for acknowledging the truth of the thought expressed by a sentence that contains it. Frege writes in *Begriffsschrift* §5:

stands for the judgment that the third of these possibilities [the possibility that A is denied and B affirmed] does not occur, but one of the other three does.

In *Grundgesetze* §12 the conditional stroke is introduced with the stipulation that the value of the two-place function

"shall be the False if the True be taken as ζ-argument and any object other than the True be taken as ξ-argument, and that in all other cases the value of the function shall be the True."[8] What these elucidations provide, on our reading, is not the meaning of the conditional stroke but only the circumstances in which a *Begriffsschrift* conditional sentence is true, that is, the conditions under which it is correct to acknowledge the truth of the thought expressed by a conditional sentence of *Begriffsschrift* (on its own merits, not as the conclusion of an inference). It does not follow from the mere fact that in these passages Frege sets out necessary and sufficient conditions for the truth of a *Begriffsschrift* conditional that Frege thinks that what *Begriffsschrift* conditionals express are truth conditions as they are normally understood, that conditionals in his logic are merely notational variants of conditionals of our standard logics. In his elucidation Frege does set out necessary and sufficient conditions for the truth, and hence judgeability, of a *Begriffsschrift* conditional; on the reading pursued here, only its role in inference can fully reveal the thought it expresses.

2.3 *Begriffsschrift* Latin Italic Letters

According to our reading, sentences of *Begriffsschrift* exhibit logical relations. In simple sentences such as '——Lrj', objects and concepts are exhibited in logical relations, for instance, here, the relation of subsumption; in conditionals it is whole thoughts that are exhibited in logical relations. Both sorts of sentences are variously analyzable. But such sentences are not Frege's primary concern. As was suggested in Chapter 1, what are of utmost importance to Frege are the laws that govern modes of inference where such laws take the form of generalized conditionals. We need an account of such sentences. In particular, we need an account of *Begriffsschrift* generalized conditionals expressed using Frege's Latin italic letters. For, we will see, although *Begriffsschrift* generalized conditionals can be expressed using either Frege's Latin italic letters or his concavity and German letters, only the former sorts of expressions are "suitable to do duty in inference" (*GG* §17).

Frege's two different ways of expressing generality, one using Latin italic letters and one using the concavity and German letters, are equivalent at least to this extent: given a generality expressed using Latin italic letters, one may make the transition to the corresponding generality expressed using the concavity with widest scope, and conversely, from a generality expressed using the concavity with widest scope one may infer the corresponding generality using italic letters. That is, the transition

$$\vdash F(x)$$
$$\vdash\!\!\!\!-\!\!\overset{\mathfrak{a}}{\frown}\!\!-\, F(\mathfrak{a})$$

is valid in Frege's logic; it is legitimated by one of Frege's few fundamental rules (*PW* 39; *BGS* §11; *GG* §17). Similarly, the judgment

$$\vdash\!\!\begin{array}{c} \rule{1cm}{0.4pt}\, f(x) \\ \rule{0.5cm}{0.4pt}\overset{\mathfrak{a}}{\frown}\!\!-\, f(\mathfrak{a}) \end{array}$$

is a fundamental law of Frege's logic (Formula 58 of *Begriffsschrift* and Basic Law IIa in *Grundgesetze*). Inferentially, then, the two formulations are equivalent in the sense that anything that is (directly) provable from the one is (indirectly) provable from the other. Logically, on our reading, they are nonetheless very different.[9]

On the standard reading, Frege's concavity with German letters is his sign for the universal quantifier, the *Begriffsschrift* sentence

$$-\!\!\overset{\mathfrak{a}}{\frown}\!\!\begin{array}{c} \rule{0.5cm}{0.4pt}\, F(\mathfrak{a}) \\ \rule{0.5cm}{0.4pt}\, G(\mathfrak{a}) \end{array}$$

is taken to be merely a notational variant of '$(\forall x)(Gx \supset Fx)$' as usually understood, and Frege's rule and axiom are held to provide introduction and elimination rules for the universal quantifier. According to this reading,

Begriffsschrift Latin italic letters and German letters function as free (or, as Russell calls them, real) and bound (apparent) variables, respectively. Russell explains the difference between these variables—a difference that was, he thinks, "first emphasized by Frege"—as follows:[10]

> Given a statement containing a variable *x*, say '*x* = *x*', we may affirm that this holds in all instances, or we may affirm any one of the instances without deciding as to which instance we are affirming. The distinction is roughly the same as that between the general and particular enunciation in Euclid. The general enunciation tells us something about (say) all triangles, while the particular enunciation takes one triangle, and asserts the same thing of this one triangle. But the triangle taken is *any* triangle, not some one special triangle; and thus although, throughout the proof, only one triangle is dealt with, yet the proof retains its generality.

Suppose, for instance, one wished to prove that $(\forall x)\psi x$ given that $(\forall x)(\phi x \supset \psi x)$ and that $(\forall x)\phi x$. One could not draw the inference directly, for what '$(\forall x)\phi x$' means is that the propositional function ϕx is (as Russell puts it) *always* true, and what '$(\forall x)(\phi x \supset \psi x)$' means is that ϕx *always* implies ψx. "In order to make our inference, we must go from 'ϕx is always true' to 'ϕx', and from 'ϕx always implies ψx' to 'ϕx implies ψx', where the *x*, while remaining any possible argument, is to be the same in both."[11] That is, we must replace the apparent variables in the quantified sentences that serve as premises with real variables that function as ambiguous object names. This gives us an instance of each of the two generalities, or, as Russell puts it, "an undetermined one of all the propositions resulting from supposing [*x*] to be this or that [ϕ]."[12] Once this has been done, the inference can be drawn by *modus ponens*. Real variables are thus essential in logic as Russell understands it. One needs to be able to introduce an arbitrary instance in order legitimately to apply rules of inference, for instance, *modus ponens,* to a generalized conditional. What one proves for this instance is then taken to hold generally—so that at the end of the proof one may pass back from real to apparent variables—on the grounds that no inference is drawn in the course of the proof that could not equally well have been drawn were any other instance in the relevant class to have been considered instead. One reasons, in other words, about a particular case, but because no feature that this case does not share with all the other cases of the relevant kind is appealed to in the course of the proof, what is proven for that one case can be taken to be true generally for all members of the class. One needs real variables as well as apparent variables in such a logic because "*all deduction operates with real variables* (or with constants)."[13]

In §17 of *Grundgesetze* Frege might seem to be making essentially the same point:

from the two sentences,
  "All square roots of 1 are fourth roots of 1"
and
  "All fourth roots of 1 are eighth roots of 1"
we can infer
  "All square roots of 1 are eighth roots of 1".
Now if we write the premisses in this way:

$$\text{``} \vdash_{\!\!\!\!\!\overset{\alpha}{\phantom{.}}} \left[\begin{array}{l} \alpha^4 = 1 \text{''} \\ \alpha^2 = 1 \end{array}\right. \qquad \text{and} \qquad \text{``} \vdash_{\!\!\!\!\!\overset{\alpha}{}} \left[\begin{array}{l} \alpha^8 = 1 \text{''} \\ \alpha^4 = 1 \end{array}\right.$$

then we cannot apply our methods of inference. We can, however, if we write them thus:

$$\text{``} \vdash \left[\begin{array}{l} x^4 = 1 \text{''} \\ x^2 = 1 \end{array}\right. \qquad \text{and} \qquad \text{``} \vdash \left[\begin{array}{l} x^8 = 1 \text{''} \\ x^4 = 1 \end{array}\right.$$

Here we have a case of §15. (*GG* §17)

The relevant rule in §15 is this:

from the two propositions

$$\text{``} \vdash \left[\begin{array}{l} \Gamma \text{''} \\ \Delta\,(\alpha \end{array}\right. \qquad \text{and} \qquad \text{``} \vdash \left[\begin{array}{l} \Delta \text{''} \\ \Theta\,(\delta \end{array}\right.$$

we may infer the proposition

$$\text{``} \vdash \left[\begin{array}{l} \Gamma \text{''} \\ \Theta. \end{array}\right.$$

Now Frege uses uppercase Greek letters to stand for objects in his elucidations, truth-values, for instance, though it is left undetermined which are designated.[14] (Because these letters have a role to play only in Frege's elucidations, no logical difficulty attaches to the fact that these signs have no determinate meaning.) Because uppercase Greek letters stand for objects, the rule given in §15 would appear to be the rule of hypothetical syllogism; that is, it applies to conditionals, sentences that have sentences designating truth-values in antecedent and consequent. A sentence such as '$x^4 = 1$' occurring to the right of a content stroke would have a truth-value, however, just if 'x' designated an object. Hence if the inference

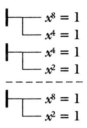

is indeed a case of the rule given in §15, then, it would seem, the quasi-sentences listed on the right must have truth-values. But then the occurrences of 'x' in these sentences must designate an individual, though it is left undetermined which one: "what we need here is the notion of a *simultaneous assignment* of objects to free variables in different propositions."[15] If that is right then Frege's Latin italic letters are functioning as free variables.

It is easy to read *Grundgesetze* §17 as making Russell's claim that free (real) variables are needed in logic because without them the logic of truth-functions could not be brought to bear on logically general sentences. Other passages can seem to reinforce the point. But there is also a great deal of evidence in Frege's writings that contrary to his claim in *Begriffsschrift* that his Latin italic letters serve "to signify various things" (*BGS* §1), *Begriffsschrift* Latin italic letters do not function as free variables. First, and most generally, it is Latin italic letters and not the concavity with German letters that are, for Frege, the primary, and most natural, vehicle for the expression of logical generality. Latin italic letters used in the expression of generality are first introduced in *Begriffsschrift* §1; only much later, in §11, does the concavity make its first appearance. The concavity is needed, Frege says in that later section, because *"it delimits the scope {Gebiet} of the generality signified by the letter."*[16] In the long Boole essay written shortly after *Begriffsschrift*, Frege again introduces generality, as marked by his Latin italic letters, before making any mention of his concavity. The exposition has essentially the same structure in *Grundgesetze:* in §8 it is noted, first, that a generality is distinguished from a statement of particular fact by the presence of letters that indicate *(andeute)* in addition to those symbols that signify *(bedeute)* particular objects and concepts; "but," Frege goes on, "by this stipulation the scope of the generality would not be well enough demarcated."[17] The point is made again in "On the Aim": "the purpose of the letter *x* is to make the whole judgment general in the sense that the content should hold whatever one may put in for *x* . . . It is sometimes necessary to confine the generality to a part of the judgment. Then I make use of German instead of italic letters" (*CN* 99). Similarly, we read in the "Introduction to Logic" (*PW* 190), first, that "letters . . . , like the '*a*' in our example, serve to confer generality of content upon a sentence," and only four pages later, in a note, that "in order to be able to narrow the scope over which the generality extends, I make use of gothic [that is, German] letters, and with these the concavity demarcates the scope" (*PW* 194 n). Were Frege's Latin italic letters functioning as free variables, they would not be spoken of in this way, as the principal vehicle for the expression of generality.

For the purposes of inference, a conditional that contains a variable in antecedent and consequent (and no other signs of generality) must be understood to be at once logically singular and ambiguous. It must be taken to be singular because otherwise the logic of truth-functions could not be brought to bear on it; but it must also, for the purposes of proof of a generality, be conceived as systematically ambiguous, or, as Russell puts it, "absolutely ambiguous."[18] It must refer to a particular object, but nevertheless to no object in particular. We have already seen that Frege at first writes as if Latin italic letters of *Begriffsschrift* function in just this way. He claims in §1 of *Begriffsschrift*: "I therefore divide all the symbols I employ into *those which one can take to signify various things* and *those which have a completely fixed sense.*" Frege also uses a variable name in his example in *Begriffsschrift* §8 to show why the identity sign is needed in logic.[19] In his later writings, however, Frege seems explicitly and categorically to reject the idea of such ambiguous symbols in logic: "it is absolutely ruled out that a sign be equivocal or ambiguous" (*PW* 237). "Where they do not stand for an unknown, *letters* in arithmetic have the role of conferring generality of content on sentences, not of designating a variable number; for there are no variable numbers" (*PW* 237). Nor do there seem to be any variable names, any variables, in Frege's logic on his mature understanding of it:[20] "we may perhaps seek a way out by taking the view that the letters '*x*' and '*y*' are not signs for what is variable, but are themselves the things that vary. But if we do this, we run foul of the established use of our signs" (*PW* 238); "we cannot even say that although '*a*' is not given a determinate meaning, nevertheless it is given an indeterminate one—for an indeterminate meaning is not a meaning. There must be no ambiguous signs"

(*CP* 311). In a properly logical language, Frege comes to think, a designating symbol, whether it be an object name, a concept word, or a sign for a logical function, must designate something—that is, some *one* thing—in particular. Free variables do not designate some one thing in particular, and they cannot if they are to play their logical role in proofs of universally quantified sentences.

Latin italic letters of *Begriffsschrift*, Frege comes to think, have a role that fundamentally contrasts with the role of designating symbols. Whereas an object name or concept word "has its own specific meaning" (*BGS* §1)—that is, it designates something, some particular object in the case of an object name and a certain concept in the case of a concept word—a Latin italic letter only "indicates an object, it does not have a meaning, it designates or means nothing" (*PW* 190). An italic letter "simply does not have the purpose of designating a number, as does a number sign; or for that matter of designating anything at all" (*CP* 307). "These letters . . . are not at all intended to designate numbers, concepts, relations, or some function or other; rather they are intended only to indicate so as to lend generality of content to the propositions in which they occur" (*CP* 306). A Latin italic letter of *Begriffsschrift* does not designate indeterminately or arbitrarily, for it does not designate at all. Nor does it have a sense: "a sign which only indicates neither designates anything nor has a sense" (*PW* 249)—though, as Frege immediately goes on, that "is not yet to say it could not contribute to the expression of a thought. It can do this by conferring generality of content on a simple sentence or on one made up of sentences."

But, it will be objected, Frege's concavity with German letter also serves to confer generality of content, and in that case too the letters involved only indicate. Because, as Frege clearly recognizes, the concavity is needed in all but the special case in which the generality has widest scope, it surely is really the concavity that is the principal sign for generality in *Begriffsschrift,* just as the universal quantifier is the principal sign for generality in any standard quantificational logic. Expressing generality by using Latin italic letters in the case in which the generality has widest scope is, as Frege himself says, merely an abbreviation. Because Frege takes this view even in *Grundgesetze,* it can seem clear that, contrary to the view we have begun to outline here, his concavity with German letter functions in just the way a universal quantifier does. The crucial question, however, is whether, on Frege's most carefully considered, overall view, his concavity with German letters and his Latin italic letters function, respectively, as universal quan-

tifiers and as free (or implicitly universally bound) variables. Frege himself
notes in the 1906 "Introduction to Logic" that "it was not until after
some time" that he himself became "aware of this use [that is, his own use
of German letters] as a special case" (*PW* 195 n to p. 194). On our reading, this is exactly right. Coming to clarity about the exact logical relationship between his two means of expressing generality in *Begriffsschrift* was
not at all easy for Frege, and as we will see in more detail in section 3.3, it
was not easy because that relationship is obscured in all but the most complex of cases. In the simplest cases, that is, in just those cases one is liable
to have in mind in any initial explication of the notation, the use of the
concavity notation as a special case, and so its real logical function, is essentially invisible. Frege does often describe his notation for generality in
ways suggestive of a Russellian reading, at least to anyone already familiar
with that logic, but he also often describes that notation in ways that are
incompatible with that reading. It is the latter passages we focus on here,
and we do so because, *all* texts considered, it is the latter passages rather
than the former that seem best to reflect Frege's most considered views.

On Frege's considered view, Latin italic letters have neither sense nor
meaning. They do not designate indeterminately; they do not designate at
all. Their role is to confer generality of content. The way they play this role
is indicated, if only in a preliminary way, by the fact that, according to
Frege, an expression such as (say) '*a* is greater than 2', taken out of the
context of a conditional in which it occurs as the antecedent or consequent, is senseless.

> We cannot . . . split up the sentence expressing the general thought
> without making the parts senseless. For the letter '*a*' is meant to con-
> fer generality of content upon the whole sentence, not on its clauses.
> With '*a* is greater than 2' we no longer have a part expressing a
> thought: it neither expresses a thought that is true nor one that is
> false, because '*a*' is neither meant to designate an object as does a
> proper name, nor to confer generality of content upon this part. It
> has no function at all in relation to the part. (*PW* 190; see also *CP*
> 308–311 and *PMC* 21)

If '*a*' were functioning as a variable, it would have a function in relation to
the part; indeed, that is the essential role of a variable, to confer content
on the part in a way that enables the logic of truth-functions to be applied
to a sentence containing it. Yet Frege denies that his Latin italic letters
function in this way. On his view, a conditional written using Latin italic

letters "expresses a single thought which cannot be divided into component thoughts" (*CP* 309; see also *CP* 171). Because they have no function at all in relation to the part, because they serve to confer generality only over a (conditional) sentence as a whole, Latin italic letters of *Begriffsschrift* seem not to be functioning as variables.

The logical role of Latin italic letters, as Frege understands them, is further indicated by the fact that they are modeled on the literal notation in arithmetic: "the most immediate point of contact between my formula language and that of arithmetic is the way the letters are used" (*BGS* 104). In *Begriffsschrift* itself Frege only illustrates the use of letters as they contrast with signifying symbols in arithmetic:

> the symbols customarily used in the general theory of magnitudes fall into two kinds. The first consists of the letters, each of which represents either a number left undetermined or a function left undetermined. This indeterminateness makes it possible to use letters for the expression of the general validity of propositions, as in
>
> $$(a + b)c = ac + bc.$$
>
> The other kind consists of such symbols as $+$, $-$, $\sqrt{}$, 0, 1, 2; each of which has its own specific meaning. (*BGS* §1)

Frege's thought is to *"adopt this fundamental idea of distinguishing two kinds of symbols"* and to use letters "for the expression of *generality*." But how exactly are we to read the sentence '$(a + b)c = ac + bc$'? Only much later, in "Function and Concept" and some notes written in 1910 in response to remarks by Jourdain, does Frege suggest an answer. Jourdain had written that "in universal algebra, as Russell has pointed out, . . . our signs of operation have variable meanings" (*PMC* 182). Frege responds:

> if, for example, we wish to investigate what follows from the laws $a + (b + c) = (a + b) + c$ and $(a + b) + c = (a + c) + b$ *quite independently of the usual denotation of the sign of addition*, one ought wholly to avoid the word 'addition' and the sign '$+$' and express the laws thus: $f\{a,f(b,c)\} = f\{f(a,b),c\}$ and $f\{f(a,b),c\} = f\{f(a,c),b\}$. *Now the letter 'f' serves to make the consideration general.* (*PMC* 182; emphasis added)

What Frege seems to have in mind can be illustrated for the simpler case in which it is object names (rather than function symbols) that are replaced by letters. Suppose that one wished to investigate what other sorts of arithmetical expressions may be put *salva veritate* for the expression '(2 + 3)(4 + 5)' in an arithmetical formula "quite independently of the usual denotation" of the signs '2', '3', '4', and '5'. One wishes to investigate, that is, not the particular case but, as it were, cases of this form. One wishes "to make the consideration general," so one writes instead '(a + b)(c + d)'. But now what should one do? In the particular case the task is obvious. Assuming that one knows one's basic arithmetical facts, one knows just what to do: add two and three to yield five, and four and five to yield nine, then multiply five and nine to yield the answer, forty-five. In the general case the problem is very different. One cannot add a and b, or c and d, for these signs do not designate any numbers. Because they do not, solving the problem set by '(a + b)(c + d)' requires fundamentally different resources from those needed to solve '(2 + 3)(4 + 5)'; it requires appeal to features of the functions of addition and multiplication themselves, not to the values they give for particular arguments. Having only the operations of addition and multiplication to go on, one discovers, say, that $(a + b)(c + d) = ac + bc + ad + bd$. As the manner of its derivation makes manifest, this law of arithmetic holds no matter what numerals are put in the place of the letters. Whereas in the numerical case one discovers a truth about numbers—that the sum of two and three times the sum of four and five is equal to forty-five—in the algebraic case one discovers a truth about arithmetical functions, that the product of two sums equals the sum of four products. In the algebraic case, numbers do not come into it at all; the sentence is directly about functions. Making the consideration general in this way pushes our thinking up a level, from consideration of numbers to consideration of functions. Just this point is made in Frege's closing remarks in "Function and Concept" (*CP* 155–156). To replace function symbols with letters, as Frege does in his remarks to Jourdain, is to move things up another level again; in that case one's concern is with second-level functions, and with the laws that involve them.[21]

In the late fragment "Logical Generality" Frege again appeals to the use of the literal notation in arithmetic to clarify the logical role of Latin italic letters in *Begriffsschrift*:

It is natural to copy the methods of arithmetic by selecting letters for indefinitely indicating parts of a sentence:
'If a is a man, a is a mortal.'
Here the equiform letters cross-refer to one another. Instead of let-

ters equiform with '*a*' we could just as well take ones equiform with
'*b*' or '*c*'. But it is essential that they should be equiform. However,
taken strictly, we are stepping outside the confines of a spoken language designed to be heard and moving into the region of a written
or printed language designed for the eye . . . The language we have
just indicated . . . contains two different *constituents: those with the
form of words and the* individual *letters.* The former correspond to
words of the spoken language, the latter have an indefinitely indicating role. (*PW* 260)

Indicating letters, Frege says, do not have the form of words; they are not
meaningful bits of language, as designating symbols are; their role is essentially different from the role played by words. This role, we are furthermore told, is one that can be played only in a written language, a language
designed for the eye, because all that matters to the proper functioning of
indicating letters is that they be equiform. We could, that is, use any sort
of meaningless squiggles we like as indicating letters, so long as they were
equiform. Frege's indicating letters are in this respect quite like our schematic letters. Nevertheless, unlike schematic letters, such letters contribute to the expression of a thought, and they do so, we have suggested,
by pushing everything up a level. Conferring generality of content on a
Begriffsschrift conditional by replacing an object name that occurs in the
main component and subcomponent(s) with a Latin italic letter enables
the expression of a logical relation among concepts.

The general point that genuine hypotheticals express relations among
concepts is first made in the long Boole essay (*PW* 18) and again in
Grundlagen §47:

It is true that at first sight the proposition
  "All whales are mammals"
seems to be not about concepts but about animals; but if we ask
which animal then are we speaking of, we are unable to point to any
one in particular. Even supposing a whale is before us, our proposition still does not state anything about it. We cannot infer from it that
the animal before us is a mammal without the additional premiss that
it is a whale, as to which our proposition says nothing. As a general
principle, it is impossible to speak of an object without in some way
designating or naming it; but the word "whale" is not the name of
any individual creature . . . However true it may be that our proposition can only be verified by observing particular animals, that proves

nothing as to its content; to decide what it is about, we do not need to know whether it is true or not, nor for what reasons we believe it to be true.

Aside from the conditional and horizontal strokes, the only designating symbols in the *Begriffsschrift* rendering of the judgment that all whales are mammals,

$$\vdash \!\!\!\begin{array}{l} \rule{0.5cm}{0.4pt}\; M(x) \\ \rule{0.5cm}{0.4pt}\; W(x), \end{array}$$

are the two concept words 'Wξ' and 'Mξ'. The sentence contains no object names; so, Frege suggests, it is not about any particular animals, or any other objects. The fact that the proposition is verified only by consideration of actual animals does not imply that reference to animals (or, for that matter, any other objects) is somehow involved in its content: "the question of how we arrive at the content of a judgment should be kept distinct from the other question, Whence do we derive the justification for its assertion?" (*GL* §3).

Again, we read in "Logic in Mathematics" (1914): "we must not think that I mean to assert something about an African chieftain from darkest Africa who is wholly unknown to me, when I say 'All men are mortal'. I am not saying anything about either this man or that man, but I am subordinating the concept man to the concept of what is mortal" (*PW* 213). As Frege understands it, the generalized conditional that is expressed in English as 'all men are mortal' does not say that everything that falls under the concept *man* falls also under the concept *mortal*. It instead subordinates one concept to another. Objects do not come into it at all—though, of course, given that there is a logical relationship of subordination between the two concepts *man* and *mortal*, then it follows that all actual men are mortal. If anywhere (any when) there was a man who was not mortal, this would be sufficient to show not only that the matter of factual generality, that all men are mortal, is false, but also that the concepts *man* and *mortal* are not related by subordination. Nevertheless, the generality itself, Frege suggests, in no way involves reference to objects. A genuine hypothetical exhibits two concepts in the logical relation of subordination. If that is right, then Latin italic letters function together with the conditional stroke to enable the expression of logical relations among concepts, and they do so much as (on our second reading of the formula language of arithmetic) '+' and '=' function together in, for instance, '2 + 3 = 5' to enable the expression of an arithmetical relation among numbers, one that can be analyzed in various ways.

In order to prove, in standard modern logic, that all As are C given that all As are B and that all Bs are C, one must first turn to an arbitrary instance of something that is B if A, and thereby to a hypothetical judgment whose main connective is a horseshoe. Only then can the rules of the propositional calculus be applied. In effect, for the purposes of reasoning, categorical sentences are reduced to hypotheticals. The Boolean pursues the converse strategy of assimilating hypotheticals to categoricals. As Frege puts the point, "Boole construes the hypothetical judgment 'If B, then A' as a case of the subordination of concepts, by saying 'the class of time instants at which B is included in the class of time instants at which A'" (*PW* 15). According to Boole, we are to understand a hypothetical syllogism as a case of *barbara*. Both the quantificational logician and the Boolean thus see a similarity in underlying form in the two cases; the strategy in both cases is to take one argument form to be the basic one and to fit the other somehow into that mold.[22] Frege's way, on our reading, is different from both.

Frege suggests in *Grundgesetze* §17 that just as

from the two propositions

"$\vdash\!\!\!\begin{array}{l}\rule{1.5em}{0.4pt}\ \Gamma \\ \rule{1.5em}{0.4pt}\ \Delta\ (\alpha\end{array}$" and "$\vdash\!\!\!\begin{array}{l}\rule{1.5em}{0.4pt}\ \Delta \\ \rule{1.5em}{0.4pt}\ \Theta\ (\delta\end{array}$"

we may infer the proposition

"$\vdash\!\!\!\begin{array}{l}\rule{1.5em}{0.4pt}\ \Gamma \\ \rule{1.5em}{0.4pt}\ \Theta\end{array}$ (*GG* §15),

so from the two propositions

$\vdash\!\!\!\begin{array}{l}\rule{1.5em}{0.4pt}\ x^4 = 1 \\ \rule{1.5em}{0.4pt}\ x^2 = 1\end{array}$ and $\vdash\!\!\!\begin{array}{l}\rule{1.5em}{0.4pt}\ x^8 = 1 \\ \rule{1.5em}{0.4pt}\ x^4 = 1\end{array}$

we may infer the proposition

$\vdash\!\!\!\begin{array}{l}\rule{1.5em}{0.4pt}\ x^8 = 1 \\ \rule{1.5em}{0.4pt}\ x^2 = 1.\end{array}$

But, it seemed, the latter could be an instance of the former only if 'x' was functioning as a variable, that is, as a designating symbol though it is left undetermined what is designated. For only so, we reasoned, could the expressions '$x^2 = 1$', '$x^4 = 1$', and '$x^8 = 1$' be taken to stand for objects, as required for the application of the rule in §15. But, we have since seen, Frege comes explicitly to hold that 'x' has no role to play in relation to the part. On Frege's mature view, *Begriffsschrift* judgments such as

$$\models \begin{array}{l} x^8 = 1 \\ x^2 = 1 \end{array}$$

do not express relations among thoughts (or truth-values); for, again, such a sentence "expresses a single thought which cannot be divided into component thoughts" (*CP* 309). That thought, furthermore, is a thought about concepts, that one concept is subordinate to another. If, then, the inference

$$
\begin{array}{l}
\models \begin{array}{l} x^8 = 1 \\ x^4 = 1 \end{array} \\
\models \begin{array}{l} x^4 = 1 \\ x^2 = 1 \end{array} \\
\hline
\models \begin{array}{l} x^8 = 1 \\ x^2 = 1 \end{array}
\end{array}
$$

is an instance of the rule in §15, it is so not in virtue of the (presumed) role the conditional stroke and variables play in *Begriffsschrift* (as on the standard reading) but instead in virtue of the fact that the conditional stroke together with *Begriffsschrift* Latin italic letters enables the expression of relations among concepts. *Barbara,* on this view, is an inference form that functions at the level of concepts (much as the traditional term logician argues), and hypothetical syllogism is an inference form that functions at the level of whole sentences or truth-values (much as the quantificational logician argues). What Frege shows (on our reading) is that these are nonetheless inferences of the same fundamental form. His official formulation of the rule that governs these inferences makes exactly this point: "If the same combination of signs occurs in one proposition as main component and in another as subcomponent, a proposition may be inferred in which the main component of the second is main component, and all subcomponents of either, save the one mentioned, are subcomponents. But subcomponents occurring in both need be written only once" (*GG* §15).

From the perspective of the reading pursued here, to take a genuine hypothetical of Frege's logic to express a relation between two quasi-sentences is fundamentally to misunderstand the role played by Latin italic letters in Frege's logic. In genuine hypotheticals Latin italic letters function together with the conditional stroke to enable the expression of relations among concepts. They do not, in such sentences, belong with the concept words as if the conditional stroke then related two quasi-sentences; they belong instead with the conditional stroke to enable the expression of a relation between two concepts. Though it is made at the level of relations of concepts rather than at the level of relations of truth-values, an inference in *barbara*, in Frege's logic, is an inference of precisely the form given in the rule of §15. Given the way Latin italic letters function to lend generality of content in this logic, nothing is needed to play the role that is played by real variables in Russell's logic. In Frege's logic, as in a traditional term logic, one infers directly from the sentences 'all square roots of 1 are fourth roots of 1' and 'all fourth roots of 1 are eighth roots of 1' to the conclusion 'all square roots of 1 are eighth roots of 1'. One can do this because what genuine hypotheticals express are not relations among sentences (or thoughts or truth-values) but instead relations among concepts.

2.4 The Diversity of Logical Relations

We saw in section 2.2 that Frege's two-dimensional conditional stroke enables the formation of expressions for logical relations of arbitrary complexity among (as we might put it, not, strictly speaking, correctly) sentences.[23] A simple conditional such as

$$\begin{array}{c} \vphantom{} \\ \end{array}$$
```
──┬─ A
  └─ B
```

exhibits a logical relation, and in just the same way a logically complex sentence such as

exhibits a logical relation. But such sentences seem to be of interest to Frege only indirectly. Insofar as his primary concern is with the laws that govern modes of inference, which are expressed in *Begriffsschrift* as generalized conditionals, that is, as genuine hypotheticals, mere hypothetical

compounds such as the sentences just given are of interest primarily because, in conjunction with indicating letters lending generality of content,
they can be used in the expression of relations among concepts. The significance of the two-dimensional conditional stroke lies in the fact that it
"[enables] us to designate the subordination of a concept under a concept,
and other important relations" (*GG* §12). A generalized conditional of
Begriffsschrift, something of the form

$$\vdash\!\!\!\!\!\begin{array}{l} \rule{0.6cm}{0.4pt}\ M(x) \\ \rule{0.6cm}{0.4pt}\ N(x), \end{array}$$

exhibits the concepts Mξ and Nξ in a relation of subordination. It shows
that whatever falls under the concept N is correctly judged to be also M
and in this way gives "as a formula" the rule of (material) inference that if
one judges of something that it is N, one is entitled to infer that that same
object is M. Furthermore, just as one can form sentence connectives of arbitrary logical complexity in *Begriffsschrift* as we read it here, so one can
form connectives of arbitrary complexity among concepts. The *Begriffsschrift* judgment

$$\vdash\!\!\!\!\!\begin{array}{l} \rule{0.6cm}{0.4pt}\ M(x) \\ \rule{0.6cm}{0.4pt}\ N(x) \end{array}$$

exhibits the concepts designated by 'Mξ' and 'Nξ' in the logical relation of
subordination. The *Begriffsschrift* judgment

similarly exhibits a logical relation among the two concepts designated.
The sentence shows these concepts in a certain second-level logical relation (in this case, one that holds of any two first-level concepts), and it
does so in a way that enables one to take various perspectives on the sentence as required for understanding the goodness of judgments and inferences. The fundamental expressive significance of Frege's Latin italic letters so understood is to preserve, in this way, the peculiar expressive power
of his two-dimensional conditional stroke for the case of relations among
concepts. Frege's Latin italic letters achieve their expressive purpose by
moving everything up a level, from consideration of objects and their

properties and relations to consideration of concepts and their properties and relations.

On this reading, Frege's logical language functions as a fundamentally different kind of language from that of quantificational logic. Rather than directly saying something about something, *Begriffsschrift* sentences display objects, concepts, and truth-values in logical relations of various kinds and can be analyzed in various ways.[24] In simple sentences such as '——Lrj', objects and concepts are exhibited in logical relations, for instance, the relation of subsumption. In conditional sentences such as

truth-values, the *Bedeutungen* of sentences, are exhibited in other logical relations, relations that can be arbitrarily complex in virtue of the distinctive way Frege's conditional and horizontal strokes can be combined. In genuine hypotheticals, that is, generalized conditionals expressed using Frege's Latin italic letters, it is concepts and relations that are exhibited in logical relations, for instance, the relation of subordination. None of these sorts of sentences are to be read as saying that the relevant objects and concepts stand in those logical relations; they are only exhibited as standing in those relations. What is presented says something about something, that is, involves a function and argument(s), only relative to an analysis. As we read *Begriffsschrift*, there is no essential logical difference between reading '——Lrj' as ascribing the second-level property *property of Romeo,* $\Phi(r)$, to the first-level concept $L\xi j$ and reading it as ascribing the first-level relation $L\xi\zeta$ to the (ordered) objects Romeo and Juliet. A multiply conditioned conditional of *Begriffsschrift,* similarly, can be read (analyzed) in various ways; in the conditional itself, there is no main connective. As we have just seen, Frege's Latin italic letters can be taken to function in conjunction with the conditional stroke to enable the point to be applied in conditionals (of arbitrary complexity) that are generalized. On this reading, generalized conditionals of *Begriffsschrift* expressed using Latin italic letters exhibit concepts in logical relations of arbitrary complexity in a way that is strictly analogous to the way mere conditionals exhibit sentences (or truth-values) in logical relations of arbitrary complexity. In both cases, as in the case of a table or tabular list, there are many different (one-dimensional) paths one can take through the two-dimensional array. We know already from the quantificational case that simple sentences such as

'Lrj' must be variously analyzable to account for the goodness of the variety of inferences in which they can figure. In Frege's logic the point is generalized to the case of multiply embedded truth-functions and, through the use of Latin italic letters, even to generalized (multiply conditioned) conditionals.

But even these features of Frege's logic do not exhaust its extraordinary expressive power. Indeed, they only scratch the surface. Much as the full expressive power of quantificational logic is revealed only in sentences that involve both universal and existential quantifiers, so the full expressive power of Frege's logical language is revealed only in sentences that employ both the concavity notation and German letters, and Latin italic letters lending generality of content. We turn now to an account of such sentences.

3

A More Sophisticated Instrument

> We are very dependent on external aids in our thinking, and there is no doubt that the language of everyday life . . . had first to be replaced by a more sophisticated instrument before certain distinctions could be noticed. But so far the academic world has, for the most part, disdained to master this instrument.
>
> —"INTRODUCTION TO LOGIC," 1906

Although Frege's notation remained essentially unchanged from its first introduction in 1879 to the end of Frege's life in 1925, Frege's understanding of that notation was radically revised. The best-known revisions concern the distinction between *Sinn* and *Bedeutung* first introduced in 1891, but as already indicated, there are others as well. First, the distinction between concept and object comes to be "characterized more sharply" in the mature logic, and "from this results further the distinction between first- and second-level functions" (*GG* 7). In *Begriffsschrift* Frege had characterized a function (concept) as that part of an expression "that shows itself invariant [under replacement]" (*BGS* §9); in the mature logic a first-level concept is conceived instead as a law of correlation that maps objects onto truth-values. A second-level concept is similarly a law of correlation, one from first-level concepts to truth-values. The difference between generalities expressed using Frege's Latin italic letters and those expressed using the concavity and German letters is also clarified. Whereas in *Begriffsschrift* Frege had claimed that the concavity is merely a means of delimiting the scope of a generality, that in the case in which the generality has widest scope the sentence can be abbreviated by means of his Latin italic letters, in the *Grundgesetze* logic of 1893 the two means of expressing generality are logically distinguished, and by the late 1890s the distinctive expressive role played by the concavity is fully comprehended. Finally, and in part as a result of these developments, Frege's conception of the nature and status of the laws of logic is also fundamentally revised. The laws of logic are not merely maximally general, as Frege seems at first to have thought; nor are they peculiarly formal, as is suggested in *Grundlagen*.

The laws of logic, like any other laws, have their own content; what is distinctive about them is that they concern higher-level concepts and relations. Already in the notation of the 1879 logic Frege unerringly draws the distinctions that are needed in his logic; only in the mature logic are these distinctions adequately comprehended. It is to this fine structure of Frege's "more sophisticated instrument" that we now turn.

3.1 The Advance from Level to Level

In "Function and Concept," read before the *Jenaische Gesellschaft für Medicin und Naturwissenschaft* on 9 January 1891 and published that same year, Frege first presents what he describes as "some supplementations and new conceptions, whose necessity has occurred to me since then," that is, since Frege had last presented a paper on *Begriffsschrift* before the society (*CP* 137).[1] The essay begins and ends by recalling the history of arithmetic, the advance from level to level that culminates in an adequate conception of the concept of a function. As Frege outlines that history, it has three principal stages. First, people calculated with individual numbers to produce theorems such as that $2 + 3 = 5$, that $2 \times 3 = 6$, and so on. "Then they went on to more general laws that hold good for all numbers. What corresponds to this in symbolism is the transition to the literal notation" (*CP* 155–156). That is, they began to formulate the basic and derived laws of elementary algebra. The last level is reached with the formulation of laws in higher analysis, which hold good for all functions, and the introduction of letters that serve to indicate functions indefinitely. Because, according to Frege, "the first place where a scientific expression appears with a clear-cut meaning is where it is required for a law" (*CP* 137–138), it is only at this third stage that we achieve an adequate conception of arithmetical functions. But a concept, on Frege's mature view, just is a function; it is a law of correlation whose value is always a truth-value. A similar account, then, ought to be formulable for developments in the science of logic, not an actual history perhaps, but a rational reconstruction of advances in that science highlighting the fundamental conceptions and transformations that are required to realize a logically adequate language. This reconstruction will serve to introduce all the main themes at issue here.

We begin with a very primitive language, Sellars's Jumblese, a language that contains only object names.[2] In Jumblese, instead of using predicate expressions to ascribe properties and relations to the objects named, one writes those names themselves in various ways. To say that something, the object o, is red, say, one writes its name in (say) bold: **o**. To say that Romeo loves Juliet, one perhaps writes a name for the former just before a name for the latter: rj. In this way, in Jumblese, one exhibits how things stand with objects by exhibiting names, representatives of those objects, in various ways. In such a language one does not say how things are; rather, one shows how things are. One shows that two things have something in common, that they share some feature, by writing their names the same way. Now we enrich the language slightly with the introduction of signs for properties and relations, which enables us not only to show that, say, o is red (by writing o's name in bold), but also to say that it is (Ro), not only to show that Romeo loves Juliet (in Jumblese, rj), but also to say so (Lrj), and so on. The next step is to learn to read the language in the new way already introduced in section 2.1, the sentence 'Lrj', for example, not as ascribing the relation *loving* to Romeo and Juliet, but instead as exhibiting two objects and a relation in the higher-level logical relation of subsumption. Independent of an analysis into function and argument, the sentence so read does not say anything but only shows (much as a Venn diagram does) what is the case if it is true. To formulate truth conditions for the sentence requires giving it a function/argument analysis, and many such analyses are possible.

In the language as it has been developed to this point, as in ordinary language, "logical relations are almost always only hinted at—left to guessing, not actually expressed" (*CN* 85). The next step is to make these relations explicit. We need, that is, to be able to express general laws about concepts (the corollary of the laws of elementary algebra), which requires in turn our "moving up a level" through the development of a sign for the conditional and the introduction of the literal notation. It is, for instance, always in order to judge of an object that it is (say) colored given that it is red. What we want to show in our language is that this inference is a good one whatever the object being considered. We do so by first showing that the judgment of an object that it is colored can be grounded in the judgment of it that it is red through the use of the conditional stroke and then replacing the object names with letters, or indeed any sort of squiggles so long as they are equiform, perhaps like this:

$$\vdash \begin{array}{l} C(x) \\ R(x). \end{array}$$

This sentence shows, on our reading, that its being red is a sufficient condition for the judgment of a thing that it is colored, that is, that one can judge of something that it is colored on the basis of the judgment that it is red; and it does so by presenting one concept as subordinate to another. Through its use of Latin italic letters lending generality of content and the two-dimensional conditional stroke, the sentential sign

$$\vdash \!\!\! \begin{array}{l} \text{---} C(x) \\ \text{---} R(x) \end{array}$$

exhibits the properties of being red and being colored in the logical relation of subordination, and it does so in a way that is strictly analogous, at a higher level, to the way the sentence 'rj' of Jumblese exhibits Romeo and Juliet in the relation of loving. Whereas the Jumblese sentence 'rj' exhibits a relation among objects, a *Begriffsschrift* generalized conditional exhibits a relation among concepts.

The next step is to introduce signs that enable one not only to show that one concept is subordinate to another but also to say that it is (much as before we introduced the sign 'L' to enable us not only to show that Romeo loves Juliet, rj, but also to say so, Lrj). Frege's concavity notation can be read in just this way. If it is, then the judgment

$$\vdash \!\!\!\!\! \underset{\alpha}{\cup} \!\!\! \begin{array}{l} \text{---} C(\alpha) \\ \text{---} R(\alpha) \end{array}$$

says of the concepts *red* and *colored* that the former is related to the latter by the relation of subordination. The sign

$$\text{---} \!\!\!\!\! \underset{\alpha}{\cup} \!\!\! \begin{array}{l} \text{---} \psi(\alpha) \\ \text{---} \phi(\alpha), \end{array}$$

that is, is to be read as a sign for the second-level relation of subordination, and the sentence

$$\text{---} \!\!\!\!\! \underset{\alpha}{\cup} \!\!\! \begin{array}{l} \text{---} C(\alpha) \\ \text{---} R(\alpha) \end{array}$$

as analogous to 'Lrj' (on our first reading of it) but at a higher level, as standing to its counterpart written using Latin italic letters as 'Lrj' stands to the Jumblese sentence 'rj'. Here again, we can learn to read the sentence in a new way, not as ascribing the second-level relation *subordination* to the first-level concepts *red* and *colored,* but as merely exhibiting first- and second-level concepts in a (third-level) logical relation. The sentence so read can be variously analyzed. We can, for instance, take the judgment

$$\vdash \!\!-\!\!\smile\!\!-^{\alpha}\!\!\!\!\begin{array}{c}\text{—}\ C(\alpha)\\ \text{—}\ R(\alpha)\end{array}$$

to involve the second-level function

$$-\!\!\smile\!\!-^{\alpha}\!\!\!\!\begin{array}{c}\text{—}\ \psi(\alpha)\\ \text{—}\ \phi(\alpha)\end{array}$$

for arguments Cξ and Rξ, or alternatively as involving the second-level function $-\!\!\smile\!\!-^{\alpha}\!\!\psi(\alpha)$ for argument

$$\begin{array}{c}\text{—}\ C\xi\\ \text{—}\ R\xi.\end{array}$$

We can also analyze it as involving the second-level concept

$$-\!\!\smile\!\!-^{\alpha}\!\!\!\!\begin{array}{c}\text{—}\ \psi(\alpha)\\ \text{—}\ R(\alpha)\end{array}$$

for argument Cξ, and so on. Now we are in a position to move up another level again.

We saw that the logical relationship between a simple sentence such as 'Ro' and another 'Co' could be laid bare in the judgment that exhibits *red* as subordinate to *colored* expressed using Frege's Latin italic letters and the two-dimensional conditional stroke. But this sentence, '*red* is subordinate to *colored*', similarly stands in certain logical relations to other sentences. One can correctly argue, for instance, that because *red* is subordinate to *colored* and *colored* is subordinate to *extended*, it follows that *red* is subordinate to *extended*. The final level is reached with the use of the literal notation to show that such an inference is a good one no matter what first-level concepts are being considered. The relation of subordination, which is a second-level relation of first-level concepts, is transitive; and we show that it is by replacing all first-level concept words with letters (equiform squiggles), for instance, this way:

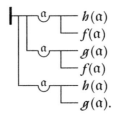

This sentence, we should be able to see, exhibits not how things stand with objects, nor even how things stand with (first-level) concepts, but instead how things stand with relations of concepts. It is analogous to the judgment

$$\vdash \begin{array}{l} C(x) \\ R(x), \end{array}$$

but at a higher level. In virtue of the peculiar expressive capacities here assigned to Frege's German and Latin italic letters, this *Begriffsschrift* sentence shows that the second-level logical relation of subordination is transitive. It exhibits a general law about concepts, and it makes essential use of the different expressive capacities of Frege's Latin italic and German letters in so doing. In this sentence, German letters together with the concavity and the conditional stroke serve in the formation of a concept name for the relation *subordination,* and the Latin italic letters enable one to show something about this designated concept, namely, that it is transitive. We are thus using a third-level concept, *transitive,* but have no sign for this concept. We show but do not say that a certain second-level concept, *subordination,* which is designated, is transitive.

In logic, as in mathematics, we can discern in this way an advance from level to level beginning with judgments about particular objects, then up a level to judgments about (first-level) concepts through the use of the literal notation, and finally, up a level again to judgments about higher-level concepts and relations. Already in Chapter 2 a reading was developed of judgments at the second level, that is, of the logical significance of Frege's two-dimensional conditional stroke, of the role his Latin italic letters play in lending generality of content, and of the way these signs of *Begriffsschrift* function together to enable the exhibition of logical relations, paradigmatically the relation of subordination, among concepts. Our interest now is in the later developments: Frege's mature understanding of the concept of a concept, of the concavity notation, and of the laws of logic as laws that hold for first-level concepts generally.

3.2 What Is a Function?

In *Begriffsschrift* a function is characterized as that part of an expression "that shows itself invariant [under replacement]" (*BGS* §9), and Latin italic letters are described as "symbols . . . *which one can take to signify various things*" (*BGS* §1). Together these remarks suggest that the expression that remains invariant in, say, '$1^2 + 3 \cdot 1$', '$2^2 + 3 \cdot 2$', '$3^2 + 3 \cdot 3$', and so on, is a function that, if the argument position is marked by, say, 'x', yields a variable name: '$x^2 + 3x$'. The impression is reinforced by the fact that

Frege appeals to just such a name in his example, in *Begriffsschrift* §8, aimed at showing why the sign for identity is necessary in logic. We are to "let a straight line rotate about a fixed point A on the circumference of a circle . . . [and to] call the point of intersection of the two lines [that is, of the circumference and the straight line] the point B corresponding to the straight line at any given time" (*BGS* §8). In that case "the name B denotes something undetermined as long as the corresponding position of the line is not yet specified." The name 'B', that is, has the form 'f(x)'; the point it signifies varies with the position of the line rotating about the fixed point A on the circumference of the circle. It is just this conception of an arithmetical function that Frege explicitly and repeatedly rejects in his later writings beginning with "Function and Concept" in 1891.[3]

Both the *Grundgesetze* account of functions and that of "Function and Concept" begin with essentially the view Frege himself takes in *Begriffsschrift*: that a function of x is a mathematical expression that contains x, an expression such as '$(2 + 3x^2)x$'. In the mature works Frege immediately rejects the formulation on the grounds that a function is not an expression any more than a number is a numeral. So, perhaps one might say, the function is what is designated by the expression '$(2 + 3x^2)x$' much as the number two is not the numeral '2' but instead what is designated by it. But what sort of entity is designated by '$(2 + 3x^2)x$'? Not any number, though if 'x' were replaced by a sign for a number (or, as we would say, assigned a value), then the resulting expression would designate a number. As it stands, then, '$(2 + 3x^2)x$' seems only indefinitely to indicate a number. In Frege's *Begriffsschrift* terminology, depending on what number one takes the 'x' to signify, the whole expression will signify various numbers. But as Frege now points out, these numbers are also not the function.

> The essence of the function manifests itself rather in the connection it establishes between the numbers whose signs we put for "x" and the numbers that then appear as denotations of our expression—a connection intuitively represented in the course of the curve whose equation in rectangular coordinates is
>
> "$y = (2 + 3x^2)x$".
>
> Accordingly the essence of the *function* lies in that part of the expression which is there over and above the "x". The expression for a *function* is *in need of completion, unsaturated*. The letter "x" serves only to hold places open for a numeral that is to complete the expression. (*GG* §1)

Neither the 'x' in '$(2 + 3x^2)x$' nor any number given as argument is part of the function. The function is what is designated by that part of the expression that is left over when the 'x' is removed; the 'x' serves *only* to mark the argument place.

The nature of the confusion Frege is concerned to dispel can be brought out by consideration of "embedded" functions, the function $(1 + x)^2$, say. Like any function, the function designated by the expression '$(1 + x)^2$' correlates numbers as arguments with numbers that are the values of the function for those arguments. The essence of the function, Frege suggests, lies in this correlation. But our function seems to be arithmetically complex. In its expression, the function designated by '$1 + x$' seems to occur as the argument for the function y^2, and yet what occurs as the argument for that function can only be a number, not a function. If we nonetheless insist on thinking of the function designated by '$(1 + x)^2$' as embedding one function in another, then, because we cannot think of $1 + x$ as itself a function in this context (because functions cannot be squared), and because it is clearly not a number, we shall have to think of it as a kind of indefinite number or variable name. Because any function can be "embedded" in this way, one comes to think that a function is a kind of indefinite number or variable (or ambiguous or arbitrary) name, one that becomes determinate when a number is supplied as the value of the variable in that variable name. In fact, as Frege comes clearly to see, '$1 + x$' does not function as a variable name in '$(1 + x)^2$'. The difference between '$1 + x$' and '$(1 + x)^2$' is merely the difference between a less complex function expression and a more complex function expression. The *signs* for functions such as that designated by '$(1 + x)^2$' are built up out of the signs for arithmetically simple (that is, primitive) functions, but the functions so designated are not complex. They, like any arithmetical functions, are laws of correlation between numbers.[4]

Frege aims in his mature writings to establish that a function is something in its own right over and above the numbers it correlates as argument and value. In "Function and Concept" he illustrates what is wanted—the notion of a function as something in its own right, albeit unsaturated—by analogy. We are to imagine a (dense) line of finite length divided by a point.

> One is inclined in that case to count the dividing-point along with both segments; but if we want to make a clean division, i.e. so as not to count anything twice over or leave anything out, then we may only count the dividing-point along with one segment. This segment thus

becomes fully complete in itself, and may be compared to the argument; whereas the other is lacking in something—viz. the dividing-point, which one may call its endpoint, does not belong to it. Only by completing it with this endpoint, or with a line that has two endpoints, do we get from it something entire. (*CP* 141)

As a line without an endpoint is lacking something, is not something complete or entire (because it only approaches the limit that is its endpoint, but never reaches it), but is nevertheless a perfectly objective entity, so, Frege now holds, a function is incomplete or unsaturated but nevertheless perfectly objective, something in its own right. It is what is designated by that part of an expression such as '$(2 + 3x^2)x$' when the two tokenings of 'x' are removed.

But why does arithmetic require such a notion? Why must we take a function to be something objective, albeit unsaturated? The answer, Frege suggests in the opening remarks of "Function and Concept," lies in higher analysis because "here for the first time it was a matter of setting forth laws holding for functions in general" (*CP* 137–138). Frege's example of such a law is this:

$$\frac{df(x) \cdot F(x)}{dx} = F(x) \cdot \frac{df(x)}{dx} + f(x) \cdot \frac{dF(x)}{dx}.$$

By contrast with a law such as '$(a + b)c = ac + bc$', which "[deals] with individual functions" but does not require "the coinage of the technical term 'function'" (*CP* 156), laws that hold for functions generally do require explicit reference to functions. Such laws, then, introduce "something essentially new"—though, Frege thinks, "to be sure, people have not always been clearly aware" of this (*CP* 144). Two key moments in the history of higher analysis will serve to highlight what it is that is new here.

In traditional accounts of derivatives, one begins with the notion of the rate of change of a straight line, that is, its slope as given by the difference quotient

$$\frac{f(x + \delta x) - f(x)}{\delta x}.$$

The rate of change of a smooth curve is then conceived as the limit, as δx approaches zero, of the difference quotient. Where $f(x) = x^2$, for example, the derivative dx^2/dx is given by

$$\lim_{\delta x \to 0} \frac{(x + \delta x)^2 - x^2}{\delta x}.$$

This, we know, is equal to $2x$. The problem is to prove the equality, and the first attempts to solve it were algebraic:

$$\lim_{\delta x \to 0} \frac{(x+\delta x)^2 - x^2}{\delta x} = \lim_{\delta x \to 0} \frac{x^2 + 2x\delta x + \delta x^2 - x^2}{\delta x} = \lim_{\delta x \to 0} 2x + \delta x.$$

If, now, it could be assumed that δx does "go to zero," then that would give the answer that is wanted: $2x$. But we cannot assume that because if δx did go to zero then the difference quotient by way of which we derived our answer would be meaningless, $\%_0$. If, however, δx does not go to zero but only approaches it indefinitely closely, then we cannot get the answer that is wanted, $2x$, but only $2x + \delta x$. The solution, Leibniz famously argued, is to take δx to be, though not equal to zero, nevertheless very, very small, infinitesimally small, so small that when it is added to any ordinary number (such as 2), the sum is just that number itself.[5] The term δx is not equal to zero, so the difference quotient is meaningful, and yet in a way δx is equal to zero because $2x + \delta x = 2x$. Problem solved. Unsurprisingly, the solution was not met with universal approval. That Newton's method of fluxions did not fare much better is suggested by Berkeley's delightful observation that "he who can digest a second or third fluxion . . . need not, methinks, be squeamish about any point in Divinity."[6]

By the mid-nineteenth century it had become clear that the problem with these early attempts to understand limit operations such as differentiation did not concern the details but instead the conception of the task as essentially algebraic. As the work of Cauchy, Bolzano, and Weierstrass showed, limit operations are fundamentally different in kind from standard algebraic operations, as different from them as algebraic operations are from calculations with numbers. As the point can be put, whereas the function ξ^2 in $(1 + x)^2$ takes as its argument not the function $1 + x$ but instead the value of this function for some argument, the function $d\phi(x)/dx$ in dx^2/dx does take the function x^2 as argument. It is just this difference that is highlighted in a law such as

$$\frac{df(x) \cdot F(x)}{dx} = F(x) \cdot \frac{df(x)}{dx} + f(x) \cdot \frac{dF(x)}{dx}$$

as it contrasts with a law of algebra such as

$$(a + b)c = ac + bc.$$

In the former case but not the latter the expression of the law requires the use of letters that indefinitely indicate functions. It shows thereby that the argument in this case is not a number but instead a function. But if functions can themselves be arguments for higher-level functions just as objects such as numbers can be arguments for first-level functions, then, despite their incompleteness, functions must be something in their own right, something objective. Because, according to Frege, a concept, as that notion is needed in logic, just is a function that gives truth-values (either the True or the False) as values, concepts similarly must be something in their own right, something objective, albeit unsaturated. Just as objects can, concepts can serve as arguments for (higher-level) concepts.[7]

3.3 The Expressive Role of the Concavity with German Letter

As the development of higher analysis reveals, arithmetical functions must be something in their own right, something objective that can serve as arguments for higher-level functions despite their being inherently unsaturated. Concepts, similarly, Frege comes to hold, are something objective, albeit unsaturated, that can serve as arguments for higher-level concepts. These higher-level concepts, in turn, he eventually comes to see, are designated by expressions that make essential use of his concavity and German letters.

In the elucidations of the 1879 logic and in the 1879 logic itself, no distinction is marked between first- and second-level concepts. Even in the 1893 logic, which does draw this distinction, the concavity with German letter is again introduced as a means of marking distinctions of scope. Were that its only role, there would be no logical justification for introducing a new sort of letter in combination with the concavity. On the other hand, already in the early logic various second-level concepts and relations are introduced and theorems about them proved. It is also possible to see (at least in hindsight) that the concavity with German letters plays an essential role in the formation of expressions for these second-level concepts and relations. Frege proves, for instance, that the second-level (unequal-leveled) relation of following in a sequence is transitive: if y follows x in the f-sequence, and if z follows y in the f-sequence, then z follows x in the f-sequence (Theorem 98). In *Begriffsschrift*:

$$\vdash \begin{array}{l} \overset{\gamma}{\underset{\beta}{\sim}}\, f(x_\gamma, z_\beta) \\ \overset{\gamma}{\underset{\beta}{\sim}}\, f(y_\gamma, z_\beta) \\ \overset{\gamma}{\underset{\beta}{\sim}}\, f(x_\gamma, y_\beta). \end{array}$$

In this judgment the second-level relation of following in a sequence is designated using a defined sign. What this sign means is given by

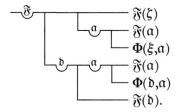

In this latter sign the Greek letters 'ξ' and 'ζ' mark the object name positions and 'Φ' the two-place relation position. The sign taken as a whole thus functions as a concept word for the second-level concept of following in a sequence, one that in the context of a judgment might be variously analyzed. Only later did Frege come explicitly to realize that it is precisely this expressive role played by the concavity with German letters in the formation of such higher-level concepts—which, it will be suggested in section 3.4, are the subject matter of logic—that provides the logical justification for the introduction of a new sort of letter in combination with the concavity.

A *Begriffsschrift* generality is correctly acknowledged to be true just in case the corresponding function "is a fact whatever we may take as its argument" (*BGS* §11). It follows, as Frege sees, that a negated generalized negation of *Begriffsschrift* is true just in case the corresponding function is a fact for at least one object as argument. The *Begriffsschrift* judgment

$$\vdash \!\!\!-\!\!\!\top\!\!\!-\!\!\!\!\!\frown\!\!\!\!\!-\!\!\top\!\!\!- \Lambda(\alpha)$$

is correctly translated 'there are Λs' (*BGS* §12). What Frege does not seem at first to have realized is that a particular affirmative, something of the form

$$-\!\!\!\top\!\!\!-\!\!\!\!\!\frown\!\!\!\!\!-\!\!\top\!\!\!\top \begin{array}{l} P(\alpha) \\ M(\alpha), \end{array}$$

can itself be construed as an instance of a negated generalized negation. Only in the long Boole essay written shortly after *Begriffsschrift* (and in subsequent writings) is the "link" between particular and existential judgments emphasized.

In

$$-\!\!\!\top\!\!\!-\!\!\!\!\!\frown\!\!\!\!\!-\!\!\top\!\!\!\top \begin{array}{l} \alpha^2 = 4 \\ \alpha^4 = 16 \end{array}$$

we may insert two negation-strokes in immediate succession, which then cancel each other out and think of this as concatenated as indicated here:

Thus the only distinction between

and

is that

takes the place of $\alpha^2 = 4$. (*PW* 20–21)

Just as

is the judgment that there is at least one square root of four, so

is the judgment that there is at least one thing that is a fourth root of sixteen and a square root of four. It is the judgment that some (at least one) fourth roots of sixteen are square roots of four. Nevertheless, Frege seems not yet (in the early 1880s) to have realized that such sentences involve a second-level concept.

Shortly after *Begriffsschrift* was written, Frege realized that in a genuine hypothetical (that is, a generalized conditional expressed using Latin italic letters) one concept is subordinated to another. In the "Dialogue with Pünjar," written sometime before 1884, Frege claims that a particular affirmative similarly puts concepts in a logical relation: "Out of context the word 'some' has no sense; it is an auxiliary like 'all', 'each', 'none' and so on, which, in the context of a sentence has a logical function to perform. This function consists in putting two concepts in a certain logical relationship" (*PW* 63). Because only one (first-level) concept would seem to be involved in a simple existence claim such as 'there are men', Frege now suggests that in such cases we should select a concept, for instance, *being identical with itself,* to enable the formulation of the sentence as a particular affirmative (thought of as putting two concepts in a logical relationship): 'there are men identical with themselves' or 'something identical with itself is a man' (*PW* 63). "The content of what is predicated," "the existence expressed by 'there is'," in such sentences, Frege thinks at this stage, is contained "in the form of the particular judgment" (*PW* 66). Only in *Grundlagen* (1884) and subsequent writings are higher-level concepts, among them the concept of existence, explicitly acknowledged as such.

In the 1893 logic Frege draws a more thoroughgoing distinction between judgments expressed using his Latin italic letters and judgments expressed instead using the concavity notation. Although a judgment expressed using Latin italic letters expresses a subordination of concepts, that same judgment expressed using the concavity and German letters has, he suggests, the form of a subsumption of first-level concepts under a higher-level concept. That is, both

$$-\underset{\alpha}{\smile}-\phi(\alpha) \qquad \text{and} \qquad -\top\underset{\alpha}{\smile}\top-\phi(\alpha)$$

designate second-level concepts, and both

$$-\underset{\alpha}{\smile}\top\begin{array}{l}\psi(\alpha)\\\phi(\alpha)\end{array} \qquad \text{and} \qquad -\top\underset{\alpha}{\smile}\top\begin{array}{l}\psi(\alpha)\\\phi(\alpha)\end{array}$$

designate second-level equal-leveled relations (*GG* §§21, 22); but neither '$-\!-\!-\psi(x)$' nor

$$\top\begin{array}{l}\psi(x)\\\phi(x)\end{array}$$

designates anything. Latin italic letters cannot be used in the formation of concept words. Nor, for the same reason, can they be used in the formation of names for truth-values. Whereas '$-\underset{\alpha}{\smile}-\alpha = \alpha$' is "a *name*, because it denotes the True" (*GG* §26), "Roman [Latin] letters, and combinations of signs in which they occur, are not *names*, because they only indicate" (*GG* §17)—though, as Frege notes in *Grundgesetze* §32, "such a mark [that is, a Latin mark of a truth-value] is transformed into a name of a truth-value by the introduction of Gothic [German] letters in place of Roman [Latin] letters and by the prefixing of concavities." If that is right, the two judgments

$$\vdash\!\underset{\alpha}{\smile}\top\begin{array}{l}\alpha^4 = 1\\\alpha^2 = 1\end{array} \qquad \text{and} \qquad \vdash\top\begin{array}{l}x^4 = 1\\x^2 = 1\end{array}$$

do not express one and the same thought; the latter is not merely an abbreviation of the former, as Frege had claimed in *Begriffsschrift*. Indeed, they do not even have the same logical form. In the first sentence a second-level concept is designated (though, as we saw in section 3.1, which second-level concept is designated is determined only relative to an analysis). The sentence has the logical form of a subsumption of a first-level concept (or concepts) under a second-level concept (or relation). In the second sentence only first-level concepts are designated. The logical form of this sentence is that of a subordination.

By the early 1890s Frege seems to have come to think that his Latin italic letters and his concavity with German letters play very different expressive roles. Nevertheless, in *Grundgesetze* §§8 and 17 he also suggests that a generality using a Latin italic letter is merely a special case of a generality expressed using the concavity notation, that the concavity notation is required only to mark distinctions of scope. That is, he both distinguishes logically between the two means of expressing generality and claims that they are not essentially, that is, logically, different. In remarks written after 1893, there is evidence that Frege finally did come to resolve this conflict in his thinking and to comprehend fully the peculiar logical role played by his concavity notation.

As already indicated, Frege remarks in a note to the 1906 "Introduction to Logic" regarding the use of letters in arithmetic that

> here and there in arithmetic there is also a use of letters which roughly corresponds to that of the gothic [that is, German] letters in my concept-script. But I have found no indication that anyone is aware of this use as a special case. Probably most mathematicians, were they to read this, would have no idea of what I am alluding to. It was not until after some time that I became aware of it myself. (*PW* 195 n to p. 194)

As Frege points out in this passage, there is a use of letters in arithmetic that corresponds to the use of his German letters, but this is a "special case"; even he himself did not recognize this use as a special case until quite late. Earlier, in the 1896 essay "On Mr. Peano's Conceptual Notation and My Own," Frege provides what seems to be an example of the use of letters in arithmetic that he has in mind:

> from the point of view of inference, generality which extends over the content of the entire sentence is [of a] vitally different significance from that whose scope constitutes only a part of the sentence. Hence it contributes substantially to perspicuity that the eye discerns these

different roles in the different sorts of letters, Latin and German. There is a similar distinction in the way the letters 'α' and 'x' are used in the formula

$$\int_0^\infty \frac{\sin \alpha x}{\alpha}\, d\alpha,$$

in which α really serves as a calculation sign. (*CP* 248)

It is not merely incidental, I think, that Frege uses such an example here rather than something much simpler such as, say, $x^n \times x^m = x^{n+m}$.

In a law such as $x^n \times x^m = x^{n+m}$, the letter 'x' functions (as we would say) as a variable and the letters 'n' and 'm' as parameters; the equation holds no matter what numbers are put for 'n' and 'm'. But of course it also holds no matter what number is put for 'x'. There is in such a law no essential difference between the two sorts of letters; the same sort of letter could be used throughout. Similarly, in a *Begriffsschrift* judgment such as

$$\vdash \begin{array}{l} x = 16 \\ \alpha\!\!\!\!\quad \begin{array}{l} \alpha^4 = x \\ \alpha^2 = 4, \end{array} \end{array}$$

there is no essential difference between the two sorts of letters. The concavity is needed to mark the scope of the generality in the subcomponent, but no further purpose is served by the choice of a different sort of letter with the concavity. The same sort of letter could have been used throughout. It would seem to be just this sort of case that Frege has in mind when he suggests that the concavity notation functions merely to mark distinctions of scope. Frege's arithmetical example is crucially different. We can illustrate how it is different by using a somewhat simpler example, for instance, the law that $dx^n/dx = nx^{n-1}$, because in this law (as in Frege's example), the different letters do serve radically different purposes, as is immediately evident by consideration of instances of it: $dx^2/dx = 2x$, $dx^3/dx = 3x^2$, and so on. In these various instances, $d\phi(x)/dx$ takes first-level arithmetical functions (that is, x^2, x^3, x^4, and so on) as arguments. In $dx^n/dx = nx^{n-1}$, by contrast, we have a general law about functions of a certain kind; 'x^n' serves in this law indefinitely to indicate not numbers but functions. This is the crucial point: though in '$x^n \times x^m = x^{n+m}$' the letters 'x', 'n', and 'm' all can be read as serving in the same way indefinitely to indicate numbers, in '$dx^n/dx = nx^{n-1}$', 'x' and 'n' cannot be read as serving in the same way indefinitely to indicate numbers; instead, the letter 'n' serves to raise everything up a level, from consideration of derivatives of particular functions to a law about functions of a certain kind generally. Just the same is true of 'α' and 'x' in Frege's example.

The arithmetical identity '$dx^n/dx = nx^{n-1}$' expresses a general law about functions. In its expression the letters 'x' and 'n' play very different roles. Because they do, it contributes substantially to perspicuity that different sorts of letters are used in the two cases. Similarly, in *Begriffsschrift* on our reading of it, German and Latin italic letters play very different roles in the expression of general laws about (first-level) concepts. As '$dx^n/dx = nx^{n-1}$' expresses a general law about functions, so, for instance,

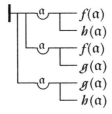

expresses a general law about concepts. In this law the Latin italic letters 'f', 'g', and 'h' serve (as the 'n' does in the law $dx^n/dx = nx^{n-1}$) to raise everything up a level; the concavity with German letters is used in the formation of a second-level concept word, and the Latin italic letters 'f', 'g', and 'h' enable one to exhibit something about the concept so designated, namely, its transitivity. It is just these logically different roles, apparent only at the level of laws that hold for concepts generally (and not at the level of laws that hold for objects generally), that are marked by Frege's use of two different sorts of letters, German with the concavity and Latin italic without it. Frege's use of two different sorts of letters in the two cases is, then, logically justified, but one can see why only by considering the most general case, the case of the laws of logic.

According to the reading just outlined, Frege came fully to comprehend the logical role of the concavity notation, and thereby the logical distinction between sentences expressed using his two notations for generality, only decades after the notation itself was developed. A *Begriffsschrift* genuine hypothetical expressed using Latin italic letters has the form of a subordination of concepts; expressed using the concavity notation, the sentence instead has the logical form of a subsumption of first-level concepts under a second-level concept. Frege explains just this distinction in the 1919 "Notes for Ludwig Darmstaedter." We begin with the basic case, that of a genuine hypothetical requiring only Latin italic letters in its expression as it contrasts with a mere conditional.

Where we have a compound sentence consisting of an antecedent and a consequent, there are two main cases to distinguish. The antecedent and consequent may each have a complete thought as its sense . . . A second case is where neither antecedent nor consequent has a sense in itself, but where nevertheless the whole compound does express a thought—a thought which is general in character. In such a case we have a relation, not between judgments or thoughts but between concepts, the relation, namely, of subordination. (*PW* 253–254)

This is just what we have already seen: Latin italic letters together with the conditional stroke enable the expression of relations among concepts.

After some clarificatory remarks, Frege turns to those cases that require the use of the concavity notation.

A general statement can be negated. In this way we arrive at what logicians call existential and particular judgments. The existential thoughts I have in mind here are such as are expressed in German by *'es gibt'* . . . In existential sentences of this kind we are making a statement about a concept. Here we have an instance of how a concept can be related to a *second level concept* in a way analogous to that in which an object is related to a concept under which it falls. Closely akin to these existential thoughts are thoughts that are particular: indeed they may be included among them. But we can also say that what is expressed by a sentence of the particular form is that a concept stands in a certain *second level relation* to a concept. (*PW* 254)

The notion of a second-level concept (relation) makes an appearance in this passage only when the case of a negated generality is considered, that is, only where the concavity notation is ineliminable. Frege marks the distinction between exhibiting (by means of the conditional stroke and Latin italic letters) two concepts in the relation of subordination, on the one hand, and showing using the concavity and German letters that a first-level concept falls under a second-level concept, on the other, by noting that in the one case, that in which Latin italic letters are used, "we have a relation . . . between concepts, the relation, namely, of subordination," and in the other, the case in which a concavity and German letters are employed, "what is expressed . . . is that a concept stands in a certain *second level relation* to another concept." The two cases, then, are essentially (that is, logically) different.[8] A judgment whose content is an unnegated generality can be expressed using Latin italic letters; these letters enable the exhibition of concepts in the logical relationship of subordination. But a judgment whose content is a negated generality can only be expressed using the concavity notation. It does not express a logical relation among concepts at the same level but instead, Frege suggests, the subsumption of a concept (or concepts) under another, higher-level concept. Such a judgment, on our reading, can serve only as a premise in an inference; it does not express an inference license, a law according to which to reason.[9]

The expressive role of the concavity, as we read it, is to enable the formation of higher-level concept words that are needed in the expression of laws at the "third" level. The second-level relations

$$-\!\!\smile^{\alpha}\!\!-\!\!\left[\begin{array}{l}\psi(\alpha)\\ \phi(\alpha)\end{array}\right. \qquad \text{and} \qquad -\!\!\top\!\!\smile^{\alpha}\!\!\top\!\!-\!\!\left[\begin{array}{l}\psi(\alpha)\\ \phi(\alpha)\end{array}\right.$$

are the basic cases. Because only the first can be used in the formation of a law, that is, in the expression of what Frege calls a genuine hypothetical, we begin with it, the second-level relation of subordination:

$$-\!\!\smile^{\alpha}\!\!-\!\!\left[\begin{array}{l}\psi(\alpha)\\ \phi(\alpha).\end{array}\right.$$

If we now replace '——$\psi(\Gamma)$' with the function

$$-\!\!\smile^{b}\!\!-\!\!\left[\begin{array}{l}\psi(b)\\ \mu(\Gamma,b),\end{array}\right.$$

another, more complex relation is formed:

$$-\!\!\smile^{\alpha}\!\!-\!\!\smile^{b}\!\!-\!\!\left[\begin{array}{l}\psi(b)\\ \mu(\alpha,b)\\ \phi(\alpha).\end{array}\right.$$

If it is further stipulated that $\psi(\xi) = \phi(\xi)$, then this expression designates the relation of following in a sequence. It is correctly ascribed to a function $f(\xi,\zeta)$ and a property $F(\xi)$ just if F follows in the f-sequence. If '——$\psi(\Gamma)$' in our original formula is replaced instead by the function

$$-\!\!\top\!\!\smile^{b}\!\!\top\!\!-\!\!\left[\begin{array}{l}\mu(\Gamma,b)\\ \psi(b),\end{array}\right.$$

we get

$$-\!\!\smile^{\alpha}\!\!\top\!\!\smile^{b}\!\!\top\!\!-\!\!\left[\begin{array}{l}\mu(\alpha,b)\\ \psi(b)\\ \phi(\alpha).\end{array}\right.$$

This is the second-level relation that is ascribed, for instance, in 'every boy loves some girl'. Where $\psi(\xi) = \phi(\xi)$, another important second-level relation is designated,

$$
\begin{array}{l}
\llcorner\!\!\!\!\!-\!a\!-\!\!\!\rceil\!\!\!\rceil\!-\!b\!-\!\!\!\rceil\!\!\!\rceil\!\!-\!\mu(a,b) \\
\qquad\qquad\llcorner\!-\psi(b) \\
\qquad\quad\llcorner\!\!-\!-\!-\!-\!-\psi(a),
\end{array}
$$

which holds, for instance, of the concept *number* and the successor relation (because every number has a successor). It is also, in a slightly more complex form, the relation that is ascribed in the density axiom of geometry. To judge that between any two points there is a third is to ascribe that second-level relation to the concepts *point* and <.

Still more logically complex second-level relations are formulable as well. If, for instance, the expression '——$\mu(\Gamma,\Delta)$' in the formula just given is replaced by

$$
\begin{array}{l}
\llcorner\!\!\!-\!c\!-\!\!\rceil\!\!-\!\rho(\Gamma,c) \\
\qquad\quad\llcorner\!\!-\mu(\Delta,c),
\end{array}
$$

the resultant concept is

$$
\begin{array}{l}
\llcorner\!\!\!-\!a\!-\!\!\rceil\!\!\rceil\!-\!b\!-\!\!\rceil\!\!\rceil\!-\!c\!-\!\!\rceil\!\!-\!\rho(a,c) \\
\qquad\qquad\qquad\qquad\llcorner\!\!-\mu(b,c) \\
\qquad\qquad\qquad\llcorner\!\!-\!-\!-\psi(b) \\
\qquad\qquad\quad\llcorner\!\!-\!-\!-\!-\!-\psi(a).
\end{array}
$$

It is this concept that is critical to limit operations. To form, for instance, the second-level unequal-leveled relation of continuity, which takes a function and a point as arguments, one puts the concept $\xi > 0$ for the two occurrences of $\psi(\xi)$, the relation $-\xi \leq \zeta \leq \xi$ for $\mu(\xi,\zeta)$, and the relation $-\xi \leq f(A + \zeta) \leq \xi$ for $\rho(\xi,\zeta)$. The result is a more determinate concept, but because it takes functions and points as arguments, it is one that is nonetheless second-level. Obviously, one could go on.

As we should furthermore expect, sentences that contain such expressions are analyzable in various ways. That *Begriffsschrift* sentences can be carved up in various ways for the purposes of judgment and inference has already been shown for the case of simple singular sentences, for the case of conditionals and genuine hypotheticals, and also for the case of generalized conditionals expressed as subsumptions using the concavity notation. We saw that a sentence such as, for instance,

$$\dashv\!\!\cup\!\!\top \begin{array}{l} \alpha^4 = 16 \\ \alpha^2 = 4 \end{array}$$

can be read either as ascribing the second-level property

$$\dashv\!\!\cup\!\!- \psi(\alpha)$$

to the first-level concept

$$\top \begin{array}{l} \xi^4 = 16 \\ \xi^2 = 4 \end{array}$$

or as ascribing the second-level relation

$$\dashv\!\!\cup\!\!\top \begin{array}{l} \psi(\alpha) \\ \phi(\alpha) \end{array}$$

to the first-level concepts $\xi^2 = 4$ and $\xi^4 = 16$, or in yet other ways. A particular affirmative such as

$$\dashv\!\!\top\!\!\cup\!\!\top\!\top \begin{array}{l} \alpha^4 = 16 \\ \alpha^2 = 4 \end{array}$$

is essentially similar, though because of its greater logical complexity even more analyses are possible. Depending on how the horizontals are taken to be amalgamated, it can be read as follows.

(1) As $\qquad \top \quad \dashv\!\!\cup\!\!\top \quad \top \begin{array}{l} \alpha^4 = 16 \\ -\ \alpha^2 = 4, \end{array}$

it is the judgment that it is not the case that the concepts *square root of four* and *not a fourth root of sixteen* are related by the (second-level) relation of subordination.

(2) As $\qquad \dashv\!\!\top\!\!\cup\!\!\top \quad \top\!\top \begin{array}{l} \alpha^4 = 16 \\ \alpha^2 = 4, \end{array}$

it is the judgment that there is something that is both a square root of four and a fourth root of sixteen.

(3) As $\qquad \dashv\!\!\top\!\!\cup\!\!\top\!\top \begin{array}{l} -\ \alpha^4 = 16 \\ \alpha^2 = 4, \end{array}$

it reads as the judgment that the property *fourth root of sixteen* has the (higher-level) property *property of some (at least one) square root of four* (that is, it is the judgment of some square root of four that it is a fourth root of sixteen).

(4) As

$$\text{———}\bigtriangledown\!\!{}^{\alpha}\text{———}\begin{array}{l} - \alpha^4 = 16 \\ - \alpha^2 = 4, \end{array}$$

that same sentence ascribes the second-level (logical) property of compossibility to the concepts *square root of four* and *fourth root of sixteen*. Just as Frege tells us already in *Begriffsschrift* §12, a particular affirmative of *Begriffsschrift* can be read either as of the form 'some S is P' or as of the form 'it is possible for an S to be a P'. Other analyses are clearly possible as well. Independent of an analysis into function and argument, this particular affirmative of *Begriffsschrift* does not "say" any one of these things to the exclusion of the others. Rather, it exhibits what Frege at first calls the "conceptual content," the *begrifflicher Inhalt*, that is common to them all. In the case of second-level relations the expression of which is more complex, even more analyses are possible.

Already in the early logic Frege employs two different sorts of letters with and without the concavity. Because he draws no distinction between first- and higher-level concepts, however, there is, in the early logic, no logical justification for using a different sort of letter with the concavity. The concavity, Frege thinks, serves only to mark distinctions of scope. For the case in which the concavity has widest scope, he (re)introduces as a mere "abbreviation" the use of Latin italic letters without the concavity. It follows that genuine hypotheticals and particular affirmatives have essentially the same logical form; so, after Frege has seen that genuine hypotheticals present concepts in relations, he supposes that particular affirmatives do so as well, in spite of the fact that in simple existentials only one logically simple concept need be involved. The confusions are not fully cleared up until after the appearance in 1893 of the *Grundgesetze* logic. As Frege says, "it was not until after some time" that he became aware of the use of German letters as a "special case" (*PW* 195 n to p. 194). What exactly it was that he became aware of was that whereas a genuine hypothetical (expressed using Latin italic letters) presents concepts in the relation of subordination, both a particular affirmative judgment and a simple existential judgment subsume a concept (or concepts) under a higher-level concept (or relation). The logical justification for the use of German letters as they contrast with Latin italic letters lies in the role the concavity plays in the formation of concept words for just such higher-level concepts.

3.4 The Formality of Logic

We have traced the emergence of two related themes in Frege's mature understanding, that of a function as something in its own right that can serve as an argument for a higher-level function, and that of a concavity with German letter as it is used in the formation of higher-level concept expressions, where a higher-level concept just is a function that takes lower-level concepts as arguments to yield truth-values as values. What we need now to see is that the subject matter of logic, on Frege's mature view, is a particular sort of higher-level concept.

In both his early and later writings, Frege takes the laws of logic to be somehow objective, that is, true or false, properly speaking, and together to form a body of knowledge the content of which is properly expressed in the form of a complete and adequate axiomatization. Nevertheless, his conception of the nature of those laws seems to have been radically revised between the early and the late logic. The developments, it will be suggested, occur in three stages. At first, in *Begriffsschrift,* Frege seems to think of the laws of logic as merely more general than the laws of the special sciences, indeed, as maximally general but not in any relevant sense different in kind from other laws.[10] In the long Boole essay written shortly after *Begriffsschrift,* and also in *Grundlagen,* Frege adopts the notion of form as it contrasts with that of content to characterize the peculiarity of the laws of logic. The laws of logic, he now suggests, are fundamentally different from the laws of the special sciences because they are formal in a way those other laws are not. The third stage is reached with the idea, explicitly formulated only in 1906 in "Foundations of Geometry II," that the laws of logic are at once contentful, just as the laws of the special sciences are, and qualitatively different from those other laws. Frege's final word on the matter thus seems to combine elements of both his earlier views.

In the Preface to *Begriffsschrift* Frege describes the laws of logic as "the laws on which all knowledge rests" (*BGS* 103), as "the laws of thought, which transcend all particulars" (*BGS* 104). Because, as we have already seen, he does not at this stage draw any sharp distinction between concept and object, or between first- and second-level concepts (though he does not, in his inferential practice, confuse them either), it seems reasonable to take him to understand the peculiar character of laws of logic in terms of a kind of maximal generality. We know that any science abstracts to some extent from the particular state of things. In mechanics, for instance, one ignores the chemical properties of objects; in topology one ignores the particular shapes of objects; and so on. The laws of a special science concern only certain properties of objects. Because in logic one ignores all (first-level) properties of objects (save for their self-identity), the laws of logic could then be thought of as most general, maximally general, but not otherwise different from other laws. Frege's conceptual notation, on this conception, is one Leibnizian "universal characteristic" among many—among, for instance, the symbol systems of arithmetic, geometry, and chemistry—and is distinguished from those other notations only by its greater centrality (*BGS* 105).

Soon after the publication of *Begriffsschrift* Frege seems to adopt instead something much more like the Boolean view of logic as distinctively formal. He begins to "distinguish the formal part [of a language] which in verbal language comprises endings, prefixes, suffixes and auxiliary words, from the material part proper" (*PW* 13). The signs of arithmetic, he now thinks, provide the material part, and his signs the formal part, "the logical cement that will bind these building stones [contained in the material part] together" (*PW* 13). His logic is to be thought of as a formal symbol system in just the sense in which Boole's is a formal symbol system—though it is also true, as Frege points out, that because his signs for logical relations are not borrowed from arithmetic as Boole's are, his symbol system alone is suited to express a content.

> When we view the Boolean formula language as a whole, we discover that it is a clothing of abstract logic in the dress of algebraic symbols. It is not suited for the rendering of a content, and that is also not its purpose. But that is exactly my intention. I wish to blend together the few symbols which I introduce and the symbols already in mathematics to form a single formula language. In it, the existing symbols [of mathematics] correspond to the word-stems of [ordinary] language; while the symbols I add to them are comparable to the suffixes and [deductive] formwords {*Formwörter*} that logically interrelate the contents embedded in the stems.
>
> For this purpose, I could not use the Boolean symbolism; for it is not feasible to have, for example, the + sign occurring in the same formula part of the time in the logical sense and part of the time in the arithmetical sense. (*CN* 93–94)

Solely in virtue of its choice of primitive signs, Frege's logical language is suitable for the expression of a content in a way in which Boole's is not.

But if, as Frege now seems to think, the signs for logical relations provide only the formal part, the logical cement that is needed to form concepts out of concepts, then concept expressions and sentences formed solely out of such signs would seem to lack all content. The purely logical "concepts" and "sentential contents" expressed thereby would have the *form* of concepts and judgments, but they would not *be* concepts and judgments, properly speaking; for they would lack all content. Frege indicates that he would concur. He writes, for instance, that "my concept-script has a more far-reaching aim than Boolean logic, in that it strives to make it possible to present a content when combined with arithmetical and geometrical signs" (*PW* 46), implying thereby that independent of its combination with those arithmetical and geometrical signs, Frege's concept-script cannot present a content. In some asides, the thought is even more explicit. Frege claims, for instance, that "disregarding content, within the domain of pure logic" his concept-script "commands a somewhat wider domain than Boole's formula language" (*PW* 46). Logic, he suggests, is a purely formal discipline, one that "disregards content." Of the theorems proven in Part III of *Begriffsschrift*, theorems that are described in *Begriffsschrift* §23 as having a content derived from pure thought, he now claims, "That my sentences have enough content, in so far as you can talk of the content of sentences of pure logic at all, follows from the fact that they were adequate for the task" (*PW* 38).

This conception of logic as peculiarly formal, as itself devoid of content, remains to the fore in *Grundlagen*. Why should we think that "the doctrine of relation-concepts . . . is, like that of simple concepts, a part of pure logic" (*GL* §70)? Frege's answer in *Grundlagen* is that the doctrine of relation-concepts belongs to pure logic because it concerns only the form of a relation, something any and all relations share insofar as they are relations.

> What is of concern in logic is not the special content of any particular relation, but only logical form. And whatever can be asserted of this is true analytically and known a priori. This is as true of relation-concepts as of other concepts.
> Just as
> "*a* falls under the concept *F*"
> is the general form of a judgment-content which deals with an object *a*, so we can take
> "*a* stands in the relation ϕ to *b*"

as the general form of a judgment-content which deals with an object *a* and an object *b*. (*GL* §70)

Logic, Frege thinks at this stage, is not concerned with the special contents of particular concepts and relations but only with the logical forms of concepts and relations and with the logical forms of the judgment-contents in which they figure.[11] Logic so conceived fundamentally contrasts with the special sciences. Whereas the special sciences have their own special contents in virtue of having their own particular concepts and relations, the science of logic has no special content of its own. Its concern is with logical form as it contrasts with content.

If, as Frege now thinks, logic is distinctively formal, then judgments in logic ought to be not merely more general than judgments in other sciences but qualitatively different, and so they are according to the author of *Grundlagen*.

> The laws of number [which, Frege thinks, are derived laws of logic] . . . are not really applicable to external things; they are not laws of nature. They are, however, applicable to judgments holding good of things in the external world: they are laws of the laws of nature. They assert not connexions between phenomena, but connexions between judgments; and among judgments are included laws of nature. (*GL* §87)

Laws of nature, Frege indicates, assert connections between phenomena; they assert, that is, not merely that this is the case and that is the case but that this is the case *because* that is the case. Similarly, the passage suggests, a law of logic asserts not merely that this law of nature holds and that law of nature holds but that this law of nature holds *because* that one holds. Of course a law of logic itself makes no reference to particular laws of nature, just as a law of nature makes no reference to particular matters of fact. Instead, much as a law of nature asserts connections between kinds of things, so a law of logic, on this view, asserts connections between kinds of judgments, that is, between judgments of this or that form. So understood, the *Begriffsschrift* judgment

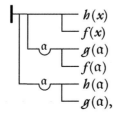

which in *Begriffsschrift* seems to have been conceived as merely more general than a law of a special science, is now taken to concern judgments that have the form of generalized conditionals and to assert a connection among judgments of that form.

Although in *Grundlagen* Frege takes logic to concern form rather than content, he is not a formalist, and he is careful to explain why. His own view—which, he thinks at this stage, is correctly described as a "formal theory"—is, as he puts it in "On Formal Theories of Arithmetic" (1885), "that all arithmetical propositions can be derived from definitions alone using purely logical means, and consequently that they must be derived in this way" (*CP* 112). The formalism he rejects is characterized as the view "that the signs of the numbers ½, ⅓, of the number π, etc. are empty signs" (*CP* 114). Interestingly enough, however, his objection to this sort of formalism, at this stage in his thinking, is not so much that the view itself is wrong as that formalist definitions of numbers are logically flawed. The formalists seek to define numbers by their properties, but the definitions they give are not definitions of objects at all. One says, for example, that √2 is something that, when multiplied by itself, yields 2. But

> so far, by means of such a definition one has merely obtained a concept, and there arises the question whether this concept is empty or fulfilled. As long as it has not been proved that there exists one and exactly one thing of this kind, it would be a mistake in logic to immediately use the definite article and say 'the number which when multiplied by itself yields 2', or 'the square root of 2' . . . The concept of a number which when multiplied by itself yields 2 no more has the property of yielding 2 when multiplied by itself than the concept of a right-angled triangle is a triangle or has a right angle. (*CP* 117)

The formalist, that is, fails "to distinguish clearly between concepts and objects" (*GL* §97) and between properties of concepts and characteristic marks of concepts. Because he fails to do so, his "theory of fractional, negative, etc., numbers is untenable" (*GL* x). The formalist "[passes] off as a definition what is only a guide toward definition" (*GL* §109). The formalist view is distanced from Frege's own, at this stage, by a technical difficulty.

Frege claims in *Grundlagen* that the demand "never to lose sight of the distinction between concept and object" (*GL* x) requires in turn that both existence and uniqueness be established if an object name is to be introduced. One must show not only that something does fall under the concept used in the definition but also that no more than one object does: "if we are to use the symbol *a* to signify an object, we must have a criterion for deciding in all cases whether *b* is the same as *a*, even if it is not always in our power to apply this criterion" (*GL* §62). Formalist theories do not meet this requirement and are therefore to be rejected. The further demand "always to separate sharply the psychological from the logical, the subjective from the objective" (*GL* x), seems intended (at least in part) to ensure that the results of Frege's investigations, though they do not concern anything that is actual (that is, spatiotemporal), are nonetheless objectively valid.

> On this view of numbers [which, Frege again notes, "too might be called formalist"] . . . we are not concerned with objects which we come to know as something alien from without through the medium of the senses, but with objects given directly to our reason and, as its nearest kin, utterly transparent to it.
>
> And yet, or rather for that very reason, these objects are not subjective fantasies. There is nothing more objective than the laws of arithmetic. (*GL* §105)

Frege's thought is perhaps this. Logic, as Frege thinks of it in *Grundlagen*, concerns itself not with any particular content but instead with the logical form of thought itself (which may be why Frege thinks, at this stage, that any objects it succeeds in introducing are thus transparent to it). Because logic concerns the form of thought, its laws must be objective, that is, "exactly the same for all rational beings" (*PW* 7; see also *GL* §27 n. 1 to p. 37). Although not in precisely the sense in which judgments in the special sciences are (objective) truths, judgments regarding the forms of thought can thus be said to be (objective) truths, even, in a sense, maximally objective.

Nevertheless, there is a problem, and Frege knows it. If, as Frege seems at first to have thought, logic were merely more general than the other sciences, then no special difficulty would attach to the idea that logic is, properly speaking, a science capable of extending our knowledge. But if logic is concerned only with form, as Frege begins to think after learning about Boole's logic around 1880, discoveries would seem to be impossible in logic. Logic, so conceived, could not be a science, properly speaking, at all.[12] The thesis of logicism compounds the difficulty. If logic is formal and arithmetic merely derived logic, then "how do the empty forms of logic disgorge so rich a content?" (*GL* §16). The author of *Grundlagen*, himself a formalist about logic, needs an answer. In *Grundlagen*, though in no earlier or later writings, Frege offers an argument to show that even analytic judgments, grounded in logic alone, can be ampliative, that is, extensions of knowledge, properly speaking. The argument, which derives from considerations first set out in the long Boole essay, aims to "put an end to the widespread contempt for analytic judgments and to the legend of the sterility of pure logic" (*GL* §17).

Both Boole's logical algebra and Frege's concept-script are designed perspicuously to represent "logical relations by means of written signs" (*PW* 14), thereby providing the "logical cement" required in the formation of new concepts out of old. But, as Frege points out in the long Boole essay, the logical relations represented in Boole's algebra enable only the simplest sort of concept formation by means of logical multiplication and addition. In Frege's imagery, concept formation in Boole's logic uses "the boundary lines of concepts we already have to form the boundaries of new ones" (*PW* 34). The much more powerful expressive resources of Frege's logic, in particular, those that involve the concavity notation, enable the formation of radically new concepts, concepts such as that of the continuity of a function at a point that do not merely trace over old boundary lines. This difference, Frege suggests in the Boole essay (though not in so many words), explains "the legend of the sterility of pure logic." "It is the fact that attention is principally given to this sort of formation of new concepts from old ones [that is, the sort that utilizes only Boolean combinations of concepts], while other more fruitful ones [the formations enabled by Frege's logic] are neglected which is surely responsible for the impression one easily gets in logic that for all our to-ing and fro-ing we never really leave the same spot" (*PW* 34). The account will not do as it stands, however. If arithmetic is merely derived logic then all its concepts are definable in purely logical terms, that is, in terms that provide only the "logical cement" and not the material part. It follows, as already noted, that the concepts of arithmetic are not really concepts at all but only forms. What needs to be explained, then, is not the fruitfulness of logic relative to a content already given, but how it is that "the empty forms of logic [themselves] can disgorge so rich a content."[13]

Frege's *Grundlagen* answer is well known: fruitful definitions (that is, those that draw new boundaries) enable fruitful proofs, that is, proofs of theorems that are not merely explicative in Kant's sense. Frege's proofs in Part III of *Begriffsschrift*, for example, involve definitions in strictly logical terms that enable derivations of theorems "which at first glance seem to be possible only on the grounds of some intuition" (*BGS* §23). In those theorems the "predicate" is not "contained in the concept of the subject," as required by Kant's conception of analyticity, and yet, as Frege shows, the predicate in the theorem proved can be shown, by logic alone, to attach to the concept of the subject. As the point is put in *Grundlagen*, such theorems "are contained in the definitions, but as plants are contained in their seeds, not as beams are contained in a house" (*GL* §88). The theorems proven are analytic, grounded in logic alone, but also ampliative in Kant's sense because the judgment is not proven solely on the basis of an analysis of the concept of the subject. They are, then, extensions of our knowledge, properly speaking—or so the author of *Grundlagen* argues.

After 1885 we hear no more about logical form as it contrasts with content, Kant's analytic/synthetic distinction is no longer invoked to demarcate the province of logic, and no further mention is made of fruitful definitions. After 1891 Frege does appeal to the distinction between the *Sinn* and the *Bedeutung* of an expression to explain how judgments of identity can constitute valuable extensions of our knowledge, but he nowhere appeals to that same distinction to explain how proofs can do so as well. The problem of the apparent sterility of logic vanishes without a trace, and the reason it does is that Frege's talk of form comes to be replaced after 1891 with talk of higher-level concepts and relations. Logic, Frege comes again to think, has its own content; it is, in this respect, like any other science, and as in any other science, discoveries are possible in logic. What is distinctive about the science of logic is that its content is higher order. We read, for instance, in "Function and Concept" (1891) that

if we use the functional letter f as an indefinite indication of a concept, then

$$\underline{\quad}\!\stackrel{\alpha}{\frown}\!\underline{\quad} f(\alpha)$$

gives us the form that includes the last examples (if we abstract from the judgment-stroke). The expressions

$$\underline{\quad}\!\stackrel{\alpha}{\frown}\!\underline{\quad} \alpha^2 = 1, \quad \underline{\quad}\!\stackrel{\alpha}{\frown}\!\underline{\quad} \alpha \geq 0,$$
$$\underline{\quad}\!\stackrel{\alpha}{\frown}\!\underline{\quad} \alpha < 0, \quad \underline{\quad}\!\stackrel{\alpha}{\frown}\!\underline{\quad} \alpha^2 - 3\alpha^2 + 2\alpha = 0$$

arise from this form in a manner analogous to that in which x^2 gives rise to '1^2', '2^2', '3^2'. Now just as in x^2 we have a function whose argument is indicated by 'x', I also conceive of

$$\underline{\quad}\!\stackrel{\alpha}{\frown}\!\underline{\quad} f(\alpha)$$

as the expression of a function whose argument is indicated by '*f*'. Such a function is obviously a fundamentally different one from those we have dealt with so far; for only a function can occur as its argument. (*CP* 153)

The form that is common to existential judgments, Frege now claims, is to be understood in terms of a higher-level function, one that takes functions as arguments. Similarly, whereas in *Grundlagen* Frege takes logic to concern the "general form of a thought-content," for instance, the form '*a* falls under the concept *F*', in *Grundgesetze* he thinks of this form (that is, the form of a simple singular sentence involving a monadic predicate) in terms of an unequal-leveled function of two arguments, namely the function ——$\phi(\xi)$, "where 'ξ' occupies and renders recognizable the place of the object-argument and '$\phi(\ )$' that of the function-argument" (*GG* §22). This function is "the relation of an object to a concept under which it falls"; it is the relation of subsumption. The concern of logic is not form, as Frege, following Boole, had thought, but instead higher-level concepts such as that of existence and higher-level relations such as that of subsumption.

In *Begriffsschrift* Frege takes judgments in the science of logic, which in *Grundlagen* he describes as "empty forms," to be properly contentful. Axioms and theorems of logic on that early view are not empty forms into which content might be injected any more than air is merely an empty space into which objects can be put. Laws of logic, the author of *Begriffsschrift* seems to think, are merely more general than other laws. By 1884 Frege had come to think that the laws of logic are qualitatively different from other laws; they are not laws of nature (albeit maximally general) but instead laws of the laws of nature. But because, at this second stage in Frege's thinking, this qualitative difference between the two sorts of laws is conceived in terms of the difference between form and content, Frege loses sight of the contentfulness of the laws of logic. Frege's mature conception of the formality of logic effects a synthesis: as Frege understands them after 1891, the laws of logic are at once fully contentful and also qualitatively different from the laws of the special sciences. As Frege puts the point in "Foundations of Geometry II" (1906), logic is formal if by that we mean that "as far as logic itself is concerned, each object is as good as any other, and each concept of the first level as good as any other and can be replaced by it." But even logic is not "unrestrictedly formal"; "if it were, then it would be without content" (*CP* 338). "Just as the con-

cept *point* belongs to geometry, so logic, too, has its own concepts and relations; and it is only in virtue of this that it can have a content. Toward
what is thus proper to it, its relation is not at all formal . . . To logic, for example, there belong the following: negation, identity, subsumption, subordination of concepts. And here logic brooks no replacement" (*CP* 338).
Like any science, Frege now suggests, logic has its own concepts and relations and its own laws regarding those concepts and relations. What is distinctive about it is that its concepts and relations, by contrast with those of
the special sciences, are second-level; they are concepts and relations under
which fall the concepts and relations of the special sciences. Even "formal"
rules of inference, then, are not formal in any sense that would contrast inferences governed by them with those inferences that are good in virtue
of the meanings (contents) of the concepts involved. What distinguishes
the laws that govern formally valid inferences from those that belong to
the special sciences, which govern instead inferences that are "materially"
valid, is that they concern concepts that are one and all higher order.

But, it will perhaps be objected, the concepts and relations of Frege's
logic are not one and all higher order. Identity, for instance, takes objects
as arguments; it is not a higher-order relation. Nor are the conditional and
horizontal strokes higher order; for they take truth-values, among other
objects, as arguments. The objection is based on a confusion the nature of
which can be illustrated by appeal (yet again) to the formula language of
arithmetic. Suppose one said that the laws of higher analysis concern not
numbers or arithmetical functions but instead kinds of arithmetical functions, that is, second-level functions (for example, the second-level function $f(x) \cdot F(x)$, which takes functions as arguments), and it was then objected that among the signs of higher analysis are, for instance, '+' and '·',
which take numbers as arguments. The right response would be to point
out that in a law of higher analysis the sign '+' does not serve any function
on its own, as, for instance, it might be thought to in '2 + 3'. Instead, it
functions, together with the other signs and indicating letters, in the formation of expressions that designate higher-level functions. The fact that
primitive signs of *Begriffsschrift* occur in the laws of logic, signs that in
other contexts can be understood as taking objects as arguments, similarly
does not show that Frege is wrong to say that the concern of logic is
higher-order concepts and relations. In calculus the primitive signs of
arithmetic, signs that in other contexts can be read as taking numbers as
arguments, are used to form expressions for higher-order functions, and in
logic, the primitive signs of *Begriffsschrift* that in other contexts can be

read as taking objects as arguments are used similarly to form expressions that designate higher-level concepts and relations.

Already in *Grundlagen* Frege indicates that the sign for identity can be dispensed with. Following Leibniz, he adopts as his "definition" of identity the principle of the substitutivity *salva veritate* of identicals: "things are the same as each other, of which one can be substituted for the other without loss of truth" (*GL* §65).[14] To say that a = b, then, is to say that the second-level properties

$$-\!\!\!\!\!\begin{array}{l}\phi(b)\\ \phi(a)\end{array} \qquad \text{and} \qquad -\!\!\!\!\!\begin{array}{l}\phi(a)\\ \phi(b)\end{array}$$

have a certain third-level property, namely, the property

$$-\overset{\mathfrak{i}}{\smile}\!\!-\mu_\beta(\mathfrak{f}(\beta)).$$

On the reading adopted here, the concept of identity is properly thought of as a logical concept for just this reason. So, we can say, laws of logic are distinctive insofar as only indicating letters occur to the right of rightmost horizontals in the laws of logic. That by itself does not show that the concepts and relations of logic are one and all higher order, however. The conditional stroke seems to be a distinctively logical sign; nevertheless, what it designates is a first-level relation. Is it, then, somehow exempt from Frege's rule that in logic "each concept of the first level [is] as good as any other and can be replaced by it"? The answer is no because, contrary to appearances, this sign will not occur in isolation in actual applications of any law of logic but only as a constituent of a higher-level concept.

Consider, for instance, the first law of *Begriffsschrift*,

This law exhibits something that is the case no matter what truth-values are taken as arguments. So, it would seem, the indicating letters here fill the argument places of the first-level relation

That is not, however, the best way to conceptualize this law in applications of it (for example, as applied in connection with the laws of the special sciences). We know that any *Begriffsschrift* sentence can be given a function/ argument analysis; that is, it can be conceived as involving an ascription of a concept. Because it can, we can construe this first law of *Begriffsschrift* as an ascription of a third-level property to a second-level relation, say,

On this reading, it is such a second-level relation, not the first-level relation previously considered, that is the argument for the law. What the law says, so analyzed, is that this second-level relation holds of any two concepts and two objects. Clearly, in the sign used to designate this second-level relation, the conditional stroke does not function as a first-level relation but is instead a constituent of a sign designating a second-level relation. In this way, instead of construing the axiom as a truth-function, we construe it as involving the ascription of a third-level concept to a second-level relation. Obviously we can do the same for any other axiom or theorem of *Begriffsschrift* that seems to involve the conditional stroke functioning as a first-level relation sign. Among the primitive signs of *Begriffsschrift* are signs for first-level concepts; nevertheless, their role in logic, according to Frege's considered view, is to enable the formation of expressions that designate higher-level concepts and relations.

In the 1879 *Begriffsschrift* the first logical symbol to be introduced after the content and judgment strokes is the sign for the conditional, followed by the negation stroke and the sign for identity. The last sign to be introduced is the concavity. In *Begriffsschrift*, that is, Frege follows the ordering of any standard textbook of logic; he begins with truth-functions, that is, the propositional calculus, and then moves on to the predicate calculus. In *Grundgesetze* the order of presentation is very different. There the first signs to be introduced are, again, the judgment stroke and the horizontal (as it is now called), but these are now followed by the negation stroke, the sign for identity, and the concavity. The last primitive sign to be introduced in *Grundgesetze* is the conditional stroke, and it is introduced, as we have already seen, "in order to enable us to designate the subordination of a concept under a concept, and other important relations" (*GG* §12). As far as logic is concerned, the author of *Grundgesetze* suggests, the conditional stroke has no significance in isolation, no significance independent of the other logical signs that together with it enable the formation of higher-level concepts. The logical significance of the conditional stroke is revealed only in combination with Frege's signs that express generality of content (that is, the concavity with German letters and Frege's Latin italic letters), and the conditional stroke itself has a role in logic only in such combinations. Its role in logic is to enable the expression of higher-level relations such as subordination.

3.5 Mastering the Instrument

Already in Chapter 2 an account was developed of the logical justification for Frege's two-dimensional notation and of the peculiar expressive function his Latin italic letters play in lending generality of content despite their having neither sense nor meaning. *Begriffsschrift* Latin italic letters, it was argued, preserve the expressive power of the two-dimensional conditional stroke by driving everything up a level. As Frege already saw shortly after the completion of *Begriffsschrift*, genuine hypotheticals of his logical language exhibit (first-level) concepts in logical relations such as that of subordination. Only more than a decade later did he come fully to appreciate the role of the concavity with German letters in driving things up yet another level. The three developments in Frege's thinking that have been traced here—that concepts are something objective, something in their own right that can serve as arguments for higher-level concepts, that the concavity notation serves in the formation of concept words for higher-level concepts, and that the laws of logic concern just such higher-level concepts—are, on our reading, one and all aspects of this hard-won insight.

Beginning with the thought that the fundamental idea of *Begriffsschrift* is to express laws governing modes of inference as formulae, we have been led to a conception of logic according to which its topic is the higher-order concepts and relations under which the concepts and relations of the special sciences fall. The task of logic on this conception is to discover the laws that govern such concepts, that is, the laws of the laws of the special sciences, where sentences expressing such laws make essential use of the distinctive expressive capacities of Frege's concavity with German letters used in the formation of higher-level concept words and of Frege's Latin italic letters lending generality of content. These sentences, furthermore, exhibit the peculiar virtue of the simpler sentences already considered. They, like any other sentences of *Begriffsschrift* on our reading, are variously analyzable into function and argument for the purposes of judgment and inference. They are essentially two-dimensional. As Frege finally came explicitly to realize, his formula language was a radically different sort of language than he had at first thought. As we will soon see, sentences of that language do not express contents of possible judgment, the circumstances that obtain if they are true, as Frege at first thought. That notion of sentential content is to be "split" in the mature logic into the thought expressed *(Sinn)*, on the one hand, and the truth-value designated *(Bedeutung)*, on the other.

4

The Work Brought to Maturity

It will be seen that the years have not passed in vain since the appearance of my *Begriffsschrift* and *Grundlagen:* they have brought the work to maturity. But just that which I recognize as a vital advance stands, as I cannot conceal from myself, as a great obstacle in the way of the dissemination and the effectiveness of my book . . . I have moved farther away from the accepted conceptions.

—GRUNDGESETZE, 1893

Frege's understanding of the logical language first presented in *Begriffsschrift* in 1879 and then again in the first volume of *Grundgesetze* in 1893 was radically revised in the intervening years. His conception of a concept, of the distinction between objects and concepts (and so of the distinction between first-level and higher-level concepts), of the laws of logic, and of the roles played by the various primitive signs of his logic all were fundamentally rethought in the 1880s. But though we have traced these developments, the guiding thread that underlies and connects them one to another has thus far figured only implicitly. We need to understand the "vital advance" that brought Frege's logic to maturity. We need an account of the *Sinn/Bedeutung* distinction.

4.1 The Shape of Frege's Discovery

Although we find it natural to construe Frege's introduction of the *Sinn/Bedeutung* distinction in the early 1890s as the discovery of an extralogical theory of the cognitive aspect of language use, Frege himself takes the discovery of the distinction between *Sinn* and *Bedeutung* to be a properly logical advance. He indicates why in the opening sentences of his "Comments on Sense and Meaning":

> In an article (*Über Sinn und Bedeutung*) I distinguished between sense and meaning in the first instance only for the case of proper names (or, if one prefers, singular terms). The same distinction can also be drawn for concept words. Now it is easy to become unclear about this by confounding the division into concepts and objects with

the distinction between sense and meaning so that we run together sense and concept on the one hand and meaning and object on the other. To every concept-word or proper name, there corresponds as a rule a sense and a meaning, as I use these words. (*PW* 118)

We tend to confound the distinction between sense and meaning with the distinction between concept and object, Frege suggests, and as a result confuse the notion of a concept with that of sense and the notion of an object with that of meaning. We think, that is, that only object names function referringly in language, that all cognitive content is predicative. Although he does not explicitly say so, Frege appears here to be diagnosing his own earlier mistake.[1] If he is, then his discovery is not the discovery of a notion of *Sinn* to supplement a semantic notion of *Bedeutung* present already in the early logic. Nor even is it simply the discovery of the distinction between *Sinn* and *Bedeutung*. It is the discovery of a distinction between two different distinctions. Much as a traditional term logic conflates the logical distinction, drawn in a modern logic, between referring and predicative expressions, so, Frege seems to have come to think, the logical distinction between referring and predicative expressions, as he had understood it in the early logic, rests on a conflation of two logical distinctions, that between object and concept with that between meaning and sense. As we will see, the relevant texts, early and late, support precisely this thought, that in the years between 1884 and 1893 Frege came fundamentally to reconceive the way a properly logical language functions as a language.

According to Frege's early view, object names function in language as referring expressions, as representatives of objects. It follows that a sentence containing an object name that is not representative of any object cannot have any meaning. "The sentence 'Leo Sasche is a man' is the expression of a thought only if 'Leo Sasche' designates something" (*PW* 174). It would also seem to follow on this view of the logical role of object names that identities are logically useless, that where 'j' and 'k' are representative of the same object, the identity 'j = k' is trivial in just the way 'j = j' is.[2] Frege resists the conclusion. Certainly it is true that if object names were merely representatives of objects, then, assuming that 'j' and 'k' are representatives of the same object and are functioning normally, the sentence 'j = k' would have the same judgeable content as the sentence 'j = j'. We know, however, that the former can require proof whereas the latter is trivial, merely an instance of the law of identity. "The same content can be fully determined in different ways; but, that the *same content*, in a particular case, is actually given by *two* [*different*] *modes of determination* is the content of a *judgment*" (*BGS* §8). So, Frege concludes in the 1879 *Begriffsschrift*, "symbols . . . usually only representatives of their contents . . . at once appear *in propria persona* as soon as they are combined by the symbol for identity of content, for this signifies the circumstance that the two names have the same content." The account is hopeless. In the first place, it requires an ambiguity in the meanings of symbols: "a bifurcation is necessarily introduced into the meaning of every symbol, the same symbols standing at times for their contents, at times for themselves" (*BGS* §8), and this contravenes Frege's requirement, set out in §1 of *Begriff-sschrift*, that symbols "have a completely fixed sense." But even if such systematic ambiguity were admitted, the proposed solution to the problem of the contentfulness of some identities would fail. Suppose that it is true that j = k, that is, that 'j' and 'k' have the same content. It follows that 'Fj' and 'Fk' too must have the same content because in this context the symbols 'j' and 'k' "[stand] for their contents," not for themselves. But, we are told in §3, Frege's *Begriffsschrift* does not "distinguish between propositions which have the same conceptual content." Indeed, it is clear that even if j = k, nevertheless 'Fj' and 'Fk' do not have the same conceptual content (*begrifflicher Inhalt*); for not all consequences derivable from the one combined with certain other judgments can be derived from the other combined with those same judgments. Consider, for example, the premise 'if Fj, then Gm'. Frege's *Begriffsschrift* solution to the problem of the logical significance of identities is no solution at all.

Because the same object (content) "can be fully determined in different ways" and it can be the content of a judgment that it is the same object that is designated in both cases, identities are necessary in logic. It would seem to follow that what matters to the correctness of an inference is something more fine grained than what matters to the correctness of judgment. We know that if j = k, then 'Fj' is true just in case 'Fk' is true, that it is the same circumstance that obtains if 'Fj' is true and if 'Fk' is true. But, as Frege's reflections on identity indicate, the sentences 'Fj' and 'Fk' nevertheless seem not to have the same content in the sense of *begrifflicher Inhalt*. In the case in which the names are associated with different modes of determination, "the judgment as to identity of content is, in Kant's sense synthetic" (*BGS* §8). Close as he comes, however, Frege does not, in *Begriffsschrift*, conclude that the *begrifflicher Inhalt* of a sentence containing an object name, its content as it matters to correct inference, is different from its truth conditions, the circumstance that obtains if the sentence is true.

Frege's first extended discussion of object names after 1890 is in "On Sense and Meaning." The similarity between his early *Begriffsschrift* discussion of identity and this later discussion is remarkable. As in the earlier work, Frege rejects the idea that a sentence of the form 'a = b' can be understood to express a relation among objects because sentences of this form "often contain very valuable extensions of our knowledge and cannot always be established *a priori*" (*CP* 157). He again rejects the idea that considered independently of "the manner in which [the sign] designates something" (*CP* 157–158), such a sentence expresses the thought that is wanted because "in that case the sentence *a = b* would no longer refer to the subject matter, but only to its mode of designation [that is, the sign used]; we would express no proper knowledge by its means" (*CP* 157). As the point is put in *Begriffsschrift*, the case of interest to logic is not the case in which the "different names for the same content are . . . merely an indifferent matter of form," but instead the case in which the different names "are associated with different modes of determination" (*BGS* §8). Frege does have a new example, however, one that differs from the earlier example in two important respects. In the *Begriffsschrift* example Frege employs one name, '*A*', that involves only a trivial mode of determination, and another, '*B*', that is a variable name because what it designates is a function of the position of the line in the example. In Frege's example in "On Sense and Meaning," both object names, 'the point of intersection of *a* and *b*' and 'the point of intersection of *b* and *c*', clearly contain a mode of presentation, and neither is a variable name. "The statement [that the objects so signified are identical] contains actual knowledge"; so, Frege immediately concludes, "it is natural, now, to think of there being connected with a sign (name, combination of words, written marks), besides that which the sign designates, which may be called the meaning of the sign, also what I should like to call the *sense* of the sign, wherein the mode of presentation is contained" (*CP* 158). An object name is not merely representative of an object, Frege now claims; rather, it expresses a sense (*Sinn*) and designates a meaning (*Bedeutung*). Appealing to essentially the same considerations as are rehearsed in *Begriffsschrift*, Frege now draws a very different conclusion, remarking only that it is "natural" to do so.

Although Frege at first thinks that object names function logically as representatives of objects, already in the 1879 logic he raises a difficulty for that conception. In identities, which (he argues) are necessary in logic, object names do not seem to function logically as representatives of objects. Frege's early view of the logical role of concept words faces a correlative difficulty, though it is not explicitly recognized. Frege thinks (at first) that concept words function predicatively, that is, that their role in language is to characterize objects independently given. But, as he also sees (though not quite in *Begriffsschrift* itself), a genuine hypothetical expresses a relation among concepts. The problem, quite simply, is that if concept words function merely predicatively then there can be no relations among concepts that are not mediated by the objects they characterize.

Object names, we have already seen, are understood in the early logic merely as representatives of objects; they represent objects, but not *as* anything. Concept words, correspondingly, do not function as representatives of objects—they are not "general" or "common" names of objects—but are essentially predicative. The role of a concept word, on Frege's early view, is to characterize an object (or objects) otherwise given. It provides a way of thinking about an object and has no independent existence. As Frege himself puts the point in a letter, apparently to Anton Marty, dated 29 August 1882, "a concept is unsaturated in that it requires something to fall under it; hence it cannot exist on its own. That an individual falls under it is a judgeable content, and here the concept appears as a predicate, and is always predicative" (*PMC* 101). A concept, Frege seems at first to think, cannot exist on its own any more than a particular instance of a property such as redness can, and for much the same reason.[3]

If, as Frege seems at first to have thought, a sentence constitutively involves two fundamentally different sorts of expressions playing essentially different logical roles, the one (an object name) to give an object or objects and the other (a concept word) to present those objects as thus and so, then in the case in which no object is given, no thought can be expressed. There can be no characterizing, no presentation of things as thus and so, if nothing is given to be so characterized or so presented. There cannot, then, be a sentence that is about concepts in just the way in which a singular sentence is about objects. But how, then, are we to understand the subordination of concepts in general sentences? A general sentence contains no object names and seems not to be about objects but instead about concepts; nevertheless, if a concept "cannot exist on its own," if it is "always predicative," then even a general sentence, if it is to have any content, must in some way be about objects. In *Begriffsschrift* Frege suggests exactly that. The difference between a singular sentence and a general sentence, as it is explained in the 1879 logic, is the difference between a sentence with a "determinate" content and one with an "indeterminate" content.

The basic case is that of a singular sentence *of* something (referred to using an object name) *as* something (that is, as characterized using a predicative expression). Such a sentence is nonetheless variously analyzable into function and argument and, independent of an analysis, merely presents "a combination of ideas."[4] To obtain a general sentence, one first gives an analysis; that is, one imagines the sentence divided up into a constant part (the function expression) and a variable part (the argument name). The variable part, the argument name, is then replaced by a letter "which one can take to signify various things" (*BGS* §1). "The argument [in this way] becomes *indeterminate*, as in the judgment: 'Whatever arbitrary positive integer we take as argument for "being representable as the sum of four squares", the [resulting] proposition is always true'" (*BGS* §9). Instead of a singular sentence characterizing a determinate object as thus and so, we now have a general sentence involving indeterminate reference, and here "the distinction between function and argument acquires a *substantive* {*inhaltlich*} significance" (*BGS* §9). What a general sentence expresses is the thought that the relevant predicative expression is correctly applied not merely to this object or that object but to any object. A general sentence that expresses the subordination of one concept to another is thus not to be conceived (according to Frege's *Begriffsschrift* account) as about concepts in the way a singular sentence is about objects. It is instead to be distinguished from a singular sentence as the indeterminate is distinguished from the determinate: a singular sentence is determinately about objects; a general sentence is indeterminately about objects—or so Frege suggests in *Begriffsschrift*.

But, as Frege also sees, the validity of some inferences is explicable only if concepts too can serve as arguments.

> *in order to express an indeterminate function of the argument A, we put*
> *A in parentheses following a letter,* for example:
>
> $\Phi(A)$.
>
> *Similarly,*
>
> $\Psi(A,B)$

represents a function (not more explicitly determined) of the two argu-
ments A and B . . .

We can read

$$\vdash \Phi(A)$$

as: "*A* has the property *Φ*."

$$\vdash \Psi(A,B)$$

can be translated by "*B* stands in the *Ψ*-relation to *A*" . . .

Since the symbol *Φ* occurs at a place in the expression

$$\Phi(A)$$

and since we can think of it as replaceable by other symbols [such as]
Ψ, *X*—which then express other functions of the argument *A*—we
can consider *Φ*(*A*) as a function of the argument *Φ*. (*BGS* §10)

Although '*Φ*' in '*Φ*(*A*)' functions predicatively, it can nonetheless be
thought of as replaceable and hence as the argument in a function/argu-
ment analysis. The point is reinforced by Frege's remark, in his discussion
of generality in §11, that "since a letter which is used as a function symbol,
like *Φ* in *Φ*(*A*), can itself be considered as the argument of a function, it
can be replaced by a German letter in the manner just specified"; it can,
that is, be replaced by a German letter and a concavity containing the letter inserted into the content stroke. In that case, as Frege puts it in §9,
which provides the first discussion of the notion of a function, "the argument is determinate, but the function is indeterminate." This, however, is
incoherent by Frege's own lights because an argument is by definition that
which is indeterminate and a function that which is determinate. The
source of the difficulty is manifest: in *Begriffsschrift* Frege thinks of an argument both as "the symbol which is regarded as replaceable by others"
and as that "which denotes the object which stands in these relations"
(*BGS* §9). An argument is that which is indeterminate (taken to be variable or replaceable) in a function/argument analysis, and a function is that
which is determinate, held invariant, in such an analysis. Clearly, then,
the function is always "predicative" or unsaturated. But as Frege himself
notes, contrary to his official account of an argument, the argument need
not in every case be saturated, that is, an object. It can be a concept. But
how can a concept provide the argument for a function if a concept "is
always predicative" and "cannot exist on its own" (*PMC* 101)? Given

Frege's early conception of concepts, and thereby of first-order generalities as indeterminately about objects, Frege can achieve no satisfactory account of higher-order generalities, generalities in which "the function is indeterminate."

In a letter to Husserl dated 24 May 1891, Frege sets out a schema to clarify his mature view.

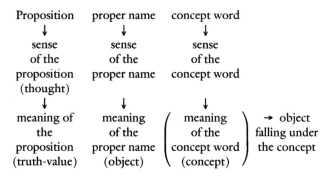

With a concept word it takes one more step to reach the object than with a proper name, and the last step may be missing—i.e., the concept may be empty—without the concept word's ceasing to be scientifically useful. I have drawn the last step from concept to object horizontally in order to indicate that it takes place on the same level, that objects and concepts have the same objectivity. (*PMC* 63)

Husserl's view of concepts, Frege suggests, would be given by the schema

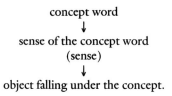

Husserl has no conception of the *Bedeutung* of a concept word.

Nor is it only Husserl who lacks this conception. Both intensional and extensional logicians do so as well, Frege thinks. Indeed, he suggests in his "Comments on Sense and Meaning" that we can understand familiar debates between intensionalist and extensionalist logicians by reference to just this lack. Both have achieved an insight, but lacking the notion of the *Bedeutung* of a concept word, they oscillate between two equally unacceptable positions: the intensionalist takes the sense to be the meaning of a concept word, and the extensionalist takes instead the extension, the objects that fall under it, to be the meaning.

> The intensionalist logicians are only too happy not to go beyond the sense; for what they call the intension, if it is not an idea, is nothing other than the sense. They forget that logic is not concerned with how thoughts, regardless of truth-value, follow from thoughts, that the step from thought to truth-value—more generally, the step from sense to meaning—has to be taken. They forget that the laws of logic are first and foremost laws in the realm of meanings and only relate indirectly to sense. (*PW* 122)

The extensionalist, then, is right to reject the sense as the meaning of a concept word. But the extensionalist is wrong to think that it is instead the extension that is the meaning: "we concede to the intensionalist logicians that it is the concept as opposed to the extension that is the fundamental thing" (*PW* 123). But again, the concept is not, *pace* the intensionalist logician, the sense. What both the intensionalist logician and the extensionalist logician fail to see is that the meaning of a concept word is neither the sense expressed nor the objects to which the concept word is correctly applied. It is a concept, that is, a law of correlation, objects (or in the case of higher-level concepts, lower-level concepts) to truth-values. Whereas in the case of an object name the mistake is to think that the name only designates an object, that it does not also express a sense, in the case of a concept word the mistake is to think that the word only expresses a sense (a way of thinking about something, a way of characterizing it), that it does not also designate something—or, if it does, that it designates a class or collection of objects. As Dummett says, "whereas [Frege's] task, with proper names, was to argue that they have *Sinn,* in the case of predicates the whole interest lies in their having *Bedeutung*."[5]

According to Frege's early conception of the way a properly logical language functions, the logical role played by object names is essentially different from that played by concept words. Object names serve a referring function; they give objects as that about which a judgment is made. Concept words, by contrast, are essentially predicative; a concept provides a way of regarding an object, a way of taking it to be. A whole sentence, then, can be thought of as a kind of picture *of* something (referred to) *as* something (characterized as thus and so through the application of a predicate); it is a kind of picture of a state of affairs, a picture of the circumstance that obtains if the sentence is true (*BGS* §2). It is just this conception of the functioning of language that is superseded in the mature logic. In the mature logic both sorts of expressions (that is, both object names and concept words) function in the same way: both sorts of expressions designate something in much the way object names were originally thought to refer to something, and both involve a kind of characterization, a way of thinking about that which is designated. The sense of an expression presents the entity meant, whether it be an object or a concept, under an aspect, as conceived in a particular way. Frege's early conception of the distinction between referring expressions (that is, object names) and predicative expressions (concept words), which grounds his early conception of a content of possible judgment as a state of affairs, the circumstance that obtains if the sentence is true, conflates the logical notion of *Bedeutung*, that which is designated, with the notion of an object, and the logical notion of *Sinn*, that which is expressed, with the notion of a concept. His early conception of a content of possible judgment is to be "split" in the mature logic into the thought expressed, on the one hand, and the truth-value designated, on the other (*GG* §5 n. 14; *GG* 6–7; *PMC* 63).

4.2 The Formula Language of Arithmetic

Frege says in his "Comments on Sense and Meaning" that it is easy to "run together sense and concept on the one hand and meaning and object on the other" (*PW* 118). Frege himself, we have suggested, does just that in the early logic. He thinks that object names serve only to refer to objects and concept words only to characterize objects (otherwise given) as thus and so, and as a result, he thinks of the content of a sentence in terms of its truth conditions, the circumstance that obtains if the sentence is true. On his mature conception of the way object names and concept words function in a properly logical language, the notion of meaning, *Bedeutung,* is not confused with that of an object. Just as object names do, concept words have meaning, not, as on a traditional conception, in virtue of their being general or common names for objects, but in virtue of serving to designate concepts, which (we saw in section 3.2) are unsaturated or incomplete but nevertheless fully objective. A concept, on Frege's mature view, is something in its own right that can serve as an argument for a (higher-level) function. Correlatively, in the mature logic, the notion of sense, *Sinn,* is not confused with that of a concept. Just as concept words do, object names express senses, not, as Russell thought, in virtue of their being disguised descriptions (that is, really predicative rather than referential), but by presenting an object (if there is one) under a mode of determination. According to Frege's mature understanding, both object names and concept words function in language both to designate something (at least in favored cases) and to express something.[6] The fundamental logical difference between them is to be understood not in terms of a difference in how they function but instead in terms of a difference in what is expressed and thereby designated in the two cases, something saturated or complete in the case of object names and something unsaturated or incomplete in the case of concept words. Frege's formula language functions as a language in a way that is radically different from that he had at first thought. As he does, we can further clarify this conception of how a properly logical language functions, and in particular the notion of *Sinn*, by reflecting on how, according to Frege, the formula language of arithmetic functions.

As Frege understands it, a true conceptual notation is at once a *lingua characterica* and a *calculus ratiocinator;* that is, it at once expresses a content in a way "which fits the things themselves" (*BGS* 105) and is completely rigorous "in the sense that there is an algorithm . . . i.e. a totality of rules which govern the transition from one sentence or from two sentences to a new one in such a way that nothing happens except in conformity with those rules" (*CP* 237). At least up to a point, Frege thinks, the formula language of arithmetic is such a language, for "it directly expresses the facts without the intervention of speech" and in calculations "the deduction is stereotyped {*sehr einformig*} being almost always based upon identical transformations of identical numbers yielding identical results" (*CN* 88). In the formula language of arithmetic, one can "operate the figures mechanically" because "the mathematical notation has, as a result of genuine thought, been so developed that it does the thinking for us, so to speak" (*GL* iv). Because "it is not a matter simply of assigning names, but of symbolizing in its own right the numerical element" (*GL* §28), the direct isomorphism between the numerical element represented and the representation of it ensures that the mere manipulation of (appropriate) symbols according to (valid) rules preserves truth. But what is the numerical element symbolized in the formula language of arithmetic? In *Grundlagen* Frege provides an answer.

In the early logic, we have seen, Frege understands identities as expressions not of complete equality but of sameness in a respect. As two objects can be the same in color or length, so two names can be the same in content, in that of which they are representative. An identity of the form 'a = b', where two different modes of determination correspond to the two names, signifies the circumstance that the two names are in this way in partial agreement. By the time he had finished *Grundlagen*, Frege had come to think that this view is mistaken, that it is instead the Leibnizian conception of identity as complete equality that is the right conception: two things are identical just if the one can be substituted for the other *salva veritate*. Nor was this an isolated insight. Frege's realization that the equal sign in arithmetic expresses complete equality, that is, identity, was at the same time a realization about all the signs of arithmetic. The thought that numbers are collections of objects, that the plus sign means 'putting together', and that the equal sign signifies agreement in a respect are, he came to see, fundamentally related one to another—and also completely mistaken.

> The conception of number as a series of things of the same kind, as a group, heap, etc. is very closely connected with the view which takes the sign of equality to designate partial agreement only, and with the view of the plus sign as synonymous with 'and'. But these views collapse at the first serious attempt to use them as a foundation for arithmetic. If we make such an attempt, we are always obliged to smuggle in something which is in conflict with these views. (*PW* 228)

Even Frege himself may have at first seriously attempted to use these views as a foundation for arithmetic. By the time *Grundlagen* was completed, they had collapsed. The formula language of arithmetic functions in a way that is very different from that one might naturally assume.

As presented in *Grundlagen*, the problem is to give an account of statements of identity in arithmetic, statements such as, for instance, that 1 + 1 + 1 = 3, and the view to be rejected is one according to which the tokenings of the numeral '1' in '1 + 1 + 1 = 3' designate units which are put together to form a collection that is then identified (partially, in a respect) with the collection designated by '3'. The question whether the units so combined are identical or different reveals the flaw in this conception of number. We suppose, to begin with, that a number is a collection of units. Were it such a collection, the units collected would have to be either the same or different. Assume, first, that the units are different, as it would seem they must be if a plurality is to be reached. Then, as Jevons argues, a sum such as '1 + 1 + 1' is more perspicuously represented as '1′ + 1″ + 1‴', thereby making manifest our otherwise tacit understanding that "each of these units is distinct from each other" (*GL* §36). Subtracting one from such a collection would be a matter of literally taking away, and taking away different units (for example, now the leftmost, now the rightmost) would leave different collections, different twos. "There would be not only distinct ones but also distinct twos and so on" (*GL* §38). As a result, one would be left with a "chaos of numbers." "There would be not a single number which was the first prime number after 5, but infinitely many: 7, 8 − 1, (8 + 6):2, etc. We should not speak of 'the sum of 7 and 5' with the definite article but of 'a sum' or 'all sums', 'some sums', etc.; and hence we should not say 'the sum of 7 and 5 is divisible by 3' but 'all sums of 7 and 5 are divisible by 3'" (*PMC* 127). If the units were different, we would be left with a chaos of numbers. Indeed, if the units were different, no numbers would be reached at all because any collection of distinct units can be assigned different numbers depending on "the way in which we have chosen to regard it" (*GL* §22). Regarding each stroke in a collection of, say, nine strokes as a unit to be counted, we assign to the collection the number nine. We can, however, as easily regard each triplet as the unit relative to which to count, and in that case the number assigned is not nine but three. In conceiving the number nine as a collection of units representable as a series of strokes, we put together different things, different units or strokes; "the result is an agglomeration in which the objects contained remain still in possession of precisely those properties which serve to distinguish them from one another; and that is not number" (*GL* §39).

Well then, the units must be identical. But if they were identical then '1 + 1 + 1' would be the same as '1' "just as gold and gold and gold is never anything else but gold" (*GL* §38). Were the units to be combined identical, they would collapse into one another; we could not get beyond the single unit. Again the notion of number eludes us.

> If we try to produce the number by putting together distinct objects, the result is an agglomeration in which the objects contained remain still in possession of precisely those properties which serve to distinguish them from one another; and that is not number. But if we try to do it in the other way, by putting together identicals, the result runs perpetually together into one and we never reach a plurality. (*GL* §39)

The units put together in a sum must be identical and yet they cannot be. There is only one number one, and yet 1 + 1 + 1 = 3. Number, Frege concludes, cannot be a collection of units; '+' cannot mean the same as 'and'; '=' does not signify identity in a respect. "It is nonsense to make numbers result from the putting together of ones" (*GL* §45).

Frege's investigations reveal that the notion of a unit involves a confusion of two different notions, that of a concept relative to which the items in a collection are identical one with another and are to be numbered, and that of the particular objects that fall under that concept. For example, "in the proposition 'Jupiter has four moons', the unit is 'moon of Jupiter'. Under this concept falls moon I, and likewise also moon II, and moon III too, and finally moon IV. Thus we can say: the unit to which I relates is identical with the unit to which II relates, and so on. This gives us our identity. But when we assert the distinguishability of units, we mean that the things numbered are distinguishable" (*GL* §54). A statement of number, we are now to see, assigns a number to a concept. "If I say 'the King's carriage is drawn by four horses', then I assign the number four to the concept 'horse that draws the King's carriage'" (*GL* §46). The logical form of the sentence, Frege argues in *Grundlagen* §57, is that of an identity. A statement of number has the form 'the number of $F = n$', where F is the concept to which the number is assigned and n is the number of objects that fall under F, the number assigned to F. What we had taken to be the number itself, namely, a collection, is only that which is counted. The notion of a collection in terms of which we had tried to understand the notion of number is split in this way into the more fine-grained notion of the concept relative to which things are counted, on the one hand, and the less fine-grained notion of the number assigned to that concept, on the other.[7] Of course there are collections of objects. What Frege has shown is that what is needed to understand a statement of number regarding a collection is not reference to the collection itself but instead reference to the relevant concept and to the number assigned to that concept in light of the objects that fall under it.

Although Frege shows that the conception of number as a collection of units is fundamentally misguided, it is nonetheless one that can seem very natural. It is very easy to think of the numerical element in terms of the idea of relative magnitude. Were that conception correct, the Roman numeration system would be a perspicuous language of arithmetic, a Leibnizian *lingua characterica* of number, because expressions in that language directly exhibit relations of relative magnitude. Two is twice as many as one, so, supposing we depict one as 'i', we should express two as 'ii'. Three is three times as many as one and one more than two, so it is symbolized 'iii'. For convenience, abbreviations are introduced, five, for instance, as 'v' to abbreviate 'iiiii'. Then we can express four as 'iv' on the grounds that four is one less than five, and six as 'vi' because it is five and one more.[8] In such a numeration system "bigger" numbers are represented by symbols that are bigger (composed of a greater number of tokenings of 'i'), and bigger by as much as the numbers themselves are bigger. Three as represented in a Roman numeral is literally and manifestly two and one; one can see in the symbols themselves that two and one make three. The Roman numeration system is in this way a *lingua characterica* of the numbers conceived as collections of units.

If, furthermore, the Roman numeration system were a perspicuous notation of arithmetic, a *lingua characterica,* then the Arabic numeration system would be a remarkably unperspicuous symbol system of arithmetic. It would be unperspicuous precisely because the symbols, '1', '2', '3', and so on, do not themselves exhibit relative magnitudes. It is inscribed in the symbols themselves that iii is greater than ii, and by how much; it is not inscribed in the symbols themselves that 3 is greater than 2. To know which of these two Arabic signs represents the larger number requires knowing what they mean. The number 222 is smaller than the number 999, but the numeral '222' does not look any smaller than the numeral '999'. From the perspective according to which Roman numerals perspicuously represent the numbers, the ten digits of the Arabic notation are quite like the convenient abbreviations 'v', 'x', and so on that we find already in the Roman system. Larger numbers, which in the Arabic system are given by the relative positions of digits in combinations of them, give the numbers through a kind of a code. Knowing the code is being able to get back to the numbers themselves, perspicuously represented in Roman numerals, as needed.

Were numbers collections of units, the Arabic system would be an unperspicuous notation of arithmetic because it does not map relative magnitudes. It would not be a *lingua characterica* of arithmetic. Nevertheless, that symbol system is enormously powerful. Because algorithms can be formulated in the Arabic numeration system for all the basic arithmetical operations, one can formalize (that is, rigorize) arithmetic using Arabic numerals. Simply by manipulating Arabic symbols according to rules, anyone who knows this formula language can in principle perform calculations of any degree of complexity. It is as if, as Frege says, "the mathematical notation . . . does the thinking for us" (*GL* iv). This is, furthermore, all but impossible in the Roman numeration system. The results of calculations can be recorded in Roman numerals, but one cannot calculate in the language.[9] Only the Arabic numeration system is a language within which to calculate; only that system is a *calculus ratiocinator*. Relative to the system of Roman numerals conceived as a Leibnizian *lingua characterica* of number, the Arabic numeration system would be, however, merely an abstract calculus. We would then have to ask what the relationship is between the rules that govern our calculations using Arabic numerals and the arithmetical truths proved thereby, what the relationship is between calculability in the Arabic notation and arithmetical truth perspicuously representable only in the Roman system, between, as it were, the proof theory of arithmetic and its semantic notion of truth. Fortunately, the question needs no answer because, as we have seen, a number is not a collection of units. The Roman numeration system is not a *lingua characterica* of arithmetic.

There is only one one, and yet $1 + 1 + 1 = 3$. How are we to understand this? Although it is not yet explicit in *Grundlagen*, Frege's way is in terms of the distinction between sense and meaning: the expressions that flank the identity sign designate the same number but differ in sense. As Frege puts the point in "On the Concept of Number" (1891/1892), after complaining that the problems he is discussing had already "been essentially resolved in *Grundlagen*":

> there are various designations for any one number. It is the same number that is designated by '1 + 1' and '2' . . . It is inevitable that various signs should be used for the same thing, since there are different possible ways of arriving at it, and then we first have to ascertain that it really is the same thing we have reached. $2 = 1 + 1$ does not [as Frege himself would have claimed in 1879] mean that the contents of '2' and '1 + 1' agree in one respect, though they are otherwise different . . .
>
> Numerical signs, whether they are simple or built up by using arithmetical signs, are proper names of numbers . . . The plus sign does not mean the same as 'and'. In the sentences '3 and 5 are odd', '3 and 5 are factors of 15 other than 1' we cannot substitute '2 and 6' or '8' for '3 and 5' [that is, in these contexts 'and' does mean and]. On the other hand, '2 + 6' or '8' are always substitutable for '3 + 5'. It is therefore incorrect to say '1 and 1 is 2' instead of 'the sum of 1 and 1 is 2'. It is wrong to say 'number is just so many ones'. (*PW* 85–86)

Both in "Function and Concept" and in *Grundgesetze*, Frege develops these points using his technical notions of *Sinn* and *Bedeutung*: "'$2^4 = 4^2$' and '$4 \cdot 4 = 4^2$' express different thoughts, and yet we can replace '2^4' by

'4 · 4', since both signs have the same meaning [*Bedeutung*]. Consequently, '$2^4 = 4^2$' and '$4 · 4 = 4^2$' likewise have the same meaning" (*CP* 145). "I call the number four the denotation [*Bedeutung*] of '4' and of '2^2', and I call the True the denotation of '3 > 2'. However, I distinguish from the *denotation* of a name its *sense*. '2^2' and '2 + 2' do not have the same *sense*, nor do '$2^2 = 4$' and '2 + 2 = 4' have the same *sense*. The sense of a name of a truth-value I call a *thought*" (*GG* §2). To the end of his life Frege was convinced that his conception of the *Sinn* and *Bedeutung* of an expression provides precisely what is needed to understand the formula language of arithmetic.[10]

The sense of an expression, as Frege understands it, is what is grasped by a thinker who understands the expression. So, we should ask, what is it that one needs to know in order to grasp the sense of, say, '375' or '58 + 62' or any other expression in the formula language of arithmetic? The answer seems obvious. One needs to know, first, the rules that govern the formation of the numerals (that is, that in '375' the '3' is in the hundreds place, the '7' in the tens position, and so on) and of more complex expressions such as '$(27 + 33)^7$'. One needs also to know that the number designated by '0' is assigned to concepts under which nothing falls, that the number one is assigned to concepts under which only one thing falls, and so on. Finally, one needs to know the algorithms of arithmetic, the algorithms of addition, subtraction, multiplication, and so on. To know all of this is to grasp (more exactly, have everything required to grasp) the sense of expressions such as '375' and '58 + 62'. The rules and algorithms of the formula language of arithmetic in this way exhaustively fix the content, the sense or *Sinn,* of such signs. This content is, as we might think of it, the *computational content* of such expressions in the Arabic numeration system—with the proviso that computational content in this sense cannot be understood in abstraction from counting, that is, assignments of numbers to concepts. Computational content, as it is to be understood here, can no more be understood to involve only computations (as if numbers were not constitutively involved in counting) than, on Frege's view, inferential content can be understood to involve only inference as contrasted with judgment. Because inferences, on Frege's view, can be drawn only on the basis of premises that are acknowledged to be true, the notion of inference, and so of inferential content, *begrifflicher Inhalt,* cannot be understood independently of the notion of judgment; and the notion of computational content that is wanted here similarly cannot be understood independently of the notion of counting, that is, of judgments of the form 'the number of $F = n$'.

An expression such as '58 + 62' of the formula language of arithmetic *expresses* its sense, its computational content. That is, it pictures, not relative magnitudes (as the Roman numeration system does), but instead senses; and where the signs are different, as they are in, say, '80 + 40', the sense, the computational content, is also different. This is the essential point: the Arabic numeration system is a *lingua characterica,* a notation that fits the things themselves, not in virtue of picturing relative magnitudes but in virtue of picturing computational content, the senses of expressions as they are fixed by the three sorts of rules just mentioned that govern the employment, in counting and calculating, of the symbols they involve. It is for just this reason that computations can be fully rigorized in this notation, that one can compute in the Arabic numeration system by (as it were, mechanically) manipulating the symbols according to the rules and algorithms that fix the senses of the symbols and of combinations of them.

But, as already indicated, Arabic numerals such as '37' and '58 + 62' do not express computational contents in abstraction from the numbers they designate. Such contents contain modes of presentation of numbers; the numerals that express such contents constitutively designate numbers (even though, as we will see, there can be instances in which a sense is expressed though no number is designated). What does '58 + 62' designate? It designates the sum of fifty-eight and sixty-two, and the rules that govern the use of the signs enable a canonical determination of what number that is: the positions of the '8' and the '2' determine (in light of the '+') that we need to write a '0' in the ones column and carry a '1' over to the tens, where the number it signifies is added to the sum of five and six to give twelve, and so we write a '1' in the hundreds column and a '2' in the tens, and there is our answer: 120. Computing, guided by the computational content that is expressed in the notation of Arabic numerals, enables the advance from that content to a canonical representation of the number designated. The expression '58 + 62' designates precisely the same number as that designated by '120', but it gives that number in a different way. That is, it gives it by way of a computational content that is different from that exhibited in '120'. One can, furthermore, readily see that the computational contents are different, for the signs are different; they involve different primitive symbols in different arrangements and thereby exhibit distinct computational contents. The sentence '58 + 62 = 120' is, then, a recognition judgment, properly speaking, a judgment in which the same object is recognized as the same again although it is given in a different way. This is, moreover, a perfectly objective matter; the rules of arithmetic themselves fully determine the truth-value of this identity. To say that it is a recognition judgment is not to say that anyone does recognize these numbers as the same. No one need have worked the problem out, and no one need ever do so. All the same, the identity is a recognition judgment because in it a number, that is, some one number, is given in two different ways.

If it is the Arabic numeration system rather than the Roman that is a proper conceptual notation of arithmetic expressing in its own right the numerical element, then it is not counting, tallying the number of objects in a collection, that is the essence of number but instead computation, that is, calculations with numbers, where (again) numbers are in turn constitutively applicable to concepts in counting.[11] Already in his *Habilitationsschrift* Frege suggests that "no beginner will get a correct idea of an angle if the figure is merely placed before his eyes . . . If a beginner is shown how to add angles, then he knows what they are" (*CP* 56). Similarly, no beginner will get a correct idea of a number if a collection is merely placed before his eyes and counted. The beginner must be shown how to add numbers; then he knows what they are. Frege makes the point in *Grundlagen* §104:

> Have we really no right to speak of $1000^{1000^{1000}}$ until such time as that many objects have been given to us in intuition? Is it til then an empty symbol? Not at all. It has a perfectly definite sense, even although psychologically speaking and having regard to the shortness of human life, it is impossible for us ever to become conscious of that many objects; in spite of that, $1000^{1000^{1000}}$ is still an object whose properties we can come to know, even though it is not intuitable. To convince ourselves of this, we have only to show, introducing the symbol a^n for the nth power of a, that for positive integral a and n this expression always refers to one and only one positive whole number.

We do not need to produce a collection of $1000^{1000^{1000}}$ objects in order to have a means of designating this number and discovering its properties. What is needed is only that we fix the sense of this form of expression, that is, that we fix the rules that govern its use in calculations. To understand that this is all that is required is to understand how "it is possible for a mathematician to perform quite lengthy calculations without understanding by his symbols anything intuitable, or with which we can be sensibly acquainted . . . All we need to know is how to handle logically the content as made sensible in the symbols, and, if we wish to apply our calculus to physics, how to effect the transition to the phenomena" (*GL* §16).

An arithmetical expression such as '$2^4 + 23$' expresses a sense, a computational content, and thereby designates an object, that is, a number (which, among other things, can be assigned to a concept). We can furthermore see in this example just how it is that the sense of the expression contains a mode of determination of the object designated. Rules govern both the calculations to be performed given such an expression and the correct application of the primitive object names involved in it. To grasp the sense of the expression is to know those rules, to be able to perform those calculations, and to apply those object names. By substituting identicals for identicals according to rules, one thus can arrive at a canonical name for the number designated. As should also be evident, even the simple object names of arithmetic, the ten digits, are not merely arbitrary signs for numbers, for they too are caught up in the web of interconnected rules and algorithms that fix the contents of the signs in the formula language of arithmetic. That we use the sign '3' to designate the number three is indeed arbitrary; "we realize perfectly that other symbols might have been assigned to stand for the same things" (*GL* §16). But the sign '3' is not merely an arbitrary name for the number three. In virtue of its role in the Arabic numeration system as a whole, in the formula language of arithmetic, it expresses a sense, and like any sense, this sense contains a mode of presentation of the number designated.

It was suggested in Chapter 2 that a sentence of the formula language of arithmetic such as '$2 + 3 = 5$' should be read as merely presenting the numbers two, three, and five in an arithmetical relation, one that can be variously analyzed. On that account, the numeral '2' designates the number two independent of any analysis. In fact, as we should by now be able to see, independent of their use in equations, the primitive signs of arithmetic *only* express senses. In a particular use, relative to some analysis, a digit such as '3', say, does designate the number three, but independent of any context of use it only expresses a sense. Like any other primitive sign of the formula language of arithmetic, the numeral '3' contributes a sense, that is, what we are calling computational content, to an arithmetical expression that in turn expresses a sense and designates some object. It is this latter expression that is variously analyzable into function and argument. For example, we use the primitive signs '2', '3', '5', '=', and '+' to form the equation '$2 + 3 = 5$', which expresses a sense and designates the truth-value True. This sentence can then be analyzed into function and argument in various ways, for example, into the relation $\xi = \zeta$ for the number five, determined in two different ways, as argument. Relative to this analysis, the numeral '5' does designate the number five, but the numeral

'2' (for example) does not designate the number two. Rather, it serves as a part of the expression '2 + 3' which (relative to the given analysis) forms an object name for the number five. Independent of such a context of use and of some particular analysis, a primitive sign of arithmetic does not designate anything; it only expresses a sense that can contribute to the sense of a sign in use and thereby to the determination of a meaning. It is just this insight that is expressed in Frege's context principle according to which we are "never to ask for the meaning of a word in isolation, but only in the context of a proposition" (*GL* x). Number words, as Frege almost says in *Grundlagen* §60, signify something only in the context of a proposition. Independent of a proposition they only express a sense.

On this account, the object names that we use in the formula language of arithmetic (relative to an analysis) are constitutively such as to designate objects, that is, numbers. It nevertheless does not follow that every object name expression in the language is guaranteed to designate a number. The expression '2/0', for instance, has a definite sense (because all the constituent signs express senses), but it designates nothing. It has sense but no meaning. The notion of sense, computational content, cannot be understood independently of the notion of meaning; nevertheless, there can occur arithmetical signs that express a sense yet lack a meaning.

The positional Arabic numeration system is a conceptual notation of arithmetic, at once a *lingua characterica* and a *calculus ratiocinator*. It "[symbolizes] in its own right the numerical element" (*GL* §28), and because it does, the manipulation of symbols in this system according to its rules enables one to establish truths. As Leibniz says of a *lingua characterica* generally, "we can pass from a consideration of the relations in the expression to a knowledge of the corresponding properties of the thing expressed."[12] A conceptual notation of pure thought, similarly, ought to symbolize in its own right the logical element so that manipulations of the symbols in that system according to its rules likewise enable the establishment of truths. But what is the logical element? In the *Begriffsschrift* of 1879 Frege assumes that the logical element, everything necessary for a correct inference, that is, inferential content or *begrifflicher Inhalt*, can be given by the truth conditions of a sentence, by the circumstance that obtains if the sentence is true. It is this notion of content that is split in the mature logic. Just as a perspicuous language of arithmetic pictures, or traces, not relative magnitudes but instead computational content, so, Frege came to see, a perspicuous language of thought pictures, or traces, not truth conditions but instead inferential content (where, again, such content cannot be understood in abstraction from judgment).

4.3 The Formula Language of Pure Thought

Frege shows in *Grundlagen* that a number cannot be understood as a collection of units because if it were, the units collected would be either the same, and they could not then form a plurality, or different, and they would then form only an aggregate to which different numbers could be assigned depending on our way of looking at it. The problem arises, he argues, because we confuse the notion of a concept relative to which the items in a collection are identical one with another and are to be numbered with that of the number of the particular objects that fall under that concept. The attempt to understand sentential content by appeal to truth conditions or states of affairs, the circumstance that obtains if a sentence is true, similarly rests on a confusion, Frege comes to think. In the case of number, the problem is that a collection of units can be assigned different numbers depending on our way of regarding it. In the case of sentential content, analogously, the problem is that a picture of things as thus and so can be assigned different truth-values depending on our way of regarding it. Frege explicitly makes the point in the late essay "Thoughts." We think "that truth consists in a correspondence of a picture to what it depicts," but "if I do not know that a picture is meant to represent [say] Cologne Cathedral then I do not know what to compare the picture with in order to decide on its truth" (*CP* 352).

> When we ascribe truth to a picture we do not really mean to ascribe a property which would belong to this picture quite independently of other things; we always have in mind some totally different object and we want to say that the picture corresponds in some way to this object. 'My idea corresponds to Cologne Cathedral' is a sentence, and now it is a matter of the truth of this sentence. So what is improperly called the truth of pictures and ideas is reduced to the truth of sentences . . . when we call a sentence true we really mean that its sense is true. (*CP* 353)

A collection of objects, nine beans, say, can be represented by a kind of a picture, for instance, by nine strokes on a page, and a state of affairs, that Romeo loves Juliet, say, can similarly be represented by a picture, for instance, by marks representative of Romeo and of Juliet in a certain relation, perhaps thus: rj. But, as Frege argues in *Grundlagen*, number does not belong to the collection of strokes independent of our way of regarding it (for example, we can as easily count the strokes as three triplets); and likewise, as he points out in "Thoughts," truth or falsity does not belong to a picture such as 'rj' "quite independently of other things."[13] As Frege shows, the conception of the collection as a collection of nine strokes *presupposes* both the concept of a stroke and the number nine that is assigned to it. Similarly, he suggests in the passage just quoted, the conception of a picture, the picture 'rj', say, as a picture of Romeo loving Juliet presupposes both the thought expressed and a truth-value. Of course there are states of affairs, just as there are collections of objects, and sentences do have truth conditions—at least those that designate truth-values do. But just as understanding the notion of number requires appeal not to collections of objects but instead to the more fine-grained notion of a concept relative to which one counts and the less fine-grained notion of a number that is assigned to that concept, so to understand the content expressed by a sentence requires appeal not to truth conditions (that is, what is the case if the sentence is true) but to the more fine-grained notion of a thought, the sense expressed by the sentence, and the less fine-grained notion of truth.

It was suggested earlier that grasping the computational content or *Sinn* of an expression in the formula language of arithmetic involves three different capacities. First, one needs to know how to form and to recognize individual numerals such as '37' and '64722' and also more complex arithmetical signs such as '37 + 642' and '37^{47}'. One also needs to know how to apply such signs, in particular that zero is assigned to concepts under which nothing falls, and so on. Finally, one needs to know the algorithms of arithmetic, how to perform calculations according to the rules of arithmetic in order to prove identities. Grasp of the cognitive content or *Sinn* of an expression in Frege's formula language of thought involves three strictly analogous capacities.

First, one needs to know how to form and to recognize simple and logically complex sentences of the language. One needs, that is, to be able to distinguish well-formed complexes of expressions from those that are not well formed. One needs to know, for instance, that "the Gothic [that is, German] letter '$\mathfrak{a}$' may not occur without

$$-\!\!\!\backslash\!\mathfrak{a}\!\!\!\!-$$

prefixed, save in

$$-\!\!\!\backslash\!\mathfrak{a}\!\!\!\!-$$

itself" (*GG* §8), that "in

$$\begin{array}{c} -\!\!\!\!\!\!\top\!\!-\xi \\ \llcorner\!\!-\Delta, \end{array}$$

any proper name may be substituted for 'ξ'" (*GG* §12). Of course, one also needs to know that object names and concept words are no more intersubstitutable one for the other than the numerals and function signs of the formula language of arithmetic are.

Second, one needs to know how to apply the signs of the formula language of thought in correct judgments. One needs to know, for instance, that "the value of the function

$$\top \xi$$

shall be the False for every argument for which the value of the function

$$- \xi$$

is the True; and shall be the True for all other arguments" (*GG* §6), and that the value of the relation

$$\top \begin{matrix} \xi \\ \zeta \end{matrix}$$

"shall be the False if the True be taken as ζ-argument and any object other than the True be taken as ξ-argument, and that in all other cases the value of the function shall be the True" (*GG* §12). Knowing in this way the conditions under which a sentence of *Begriffsschrift* composed of such signs designates the True, one knows how correctly to apply the language, how to employ it in making correct judgments about how things are.[14] Having grasped in this way the functions designated by the basic combinations of the primitive signs (that is, the horizontal, conditional, and negation strokes and the concavity with German letter) and the role Latin italic letters play in lending generality of content, one ought to be able to see, for instance, that

$$-\mathfrak{t} \begin{matrix} \vphantom{} \\ \end{matrix} \begin{matrix} \mathfrak{f}(\Gamma) \\ \alpha - \mathfrak{f}(\alpha) \end{matrix}$$

designates the truth-value True whatever object Γ denotes and hence that

$$\vdash \mathfrak{t} \begin{matrix} \vphantom{} \\ \end{matrix} \begin{matrix} \mathfrak{f}(a) \\ \alpha - \mathfrak{f}(\alpha) \end{matrix}$$

is a correct judgment, and so on for all the basic laws of *Begriffsschrift* (save for Law V, which does not designate the True). Much as the simple truths of arithmetic form the basis for calculations in the formula language of arithmetic, so these basic truths of logic form the basis for inferences in the formula language of pure thought.

The third and last thing one needs to know is how to draw valid inferences, that is, the rules that govern correct inferences from *Begriffsschrift* judgments. Frege summarizes these rules in *Grundgesetze* §48. All and only these three capacities are required to grasp the content, that is, the thought or *Sinn* expressed by a *Begriffsschrift* sentence as understood here. Much as an expression in the formula language of arithmetic expresses computational content in virtue of the various rules governing the use of the symbols of that language in counting and calculating, so an expression in the formula language of thought expresses cognitive content in virtue of the various rules governing the use of the symbols of that language in judging and inferring.

An expression in the formula language of arithmetic such as '2 + 1' does not picture (map or trace) relative magnitude; it is not, as the Roman numeral 'iii' is, a picture of a collection of objects. What an expression in that notation pictures is the numerical element, everything necessary for a correct calculation, what we have called its computational content. An expression in the formula language of pure thought, similarly, pictures not truth conditions but instead everything necessary for correct judgment and inference, what we have called cognitive content. Sameness and difference in sign, on this view, correspond not to sameness and difference in truth conditions but instead to sameness and difference in the thought expressed, in cognitive content, that is, in content as it matters to judgment and inference.

Furthermore, just as in the case of the formula language of arithmetic, object names in the formula language of thought can designate one and the same object under different modes of presentation. In such cases sentences that contain those object names express different thoughts despite the fact that they have identical truth conditions. To take a familiar example, the sentences 'The Morning Star is a planet' and 'The Evening Star is a planet' have exactly the same truth conditions because in both cases what is referred to is Venus and the property ascribed is that of being a planet. But the two sentences do not express one and the same thought because the mode of presentation of Venus is different in the two cases; Venus is "arrived at" in two different ways in this case just as the number four is arrived at in different ways in the expressions '2²' and '7 − 3'. Because, as we will see, judgment on Frege's considered view is an advance from a thought to a truth-value, it follows that judging that the Morning Star is a planet (acknowledging the truth of that thought) is different from judging that the Evening Star is a planet. Because the thoughts are different, the acts of judgment are different, even though it is one and the same object about which the judgment is made and one and the same property that is ascribed. For just the same reason, the inference 'The Morning Star is a planet; therefore, the Evening Star is a planet' is invalid as it stands, even though the truth of the premise is sufficient to ensure the truth of the conclusion. The (correct) judgment that the Evening Star is a planet does not immediately follow from the (correct) judgment that the Morning Star is a planet, any more than that $2 + 3 = 7 - 2$ follows immediately from $2 + 3 = 5$; in both cases a recognition judgment is required, that the Morning Star = the Evening Star in the first case and that $7 - 2 = 5$ in the second. Furthermore, we can see in the notation itself that this is so because in the notation differences in sign correspond to differences in sense (save in certain well-demarcated cases already discussed in section 2.2).

Comparison with yet another symbol system will further clarify the point. As pictured in a standard language of chemistry, phenylalanine is given thus.[15]

$$\langle\bigcirc\rangle\ CH_2 - \overset{\displaystyle H}{\underset{\displaystyle NH_2}{C}} - COOH$$

This is not what a molecule of phenylalanine "looks like," and yet the picture is enormously useful because it traces the chemical bonds that matter to the synthetic pathway through which such a molecule might be constructed, and it reveals biochemically significant similarities and differences between this amino acid and other organic molecules. Furthermore, the picture simply presents this structure, that is, various atoms in a particular molecular arrangement. Because it does, it can be regarded in various ways, for instance, as a benzene ring with a complex in place of one hydrogen, or as an amino acid distinguished from, say, alanine in having the group

$$\langle\bigcirc\rangle\ CH_2 -$$

in place of CH_3—. We can divide it, that is, into a "main component" and "subcomponents" in various ways. Furthermore, there are, in the picture, clearly significant subunits: the benzene ring, obviously, but also 'CH_2',

'NH$_2$', and 'COOH' are all treated as units in our depiction relative to the main bonds. Like any defined signs, these signs are easily unpacked to reveal in turn the bonds they involve; and the defined signs might well need to be so unpacked to account for a particular synthetic pathway.

Sentences of *Begriffsschrift* (as we read them) similarly picture not what a sentential content, with all its tone and coloring, "looks like" but only its sense, that is, its content as it matters to the correctness of judgments and inferences it can figure in, as well as its (logically) significant similarities to and differences from other contents. For instance, the judgment that would be rendered in (a slightly modified) English as the judgment that every result of an application of a procedure f to an object x follows this x in the f-sequence has its content pictured in Frege's formula language thus:

$$\vdash\quad \overset{\gamma}{\underset{\beta}{\backsim}}\, f(x_\gamma, y_\beta)$$
$$f(x,y).$$

As in our sign design for phenylalanine, this sign design includes a defined sign that marks a significant unit. The same thought expressed using only the primitive signs of *Begriffsschrift* is this:

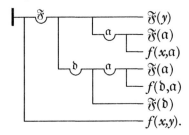

The thought so expressed reveals all the primitive logical "bonds" that are involved in it. Furthermore, just as any chemical bond may be regarded as the "last" one for the purposes of organic synthesis (though there are of course laws that govern what is and is not possible in an organic synthesis), so any of the primitive logical bonds in the thought expressed here may be regarded as the "main" one for the purposes of judgment and inference—though, again, there are laws that govern what can and cannot be judged or inferred in a proof. We know that understanding the goodness of inference can require taking any one of a variety of different perspectives on a sentence, any one of the various different pathways through it that are available, depending on what other premises are involved in the inference.

To infer, for instance, that Romeo admires Juliet on the grounds that Romeo loves Juliet and that anyone who loves Juliet admires her requires analyzing 'Romeo loves Juliet' into function and argument in a way that is different from that required in the inference 'Romeo loves Juliet; anyone who loves someone loves himself or herself; therefore, Romeo loves himself'. Frege's two-dimensional notation, which merely sets out the logical relationships among the senses of primitive object names and concept words (rather as, in our example from chemistry, the depiction of phenylalanine merely sets out the molecular arrangement of atoms), makes it easy to see just what analyses are possible and so what the inference potential of a sentence is. As we will see later, an analogous point holds also for the case of judgment.

Our example from the language of chemistry furthermore highlights both the respect in which a defined sign is, and the respect in which it is not, significant in a properly logical language. Defined signs, Frege points out, are "quite inessential . . . considered from a logical point of view" (*PW* 208); for, it is clear, nothing could be proved using the definiendum in, say, the definition of following in a sequence that could not be proved using the definiens instead. (Because the logical structure exhibited in the definiens may be integral to a proof, the reverse is not the case.) Nonetheless, as Frege also points out, "to be without logical significance is still by no means to be without psychological significance" (*PW* 209). Just as one needs conceptually to carve up the depiction of a phenylalanine molecule in one particular way in order to see that molecule as an amino acid (rather than, say, as a benzene ring with a complex in the place of one hydrogen), so one needs to carve up the thought depicted earlier in one particular way in order to see it as exhibiting the fact that every result of an application of a procedure f to an object x follows this x in the f-sequence. It is this way of looking at the sentence that reveals its importance as a theorem in the general theory of sequences, and the use of the defined sign helps to reveal this; but again, we could not make do in the proof of this theorem with the defined sign alone. As Frege says:

> we often need to use a sign with which we associate a very complex sense. Such a sign seems, so to speak, a receptacle for the sense, so that we can carry it with us, while being always aware that we can open this receptacle should we have need of what it contains . . . If therefore we need such signs—signs in which, as it were, we conceal a very complex sense as in a receptacle—we need also definitions so

that we can cram this sense into the receptacle and also take it out again. (*PW* 209)

Much as the standard symbol for the benzene ring is useful for marking out a significant part of a vast range of organic molecules, so defined signs in *Begriffsschrift* are useful in marking for us significant parts of thoughts. They impose a kind of secondary structure on the thought, one that highlights its larger significance in the body of knowledge as a whole. But that secondary structure, although it may help us to see what is important about a particular theorem, why it is worth proving at all, is not logically significant. Logically speaking, the only significant differences between the various logical bonds depicted are those marked by the axioms and rules of the language itself.

It was suggested earlier that to understand an expression in the formula language of arithmetic is to grasp its computational content as determined by the rules that govern the use in calculations and in statements of number of expressions in that language. To understand an expression in Frege's formula language of thought is similarly to grasp its cognitive content as determined by the three sorts of rules that govern the use of expressions in that language in judgments and inferences. Sense, so conceived, attaches to an expression only relative to a whole language, "a complete totality of signs" (*CP* 159). Whereas for the classical logician the smallest unit of cognitive significance is the term (either a term such as 'Socrates' intended for application to only one object or a term such as 'man' intended for application to many objects), and for the modern logician it is the sentence conceived as expressing a proposition, what is the case if it is true, on Frege's mature account, it is the whole language that is the minimum unit of cognitive significance. To grasp the sense of a sentence, on this account, it is not sufficient to know what is the case if it is true, that is, the necessary and sufficient conditions for correctly acknowledging its truth (any more than to grasp the sense of the numeral '3', say, it is sufficient to know to apply it to concepts under which fall only three objects); one must also know what follows from it with or without auxiliary premises. For users of natural language, such knowledge is largely tacit. In *Begriffsschrift* this knowledge is made explicit, at least for the fragment of language with which Frege is concerned. As Frege says of the formula language of arithmetic, so we can say of Frege's own formula language: "the . . . notation has, as a result of genuine thought, been so developed that it does the thinking for us, so to speak" (*GL* iv). One can see in the sentence itself everything necessary for a correct judgment and for a correct inference involving it just as one can see in an expression of arithmetic everything necessary for a correct statement of number and for a correct calculation involving that expression. From the perspective afforded by Frege's mature understanding of how *Begriffsschrift* functions as a language, a symbolic language designed perspicuously to express not inference potential so conceived but instead truth conditions would be quite like the Roman numeration system designed perspicuously to express not computational content but instead relative magnitude. In neither case is what is mapped or pictured what is needed in a conceptual notation proper, one that is at once a *lingua characterica* and a *calculus ratiocinator.*

Once Frege had come explicitly to realize that sentences of *Begriffsschrift* directly express not truth conditions, that is, the circumstance that obtains if the sentence is true, but instead cognitive content *(begrifflicher Inhalt),* that is, everything necessary for a correct inference, explaining the cognitive significance of some identities was easy. Even the simplest object name (for example, '3' or 'Socrates') expresses a sense "wherein the mode of presentation is contained," a sense that "is grasped by everybody who is sufficiently familiar with the language or totality of designations to which it belongs" (*CP* 158). Because two names that designate the same object can nonetheless differ in sense—can "arrive at" the object in different ways (*PW* 85), "lead to it from different directions" (*PMC* 152)—statements of identity can "contain very valuable extensions of our knowledge and cannot always be established *a priori*" (*CP* 157). The problem on the side of concept words is similarly resolved in the mature logic. The problem for Frege's early view of concept words, as developed in section 4.1, concerned (as we might think of it) not the cognitive significance of identities but instead the objective significance of generalities. More specifically, as long as the logical notion of a concept was confused with the logical notion of *Sinn,* it was impossible to understand generalized conditionals as expressing relations directly among concepts. If the role of a concept word were merely predicative, if it served, that is, only to characterize objects otherwise given, then even a logically general sentence, to have any content at all, would have to be in some way about objects. Frege did see, even in the early logic, that this cannot be right because understanding the goodness of some inferences requires taking not an object but instead a concept as the argument for a (higher-level) concept; but only after he had realized that his early conception of concept words as essentially predicative rested on a confusion of the concept/object distinction with the *Sinn/Bedeutung* distinction could he see why it is not right. Concept words, on Frege's mature view, do not only express senses; they also designate concepts which, although unsaturated, are fully objective entities that can stand in logical relations one to another and can serve as arguments for higher-level functions. The laws of the special sciences, and the laws of logic as well, can then be taken to be fully objective, substantive truths despite the fact that they involve no reference to any objects, and in the case of the laws of logic no reference even to any first-level concepts.

In the long Boole essay Frege takes a concept word directly to signify a concept, to be a kind of map of that concept. He does so, we can see in retrospect, because he conflates the notion of sense with the notion of a concept in the early logic. Concepts, we are told in that essay, are to be formed out of concepts just as the signs for them are formed out of primitive signs using the "logical cement" provided by Frege's concept-script (*PW* 13)—rather as the number three, on the collections conception, is to be formed out of units just as the sign for three can be formed out of 'i's. Just as, on that conception of number, different collections form different numbers, so it follows on Frege's early conception of concepts that different constructions yield different concepts, that, as Frege himself explicitly notes, one could "form concepts with different contents whose extensions were all limited to [for example] this one thing, the Earth" (*PW* 18). Indeed, Frege calls his language a *Begriffsschrift*, a concept-script, for just this reason. What his formula language (his *Formelsprache*) maps or traces is what he thinks of in the early writings as *conceptual* content; so, he at first thinks, sameness and difference in signs correspond to sameness and difference in concepts. But, as he later sees, concepts are no more formed by cementing together concepts than numbers are formed by putting together units. Concepts are functions (laws of correlation), objects to truth-values in the case of first-level concepts and concepts (and in certain cases also objects) to truth-values in the case of higher-level concepts. The senses expressed by concept words have parts (in all but the most basic cases); concepts themselves do not.[16] One and the same concept, then, can be designated by different concept words, by expressions that express different senses. To show that two concepts (or what are ostensibly two concepts) are mutually subordinate is to show just that. *Begriffsschrift*, then, is not a *concept*-script at all on our reading; it is a *Sinnsschrift*, a formula language of *thought*.[17] As Frege himself comes to see, a sentence of *Begriffsschrift* is a picture of a thought whose parts correspond to the parts of that thought. "We can regard a sentence as a mapping of a thought: corresponding to the whole-part relation of a thought and its parts we have, by and large, the same relation for the sentence and its parts" (*PW* 255). "The structure of the sentence can serve as a picture of the structure of the thought" (*CP* 390). Thoughts so conceived are variously analyzable for the purposes of judgment and inference, and are perspicuously expressed only in a two-dimensional written language of the sort we have learned to read as Frege's *Begriffsschrift*.

Frege's new conception in terms of *Sinn* and *Bedeutung* of the way a properly logical language functions also clarifies a surprisingly wide variety of features of ordinary language and its use, despite the fact that this aspect is not properly of concern to logic itself. Frege clearly takes this unanticipated explanatory power to constitute strong evidence for his view. His new conception of the way a properly logical language functions explains, for instance, the marvelous creativity of language, the fact that "with just a few sounds and combinations of sounds it is capable of expressing a huge number of thoughts, and, in particular, thoughts which have not been grasped or expressed by any man" (*PW* 225). Because, on the mature view, the primitive symbols of the language (object names and concept words) express senses that are combined in the thoughts expressed by sentences formed from these symbols, our capacity for grasping novel thoughts can be directly explained by the fact that thoughts are built up out of their parts as sentences are built up out of words (*CP* 390).[18] Understanding indirect discourse is similarly straightforward: "the thought, which otherwise is the sense of a sentence, in indirect discourse becomes its denotation." Indeed, Frege claims, "only in this way can indirect discourse be correctly understood" (*GG* 7).

> In our whole proposition ['Copernicus thought that the planetary orbits are circular'], the proper name 'Copernicus' designates a man, just as the subordinate claim 'that the planetary orbits are circular' designates a thought; and what is said is that there is a relation between this man and that thought, namely that the man took the thought to be true. Here the man and the thought occupy, so to speak, the same stage. (*PMC* 164)

Because the clause 'that the planetary orbits are circular' here designates a thought, rather than expressing one, only clauses that express (in ordinary contexts) the same sense can be substituted for it *salva veritate*. Because (as will be clarified in section 4.4) a judgment is now to be understood as an advance from a thought to a truth-value, judgments are different if the thoughts expressed are different.

> If now $a = b$, then indeed what is meant by 'b' is the same as what is meant by 'a', and hence the truth-value of '$a = b$' is the same as that of '$a = a$'. In spite of this, the sense of 'b' may differ from that of 'a', and thereby the thought expressed in '$a = b$' differs from that of '$a = a$'. In that case the two sentences do not have the same cognitive value. If we understand by 'judgment' the advance from the thought to the truth-value, as in the present paper ["On Sense and Meaning"], we can also say that the judgments are different. (*CP* 177)

From the fact that, say, Hesperus is Phosphorus and the fact that someone judges that Hesperus is Venus, it cannot be inferred that that same person judges that Phosphorus is Venus, despite the fact that the sentences 'Hesperus is Venus' and 'Phosphorus is Venus' have precisely the same truth conditions.

Light is shed also on explanations and counterfactual claims in natural language.[19] We say, for instance, that ice floats on water because it is less dense than water. This judgment, Frege now suggests, involves three different thoughts: (1) that ice is less dense than water, (2) that anything that is less dense than water floats on water, and (3) that ice floats on water (*CP* 175). It involves, that is, not only the judgment that ice floats on water and the judgment that ice is less dense than water but also the judgment that there is a lawful or causal connection between the two claims (in the sense elucidated in section 1.2). In *Begriffsschrift* this lawful connection would be expressed in a genuine hypothetical, as a relation between the concepts *less dense than water* and *floats on water,* though (as we saw in section 1.3) its status as a law proper would be revealed only by its ultimate justification, by a determination of the grounds of its truth. The account of counterfactual claims is essentially similar. To judge that if iron were less dense than water then it would float on water is to deny that iron is less dense than water but to assert an internal connection between something's being less dense than water and its floating on water. Again, the truth of the whole claim depends on the genuine hypothetical's being necessary, that is, properly lawful rather than merely accidental. Though an accidental generality is expressed as a genuine hypothetical in Frege's logic as we read it, and has thereby the status of a law for the purposes of inference, following it back to its ground would reveal that it is merely contingent or accidental, grounded in accidental facts about particular objects, and so could not properly support the counterfactual claims of natural language. But again, the light that is shed on these various aspects of our understanding and use of natural language expressions by Frege's mature understanding of the functioning of language in terms of *Sinn* and *Bedeutung* is only confirmation of the view. It is in *Begriffsschrift*, and only in *Begriffsschrift* as it is read here, that the sense of a sentence is perspicuously expressed. We must look to Frege's formula language of pure thought adequately to understand the notions of *Sinn* and *Bedeutung*.

Though Frege's logical language was originally designed to express everything necessary for a correct inference, Frege himself did not at first adequately understand the nature of such a language. He did not understand what it is that is the logical element and so confused the notion of content as it is given by truth conditions—which, in Frege's logical language as here conceived, can be given only relative to an analysis—and the logically prior notion of cognitive content as it is fixed by the rules that govern the correctness of judgments and inferences in the language. What *Begriffsschrift* expressions directly map (picture or trace) are not truth conditions but cognitive content, that is, thoughts, everything necessary for correct judgment and inference. Such content is, furthermore, essentially two-dimensional, for what matters to the correctness of judgment and inference is that sentences be variously analyzable. The extended, two-dimensional, inferentially articulated space of Frege's mature conception of the thought expressed by a sentence effectively displaces, on our account, the one-dimensional space of his early conception of a content of possible judgment in terms of truth. Relative to the thought that a *Begriffsschrift* sentence expresses, a one-dimensional representation of its truth conditions provides only a single facet of that thought. Like an image on the wall of Plato's cave, a one-dimensional representation of a thought, as Frege comes to understand thoughts, is only a shadow of the full figure.[20]

4.4 The Striving for Truth

Judgment, one is often told, is the ascription of a predicate, the endorsement of the application of a concept. Already in 1879 Frege seems to have held that this cannot be right. On the one hand, as regards what follows from it, the content expressed by a sentence must be variously analyzable into function and argument if the goodness of inferences in which it figures are to be understood; only relative to an analysis has it a subject (argument) and a concept (function) applied to that subject. On the other hand, as regards what a judgment follows from, Frege indicates, although one's basis for a judgment can be various, the content acknowledged to be true is nevertheless in each case the same. One can, for instance, arrive at the judgment that $2^4 = 16$ either by taking two to the fourth power or by finding the positive fourth root of sixteen or by calculating the logarithm of sixteen to the base two. Similarly, one can arrive at the judgment that Romeo loves Juliet by interrogating Romeo, by discovering relevant facts about Juliet, or by some other means reflected in some other function/argument analysis of the relevant sentence. Nevertheless, the judgment is in each case the same. Reflection on the case of denial, that is, on the case of acknowledging the truth of the negation of a sentence, reinforces the point. Suppose, for instance, that it is discovered that the thought expressed by the sentence 'Jane gave Jack a book for his birthday' is false. It is, then, the negation, that it is not the case that Jane gave Jack a book for his birthday, that is acknowledged as true. But the grounds for the acknowledgment can be various: that it was not Jane but Jean who gave Jack the book, that it was not Jack but John to whom Jane gave the book, that it was not a book but a boat, not his birthday but his graduation, or even that she did not give him the book at all but only lent it to him on that occasion. Any part of the sentence can be "denied" in this way, thereby indicating that in the sentence itself all parts of it are logically on a par. What is asserted (denied) is not that "the predicate" applies but that the thought as a whole is true. The judgment itself is simply an acknowledgment of the truth of the thought expressed.[21]

At first, in *Begriffsschrift*, Frege tries to register this point by thinking of judgment as an ascription of the predicate 'is a fact'. To judge, on the early view, is not to ascribe now this property, now that to a subject; but it is to ascribe a property, namely, the property 'is a fact' to the whole content. To judge, on the early view, is to endorse the whole content of a sentence as a fact. As Frege later argues, such a predicative conception of judgment is hopeless.

> One might be tempted [as Frege himself was] to regard the relation of the thought to the True not as that of sense to meaning, but rather as that of subject to predicate. One can, indeed, say: 'The thought that 5 is a prime number is true'. But closer examination shows that nothing more has been said than in the simple sentence '5 is a prime number'. The truth claim arises in each case from the form of the

assertoric sentence, and when the latter lacks its usual force, e.g., in the mouth of an actor upon the stage, even the sentence 'The thought that 5 is a prime number is true' contains only a thought, and indeed the same thought as the simple '5 is a prime number'. It follows that the relation of the thought to the True may not be compared with that of subject to predicate. (*CP* 164; see also *PW* 234)

Once Frege had given up the idea that judgment can be understood in terms of predication, that is, as an ascription of the predicate 'is true' or 'is a fact', it was quite natural for him to argue instead, as he does in "On Sense and Meaning," that the meaning, *Bedeutung*, of a sentence, assuming that it has one, is a truth-value, either the True or the False. For the question of judgment is always and only the question of the truth of a thought.

Judgment, on Frege's considered view, is an acknowledgment of truth. More exactly, it is the acknowledgment of "that sort of truth which it is the aim of science to discern" (*CP* 352); and where there is no concern for truth of this sort, there is no judgment—at least in the sense of judgment that concerns Frege. That is why the assertions of the actor, novelist, and poet "are not to be taken seriously: they are only mock assertions" (*PW* 130). "As stage thunder is only sham thunder and a stage fight only a sham fight, so stage assertion is only sham assertion. It is only acting, only fiction" (*CP* 356). Furthermore, because the assertoric force is lacking in such cases, it does not matter whether the thoughts expressed are true, or false, or have no truth-values at all: "thoughts in myth and fiction do not need to have truth-values" (*PW* 194). If, on the other hand, one adopts "an attitude of scientific investigation" (*CP* 163), the question whether a sentence has or lacks a truth-value is paramount.

> If it is the question of the truth of something . . . we have to throw aside all proper names that do not designate or name an object, though they may have a sense; we have to throw aside concept words that do not have a meaning. These are not such as, say, contain a contradiction—for there is nothing at all wrong in a concept's being empty—but such as have vague boundaries . . . For fiction the sense is enough. The thought, though devoid of meaning, of truth-value is enough, but not for science. (*PW* 122)

It is, finally, a perfectly objective matter whether a sentence has or lacks a truth-value on Frege's view. We think, for example, that there was in fact no such person as Odysseus, that Odysseus is merely a character in a story. Hence we do not take claims about Odysseus seriously; we do not concern ourselves with whether or not the claims are true. But however we take claims about Odysseus, whether seriously (in Frege's sense) or not, it is an objective matter whether they belong to the realm of fiction or to the realm of truth, that is, whether they can (properly speaking) be taken seriously. If the accounts of Odysseus's exploits were not after all fictional but were properly historical narratives, then "the thoughts would remain strictly the same; they would only be transposed from the realm of fiction to that of truth" (*PW* 191). To discover that accounts of Odysseus's exploits were historical narratives would be to discover that they belong to the realm of truth.

One can discover that sentences one had taken to be only fictional, to express only mock thoughts, are sentences that belong after all to the realm of truth. One can similarly discover that sentences that one had taken seriously as belonging to the realm of truth are after all merely fictions, not because they have not been uttered with assertoric force (though this too can happen) but because they designate no truth-values. One can, in other words, think that one is engaged in properly scientific discourse, think that one is operating in the realm of truth, when in fact one is not. Frege provides examples of this sort of case both in the Introduction to *Grundgesetze* and in the late essay "Thoughts."

> I simply mean to designate a man [when I speak of Charlemagne], independent of me and my ideating, and to assert something about him. We may grant idealists that the attainment of this intention is not completely sure and that, without wishing to, I may perhaps lapse from truth into fiction; but this can change nothing about the sense. (*GG* 20)

> By using the expression 'that lime-tree' . . . I mean . . . to designate what I see and other people too can look at and touch. There are now two possibilities. If my intention is realized, if I do designate something with the expression 'that lime-tree', then the thought expressed in the sentence 'That lime-tree is my idea' must obviously be denied [since a lime-tree is a tree, not an idea]. But if my intention is not realized, if I only think I see without really seeing, if on that account the designation 'that lime-tree' is empty, then I have wandered into the realm of fiction without knowing it or meaning to. In that case neither the content of the sentence 'That lime-tree is my idea' nor the

content of the sentence 'That lime-tree is not my idea' is true, for in both cases I have a predication which lacks an object . . . The content of the sentence 'That lime-tree is my idea' is [in that case] fictional. (*CP* 361–362)

I am convinced that the idea I associate with the words 'my brother' corresponds to something that is not my idea and about which I can say something. But may I not be making a mistake about this? Such mistakes do happen. We then, against our will, lapse into fiction. Yes, indeed! By the step with which I win an environment for myself I expose myself to the risk of error. (*CP* 367)

Judgment in this way involves both a kind of seriousness, a concern for truth that is lacking in fictional discourse, and also a moment with respect to which one is entirely passive. Because judgment is an act of acknowledging the truth of a thought, according to Frege, the thought regarding which one judges must have a truth-value. I must actually have a brother in order to make judgments about him, and if I do not, however confident I am that I do, then my "judgments" have exactly the same status as the "judgments" of the actor on the stage. They are only sham judgments, not judgments, properly speaking, at all.

When one judges truly that, say, Mont Blanc is more than 4000 meters high, one's knowledge is knowledge regarding the mountain and not one's thought of it. On the other hand, the thought acknowledged to be true in a correct judgment must be something that can be grasped in thought, by thinking, and a physical object such as Mont Blanc seems exactly the wrong sort of thing for thought to grasp. It is no more Mont Blanc itself that I grasp in thinking that Mont Blanc is more than 4000 meters high than it is the number seven that I grasp in my hand when I clutch seven coins. Indeed, it cannot be the object itself that is grasped in thinking because, again, what is grasped in thinking must be variously analyzable: "strictly speaking, it is not in itself that the thought is singular, but only with respect to a possible way of analysing it" (*PW* 187). One's knowledge, then, is not about that which one grasps in thinking. On the one hand, "proper names designate objects, and a singular thought is about objects"; but on the other hand, "we can't say that an object is part of a thought as a proper name is part of the corresponding sentence" (*PW* 187). What, then, does the object have to do with the thought? The answer depends on whether or not one adopts an attitude of scientific investigation, on whether or not one strives after truth. If one lacks that sort of seriousness, then Frege's answer is: nothing. "As far as the mere thought-content is concerned it is indeed a matter of indifference whether a proper name has a meaning" (*PW* 192). "But," as Frege immediately continues, "in any other regard it is of the greatest importance; at least it is so if we are concerned with the acquisition of knowledge. It is this which determines whether we are in the realm of fiction or truth." To adopt an attitude of scientific investigation is to expose oneself to the risk of thinking that one is making a judgment, uttering a sentence with assertoric force, when in fact one is doing nothing of the sort. For even to judge at all, whether correctly or incorrectly, depends on factors wholly outside one's control. "It is the striving for truth that drives us always to advance from the sense to the thing meant" (*CP* 163). Relative to that striving, then, the object is in a way constitutive of the thought, even though it is not a part of it, a constituent of it. One aims, for example, to pose the thought as a question, to ask whether or not the thought is true, but that question can be posed only if the relevant objects exist. If the relevant objects do not exist, then, relative to the striving for truth, the thought is merely mock, not a "real" thought at all, because it cannot be taken seriously (though, of course, one can think that it can). It cannot, in that case, be so much as posed as a question.

To say that Fregean thoughts are object dependent is to register the fact that the act of judgment (as such, that is, independent of the question whether it is correct or incorrect) involves not only the active moment of assent but also a moment with respect to which one is entirely passive. Quite simply, not all thoughts are available to be taken seriously; in particular, those that involve object names, relative to some analysis or other, that fail to designate any objects cannot be taken seriously (though it may seem to a deluded user of the name that they can). Such thoughts are merely fictions, no more to be taken seriously than the sham assertions of an actor on the stage. Just the same is true, on Frege's account, in the case of concept words. To say that thoughts are concept dependent—and all thoughts are if they so much as purport to be taken seriously—is to register the fact that we are equally passive on the side of concepts. One is free to decide whether or not to use a particular concept word in an attempted act of judgment, but only if the concept word does designate a concept will the attempted act succeed as an act of judgment. On Frege's view, it is possible to think that one has grasped a concept in the case in which there is nothing there to be grasped, just as it is possible to think that one has designated an object in the case in which there is no object there to be designated (and so no possibility either of ascribing or of denying a property). As the point is put in the "Inertia" essay, "a concept is something objective: we do not form it, nor does it form itself in us, but we seek to grasp it, and in the end we hope to have grasped it, though we may mistakenly have been looking for something where there was nothing" (*CP* 133).

There is, however, one important difference between the two cases on Frege's view. Whereas grasp of an object would seem to be an all-or-nothing affair—either the object name one uses designates an object, and it is fully determined which, or it does not—one's grasp of a concept can be more or less sure, one conception of it better or worse than another without either being fully adequate. The concept itself (assuming that there is one) is fully determinate in the sense of having sharp boundaries.[22] But although the concept itself has sharp boundaries, it is not necessary that these boundaries be clearly perceived. Especially in the early days of a science, "we do not have a clear grasp of the sense of the simple sign . . . its outlines are confused as if we saw it through a mist" (*PW* 211); "we see everything through a fog, blurred and undifferentiated" (*GL* viii). Achieving knowledge of a concept in its pure form, Frege thinks, can require "immense intellectual effort, which may have continued over centuries" (*GL* vii). In the case of concepts, "what comes first in the logical and objective order is not what comes first in the psychological and historical order" (*CP* 136). Frege's *Habilitationsschrift* begins with an example of just this phenomenon:

> According to the old conception [of quantity in geometry], length appears as something material which fills the straight line between its end points . . . The introduction of negative quantities made a dent in this conception, and imaginary quantities made it completely impossible. Now all that matters is the point of origin and the end point . . . All that has remained is certain general properties of addition, which now emerge as the essential characteristic marks of quantity. (*CP* 56)

Similarly, in the case of the concept *number*, it seemed, at a certain stage in the history of our acquisition of this concept, that a number "submits to being taken away from another number greater than itself, but to take it away from a number less than itself is ridiculous."[23] Even Euler, who saw no difficulty in the notion of a negative number, refused to admit complex numbers: "because all conceivable numbers are either greater than zero or less than zero or equal to zero, then it is clear that the square roots of negative numbers cannot be included among the possible numbers."[24] Only

after immense intellectual effort continued over centuries have we suc-
ceeded in "stripping off the irrelevant accretions which veil it [here, the
concept *number*] from the eyes of the mind" (*GL* vii). It is not obvious
that we have achieved knowledge of this concept in its pure form even
now.

As Frege claims, and as both the example of *quantity* in geometry and
that of *number* in arithmetic illustrate, the problem with our conceptions,
that which veils concepts from the eyes of the mind, is that those conceptions contain "irrelevant accretions," that is, content that does not properly belong to the relevant concepts. We once thought, for instance, that
from the concept of number itself it can be shown that negative numbers
are impossible, or that any number is greater than, or less than, or equal to
zero. We once thought, to take now an example from calculus, that from
the fact that a function is continuous it can be inferred that it is differentiable. In each case our conception of the concept seemed to justify inferences that, as we later discovered, are not in fact valid. Indeed, as Frege
claims already in the long Boole essay, "almost all errors made in inference . . . have their roots in the imperfection of the concepts" (*PW* 34);
more exactly, as the point would have been put after the distinction between concept and *Sinn* was in place, they have their roots in the imperfection of our conceptions, in the senses we attach to concept words. As
long as our conceptions are imperfect in this way, and the outlines of the
sense are thus confused, our knowledge of the concept itself is similarly
confused.

Like any expression in a properly logical language as here conceived, a
concept word expresses a sense that is fixed by the three sorts of rules governing its use in judgment and inference that are codified in the language
as a whole. The sense of a concept word in this way presents a concept (assuming that there is one) under a mode of determination, a conception of
it. The word has cognitive content for a thinker for just this reason. But
one's conception, at any given historical moment, may be flawed; one's
perception of the boundaries of the concept may be blurred (as, for instance, in the case in which the continuity of a function is taken to entail its
differentiability) or altogether illusory (as in the case of a concept word
such as 'phlogiston'). According to Frege's account in the "Inertia" essay,
we discover that our conceptions are flawed in these ways by discovering
that our conceptions and judgments involving them lead to contradictions. Contradictions, Frege thinks, are "created by treating as a concept
something that was not a concept in the logical sense because it lacked a

sharp boundary. In the search for a boundary line, the contradictions, as they emerged, brought to the attention of the searchers that the assumed boundary was still uncertain or blurred, or that it was not the one they had been searching for . . . The real driving force is the perception of the blurred boundary" (*CP* 134). Because our grasp of concepts is mediated in this way by conceptions that are constitutively inferentially articulated (by way of the rules that govern judgment and inference in the language), we can discover that what we had taken to be judgeable thoughts about (say) phlogiston or motion lead to contradictions that reveal in turn the flaws in these conceptions. It is by just such a mechanism that we are able to strip those conceptions of the irrelevant accretions that can attach to them and, on Frege's account, veil the concepts themselves from the eyes of the mind. Correlatively, when we get things right, that is, when our conceptions, the senses we attach to concept words, are adequate to the concepts themselves in setting the "boundary lines" of the concepts where they are as a matter of objective fact, then our (correct) judgments involving those concepts are wholly successful: what we judge to be so is so. "The work of science," on Frege's view, "[consists] in the discovery of true thoughts" (*CP* 368) for just this reason.

As it has been understood here, a Fregean thought, insofar as it is thinkable, available to be grasped by a thinker, is not world involving. If the signs that are involved in a sentence themselves have sense (and are appropriately combined in the sentence), then the sentence as a whole expresses a sense. It expresses something thinkable. But that same thought, we have suggested, is judgeable—available to be acknowledged as true (or its negation as true) and hence also available (or its negation available) to serve as a premise in an inference—just if the relevant objects and concepts exist. A judgeable content must designate a truth-value, either the True or the False, and is thus essentially world involving. Because it is often only after immense intellectual effort that we achieve knowledge of a concept in its pure form, it follows that we must work not only to achieve true thoughts but also, and antecedently, to achieve adequate conceptions of things and thereby thoughts that are available to be judged true (or false) at all. We must work our way into the realm of truth, and we can do so, on the account just sketched, in virtue of our inferentially articulated conceptions of things. It is by discovering the contradictions buried in our faulty conceptions that we achieve better conceptions, in geometry and arithmetic, in the natural sciences, and even in logic itself. In so doing, we come to have the eyes (as it were) to see things as they are.[25]

4.5 The Science of Logic

We have seen that Frege's early understanding of the nature of a logical language is shaped by the idea that object names and concept words serve two radically different functions, the one to refer to objects, that is, to function as a representative of objects, the other to characterize objects so referred to, or represented, as thus and so. The contents of complete sentences, then, are conceived in terms of the notion of a content of possible judgment, something as something. Already in the early *Begriffsschrift* the inadequacies of this conception are apparent. If names functioned only as representatives of objects then no account could be given of the cognitive value of some identities. If concept words functioned only to characterize objects otherwise given then no account could be given of the objective significance of laws that subordinate one concept to another. The force of these problems, combined with Frege's penetrating reflections in *Grundlagen* regarding the expression of such simple arithmetical truths as that $1 + 1 + 1 = 3$, yields, in the mature logic, a radically different conception according to which both object names and concept words function both to express senses and (in the context of a proposition and relative to an analysis) to designate objective entities, objects and concepts, respectively. From the perspective afforded by this mature logic, Frege had, in the early logic, conflated, on the one hand, the notion of *Bedeutung*, the objective, with that of an object, and on the other, the notion of *Sinn*, cognitive significance, with that of a concept.

But Frege's *Grundlagen* reflections on the formula language of arithmetic were not only a moment in the dawning realizations that came to fruition in the writings of the early 1890s. The understanding Frege achieves in *Grundlagen* of the way that language functions to express computational content provides a direct and essentially complete analogue of the way a formula language of thought functions to express what Frege, in the early logic, characterizes as *begrifflicher Inhalt*, that is, everything necessary for a correct inference—and judgment, since, as he came to see, among what is necessary for a correct inference is the acknowledged truth of the premises. To grasp the content expressed by an expression in the formula language of arithmetic requires, we suggested, first, the capacity to form and to recognize properly constructed expressions as opposed to those that are not well formed, second, the capacity correctly to assign numbers designated by expressions in the language to concepts in light of the objects that fall under them, and third, the capacity correctly to compute in the language. Grasp of the thought expressed by a sentence in the formula language of pure thought, analogously, requires, on our view, first, the capacity to form and to recognize well-formed sentences in the language, second, the capacity correctly to judge of sentences in the language that they, or their negations, express true thoughts, and third, the capacity correctly to draw inferences in the language. All and only these three capacities are required in order for a thinker to understand a properly logical language, to be capable of grasping the thoughts expressed by sentences in the language.

Because grasp of the *Sinn* of an expression requires knowing (either explicitly or only tacitly) the rules that govern judgments and inferences in the language, where judgment and inference necessarily involve in turn the notion of *Bedeutung,* the notion of *Sinn* is not, on our view, intelligible independent of the notion of *Bedeutung.* Nevertheless, locally, we have seen, there can be sentences that express thoughts though they designate no truth-values. There could be no fiction were there not also the striving for truth; but it is also the case, on Frege's account as it is here understood, that one cannot fully understand the striving for truth without recognizing the possibility that, as Frege puts it, one has wandered into the realm of fiction. Judgment, on this view, essentially involves both an active moment, the moment of assent, and also a moment with respect to which one is entirely passive, the moment of truth. If either is lacking—the active moment in stage assertion, for example, the passive moment in the case of a *bedeutungslos* thought—there is an appearance of judgment but no judgment, properly speaking. Relative to the striving for truth, *bedeutungslos* thoughts are only mock thoughts. Not only are they not revelatory of things as they are, they are not even revelatory of things as they could be. As we might think of it, they provide no window on the world at all.

On Frege's account as here developed, it is only through thoughts expressed by sentences in a sufficiently advanced scientific language that one perceives (more generally, has cognitive access to) anything at all. All our knowledge is essentially mediated by an inherently historical, learned public language. It follows that anything we think we know could in principle be called into question, that although we can have knowledge, we cannot have certainty, an unquestionable ground to which we might retreat when all else fails. This is furthermore true even in the case of our knowledge of the laws of logic, even in the case of our knowledge of a law such as that of identity, $a = a$, which seems to be *transparently* self-evident. Frege indicates just this possibility in the Introduction to *Grundgesetze:* "this impossibility of our rejecting the law in question [that is, $a = a$] hinders us not at all in supposing beings who do reject it; where it hinders us is in supposing that these beings are right in so doing, it hinders us in having doubts whether we or they are right" (*GG* 15).

We cannot ourselves find the least reason to doubt the law of identity; it seems to us to be as manifestly true as any truth could be. But whereas we ourselves can find no grounds for doubt, we can imagine beings who do have such grounds, even who reject this law. Because we cannot ourselves, now, in our particular historical moment, find any grounds for doubt, we cannot imagine that they are right. But, Frege claims, we can imagine them. His point, then, seems to be that though we cannot (now, anyway) doubt the law of identity, we can imagine someone, sometime, coming up with a reason to call that law into question. Certainly at various points in our intellectual history we have come to doubt what had before seemed true, even self-evidently true, for example, that a greater number cannot be subtracted from a lesser, that any number is greater than or less than or equal to zero, or that continuity entails differentiability. Frege's point is that our knowledge of the laws of logic is no different. Even the law of identity could, in principle, be reasonably called into question, for even this law is known only through the medium of a historical, learned public language. Because we grasp this truth by way of the thought expressed by '$a = a$', where this thought in turn is determined by the place of the sentence in the language as a whole, the possibility that we are mistaken cannot be foreclosed. Logic, on this view, is a science like any other, and no more than in any other science is it simply *given* what the basic logical concepts are or how best to conceive them. We can make mistakes, even in logic; and we do for the same reason we make mistakes in any science, namely, that we fail adequately to grasp the concepts constitutive of the domain of that science. On Frege's mature view as we have understood it here, nothing, not even the most basic truth of logic, is "utterly transparent" to reason, as he had claimed in *Grundlagen* §105. Our conceptions of things, the medium through which they are grasped by us, can become transparent to us in a fully axiomatized system, but such conceptions must be distinguished in principle from the concepts we seek to grasp by their means. We can make mistakes.

In *Grundgesetze* Frege attained, so he thought, the goal of a system, "the ideal of a strictly scientific method" (*GG* 2). In *Grundgesetze* everything on which proofs are based is "brought to light," and because it is, "if anyone should find anything defective, he must be able to state precisely where, according to him, the error lies: in the Basic Laws, in the Definitions, in the Rules, or in the application of the Rules at a particular point" (*GG* 3). Of course, someone, Russell, did find something defective, and he found it at just the place Frege had suggested one might, in Basic Law V concerning courses of values. As Russell's paradox shows, something is amiss in our conception of a course of values. Either the boundary of this concept is not where it has been taken to be or there is no boundary, no concept at all, where we had been looking for one. Frege came to think that it is the latter that is the case, that the concept word 'course of values' and expressions in *Begriffsschrift* of the form '$\acute{\epsilon}F(\epsilon)$' used to designate courses of values are meaningless, and that all sentences containing such expressions are neither true nor false. We need, finally, to understand why.

5

Courses of Values and Basic Law V

We must set up a warning sign visible from afar: let no one imagine
that he can transform a concept into an object.
—LETTER TO HÖNIGSWALD, 1925

A central insight of Frege's logic as understood here is that thoughts, the
contents of sentences as they are involved in judgment and inference, must
be variously analyzable into function and argument. Frege did at first think
that sentential content in this sense could be given by truth conditions, by
what is the case if a sentence is true, but by the early 1890s he had seen
that what a *Begriffsschrift* sentence expresses is not truth conditions but
instead *Sinn,* an inferentially articulated thought through which a truth-
value, either the True or the False, is (or at least ought to be) designated.
At the same time Frege made another, less happy move. He introduced
the notion of an extension, more exactly, that of a course of values or value
range, and the "law" that mutually subordinate concepts share a course of
values in common. As Russell's paradox shows, this "law" is not true. The
notion of an extension or course of values, Frege eventually came to think,
is a fiction. An account of why Frege's logicism required Law V, and of
why Law V must be rejected, is the essential last step in this study of
Frege's logic.

5.1 Frege's *Grundlagen* Definition of Number

The aim of Frege's logicism was to show that arithmetic is merely derived
logic, that there are no peculiarly arithmetical modes of inference, no concepts of arithmetic that are not definable in purely logical terms. The
concept *number,* in particular, was to be shown to be strictly logical. In
Grundlagen the task is conceived in explicitly Kantian terms: what is to
be demonstrated is that Kant's thesis that "without sensibility no object
would be given to us" (A51/B75; quoted in *GL* §89), although perhaps
true of actual (that is, spatiotemporal) objects, is not true of numbers,

"that in arithmetic we are not concerned with objects which we come to know as something alien from without through the medium of the senses, but with objects given directly to our reason" (*GL* §105). The demonstration is in three stages. First, the tempting but ultimately misguided idea of defining a number by its conditions of application—for instance, the number 0 as belonging to a concept "if the proposition that *a* does not fall under that concept is true universally, whatever *a* may be" (*GL* §55)—is sketched and its critical flaw revealed. The proposed definition, although it sets out adequate circumstances of application of a number, does not include the consequences of its application, that is, what follows from a number's belonging to a concept. In particular, it does not allow one to infer "that, if the number *a* belongs to the concept *F* and the number *b* belongs to the same concept, then necessarily *a* = *b*" (*GL* §56). What is defined in the first definition are not the numbers 0, 1, and so on, but instead the phrases 'the number 0 belongs to', 'the number 1 belongs to', and so on. Because, as seems obvious to Frege, numbers are "self-subsistent objects that can be recognized as the same again" (*GL* §56), the strategy must be rejected.

The lesson of the first *Grundlagen* definition is that "number words are to be understood as standing for self-subsistent objects" (*GL* §62). The second definition aims, then, to fix the sense of the sentence 'the number belonging to the concept *F* = the number belonging to the concept *G*'. Appealing to Hume's principle that "when two numbers are so combined as that the one has always an unit answering to every unit of the other, we pronounce them equal" (quoted in *GL* §63), the sense of our sentence is to be the same as the sense of the sentence 'the concept *F* is equal (*gleichzahlig*) to the concept *G*', where two concepts are equal in this technical sense if and only if the objects that fall under them can be put in a one-to-one correlation. Frege's example in *Grundlagen* of the strategy is the transformation of the sentence 'a//b' into an identity: 'the direction of a = the direction of b'. Because Frege introduces object names for courses of values in essentially the same way in *Grundgesetze*, it is critical that we have an account of just how this strategy is supposed to work.

The general strategy is to "carve up the content in a new way different from the original way" (*GL* §64), that is, to analyze a given sentence in a new way. Consider, to begin with, a different case, say, the English sentence 'two is a fourth root of sixteen'. This sentence would seem to be about the number two and to ascribe to that object the property of being a fourth root of sixteen. Contained in the predicate 'is a fourth root of sixteen' is an object name for the number sixteen and, less obviously, an object name for the number four. In virtue of that fact, the sentences 'sixteen is a fourth power of two' and 'four is a logarithm base two of sixteen' can be taken to present the same sense as that presented in the first of our three sentences, but in two different ways. Each of the three sentences so read presents one and the same sense under an analysis into function and argument, a different one in each case. In a perspicuous formula language of arithmetic, all these sentences receive the same expression: '$2^4 = 16$' expresses the computational content that is common to our three sentences of English. It presents an arithmetical thought and can be variously analyzed.

Consider now the sentence (of a slightly modified English) 'work a is same-authored with work b', where two written works stand in the same-authored relation just in case they have one and the same (unique) author. This relation is clearly symmetrical, transitive, and reflexive; the same-authored relation sorts written works into equivalence classes, each of which contains all and only the written works that have the same author. This relationship is also obviously grounded in another relation that each of the works that are same-authored bear to some other object, namely, the person who is their author. The relation *same-authored* holds between two works a and b in virtue of the fact that there is a person c such that a was written by c and b was written by c. In the sentence 'a is same-authored with b', reference to this person is buried in the relation expression much as reference to the number four is buried in the predicate 'is a fourth root of sixteen'. But just as we did before, we can bring out this reference to c by carving up the content in a way different from the way it is carved up in 'a is same-authored with b' to yield the sentence 'the author of a = the author of b'. That is, just as 'two is a fourth root of sixteen' expresses a sense that can be variously analyzed (for instance, also as 'four is a logarithm of sixteen to the base two'), so 'a is same-authored with b' expresses a sense that can be variously analyzed, for instance, also as 'the author of a = the author of b'. The strategy is clearly legitimate for this case and more generally for cases in which the relation in question is not only reflexive, symmetrical, and transitive, but also grounded in another relation that the relevant objects bear to some third object. Where R is an equivalence relation and there is an object c and a relation R* such that aRb if aR*c and bR*c, the sentence 'aRb' can be carved up in a new way to yield the sentence 'the one that is R* to a = the one that is R* to b'.

Where two objects merely share a property, for instance, the property of being a certain color, the legitimacy of the strategy is less obvious. If an object a is some color and the object b is the same color, then we can say that a is same-colored with b. Same-colored is an equivalence relation; but we would not ordinarily say that that relationship is grounded in another relation that a and b both bear to some third object c. Two objects that are same-colored are not same-colored in virtue of there being some color, some object, to which they are both related. Colors are not objects, self-subsistent entities that can be or fail to be identical to other objects; they are properties of (self-subsistent) objects. Because they are properties rather than objects, the strategy of the second definition would seem not to apply to this case.

Yet Frege clearly does seem to think that the strategy applies even in a case such as that of being same-colored: "instead of 'the segments are identical in length', we can say 'the length of the segments is identical' or 'the same', and instead of 'the surfaces are identical in color', 'the color of the surfaces is identical'" (*GL* §65). There are two possibilities. Either Frege thinks that an equivalence relation alone is sufficient for the strategy of the second definition to be applied, or he thinks that even in these sorts of cases there is an object that grounds the equivalence relation. The latter seems to be Frege's view. First, he does not think that objects can be created at will: "even the mathematician cannot create things at will, any more than the geographer can; he too can only discover what is there and give it a name" (*GL* §96). We cannot, then, simply postulate that there is something, that is, some object, to which all and only the objects standing in an equivalence relation are related. We can only discover such an object (assuming that there is one) and give it a name. For the strategy of the second definition to apply to a sentence 'aRb' (where R is an equivalence relation), there must be an object c and a relation R* such that aR*c and bR*c. All the strategy of the second definition can do is to provide a means of recognizing this object. It cannot create it.

If mathematicians cannot create things at will but only discover what is there and give it a name, then Frege, if he is to apply the strategy of the second definition to the case of parallel lines, must have independent grounds for thinking that there exists an object to which two parallel lines are related. And so he does. Taking the concept *direction* as the concept *point at infinity that parallel lines share,* Frege shows in his dissertation that points at infinity are objects, properly speaking, by producing them by "projecting the plane on a sphere from a point on the sphere which is neither the nearest nor the furthest" (*CP* 2–3). Such a projection yields us intuitions of such points, puts them "before our eyes." As the sort of beings we are, we first discover Euclidean space and only "as a result of a process of intellectual activity"(*GL* §64) discover the points at infinity of projective space. In the order of knowing, then, in the historical and psychological order, directions conceived as points at infinity are essentially derived. In the order of being, however, they are perfectly self-subsistent entities.[1] *We* only come to discover points at infinity through our understanding of parallel lines, but they are not themselves logically dependent on the concept *parallel*. In this case, then, just as in the case of being same-authored, we can know already that there is an object to which both the (parallel) lines a and b are related. Because there is such an object, it is legitimate to transform the sentence relating them (namely, 'a is parallel to b') into an identity of objects: 'the direction of a = the direction of b'.

Both in his critique of formalist theories of arithmetic and in his directions example, Frege provides grounds for our taking the strategy of the second definition to apply only in cases in which there is independent reason to think that there is something, an object, to which the relevant objects are related. The case of same-colored objects is more difficult, for surely in this case there is no third thing that two objects are related to in virtue of being same-colored. In fact, for a time, Frege thinks there is: not only can we analyze the sentence 'o is red' (say) as involving the function ξ-is-red for argument o, or as involving the second-level function Φ-is-true-of-o for argument ξ-is-red, but we can also analyze it as involving the first-level relation ξ-falls-under-ζ for the arguments o and the concept *red*, where both o and the concept *red* have the logical status of objects, that is, of complete or saturated self-subsistent entities. 'The concept *red*' does not designate the same entity as 'ξ is red' does—though, as the two expressions suggest, the two entities that are designated are related to one another—but it does designate an entity, and as its name suggests, that entity is an object, complete and self-subsistent. The point is made in "On Concept and Object":

> The concept as such cannot play this part [of the grammatical subject], in view of its predicative nature; it must first be converted into an object, or, speaking more precisely, represented by an object. We designate this object by prefixing the words 'the concept'; e.g.
>
> 'The concept *man* is not empty'.
>
> Here the first three words are to be regarded as a proper name, which

can no more be used predicatively than 'Berlin' or 'Vesuvius'. (*PW* 97)

The sentence 'the concept *man* is realized', Frege thinks (at this point), has the same logical structure as the sentence 'Julius Caesar is realized'. The latter sentence is false because "the assertion that something is realized . . . is one we can only truly make of such objects as stand in quite special relations to concepts" (*PW* 109). But it does express a sense, just as the sentence 'the concept *man* is realized' does. Both are about self-subsistent objects, in the one case the man Julius Caesar, in the other the concept *man*.

Much as an identity 'a = b', though it is most naturally analyzed as involving a relation (identity) and two objects, can also be analyzed as involving an object (a, say) and a function, $\xi = b$, so, Frege thought for a time, a simple predication, 'Fa', though it is most naturally analyzed as involving an object a and a function Fξ, can also be analyzed as involving a first-level relation and two objects. The concept F (an object) is not identical to (the concept) Fξ; one could not, for instance, take the concept F as the argument for the second-level function $\Phi(a)$. That would be nonsense. Nevertheless, Frege suggests, the sentence 'Fa' can, on the relevant analysis, reveal an object, namely, the concept F, just as, on another analysis, it reveals a concept, Fξ. Hence, in whatever equivalence relation two objects might stand, one to another, in virtue of their sharing a property (as we would naturally put the point), the content of a sentence that ascribes that relation to those objects can be differently analyzed so as to yield a strict identity. Now we apply the point to the case of equal (*gleichzahlig*) concepts, stipulating that 'the number of *F* = the number of *G*' is to have the same sense as the sentence 'the concept *F* is equal (*gleichzahlig*) to the concept *G*', where two concepts are equal in this technical sense just if the objects that fall under them can be correlated one to one. In this way we discover the number that is assigned to the concept *F* and give it a name— or rather, we could count as having done so were we able to assume already the concept *number*.

Frege rejects his second definition on the grounds that it does not settle all identities but only those of the form 'the number belonging to the concept *F* = the number belonging to the concept *G*'. If we already had the concept *number*, the definition would be adequate (that is, it would settle all identities) because if we already had the concept *number*, then we could lay it down that if for some object o (Julius Caesar, say) o is not a number then the thought expressed by the sentence 'o is identical to the number of Fs' is to be denied. But the logicist cannot take the concept *number* for granted. That *number* is a purely logical concept must be proved, and it cannot be proved simultaneously with a definition of the numbers via Hume's principle.[2] We must "try another way."

Frege's first definition fails because it does not yield names for numbers. The second definition fails because its adequacy presupposes the notion of number. What is needed, then, is a definition of the numbers conceived as self-subsistent objects that avoids any reliance on the concept *number*. Frege's third *Grundlagen* definition will, he thinks, serve: "the Number which belongs to the concept *F* is the extension of the concept 'equal [*gleichzahlig*] to the concept *F*'" (*GL* §68).[3] We are to understand numbers as extensions of second-level concepts—though, Frege notes, the definition could also be written in a way that makes no reference to extensions: "for 'extension of the concept' we could write simply 'concept'" (*GL* §68 n. 1). Because, as Frege goes on to show, both Hume's principle and a definition of the concept *number* can be derived on the basis of this definition, the definition is adequate. It also can seem to come out of nowhere. To see that it does not, to see that Frege's third definition is the natural culmination of the discussion so far, we need to set it against the background of Kant.

Frege's task in *Grundlagen* (which, as already noted, is conceived in explicitly Kantian terms) is to show that numbers, self-subsistent objects, can be given directly to reason; it must be shown, through logical concepts alone, that there are numbers having the arithmetical properties numbers are known to have. The task is to fix the sense of expressions, object names, of the form 'the number belonging to the concept F'—that is, to set out not only the circumstances but also the consequences of the (correct) use of such expressions in judgments—and to do so without appeal to the concept *number*. Two hurdles must be overcome. The first is the general point, due to Kant, that concepts, even in their singular use in definite descriptions, cannot function logically as singular representations of objects for the simple reason that objects are thoroughly determinate and concepts are inherently determinable: "even if we have a concept that we apply *immediately* to individuals, there can still be specific differences in regard to it, which we either do not note, or which we disregard."[4] It follows, Kant thinks, that "there can be thoroughly determinate cognitions only as *intuitions*, but not as concepts; in regard to the latter, logical determination can never be regarded as completed." Because a definite description determines an object by way of marks that are in principle common to many, such a description, although it may happen to be true of one and only one object, is unlike an object name in that it could as well be true of others, or of nothing at all. As Kripke would put the point, definite descriptions, unlike object names (or, as Kant would say, intuitions), are not rigid designators.[5]

On the Kantian view, one can use a concept word with the definite article as a kind of referring expression, that is, use it as a means of referring to a particular object that one has in mind; but the expression itself does not amount to, that is, function logically as, an intuition. Frege disagrees, and he does so because he distinguishes, though in *Grundlagen* only implicitly, between the inferentially articulated sense of an expression and that which it designates. Given this distinction, the fact that a definite description such as (say) 'the last great philosopher of antiquity' would designate not Aristotle but instead someone else in a different possible situation cannot be used to show that such a description functions in a way that is logically different from the way an object name such as 'Aristotle' functions. For, on Frege's mature view, the name 'Aristotle' is no more a mere label than the numeral '3' of the Arabic notation is a mere label; both object names express senses. Similarly, the description 'the last great philosopher of antiquity' is no more a mere description than the expression 'the sum of 2 and 3' is; both expressions designate objects. Provided one understands the logical functioning of the language as Frege does, in terms of the logical distinction of *Sinn* and *Bedeutung*, there is in principle no difficulty with using a definite description to fix the sense, and thereby the reference, of an object name.

If we already had the concept *number*, we could define the numbers by way of definitions of the form 'the number belonging to the concept F', the number zero, for instance, as the number belonging to the concept *not self-identical*. This is, furthermore, the most natural way to think of a definite description, as of the form 'the K that is F', where 'K' is the governing sortal that fixes the kind of thing that is being introduced and 'F' the uniquely identifying description of the particular K that is wanted. Frege's problem is that he cannot, for the purposes of logicism, assume the concept *number* as given. That concept must be derived from purely logical notions, that is, shown to be strictly logical. Frege needs another way. It is provided by his newly discovered notion of a second-level concept introduced already in *Grundlagen* §53.

Kant argues that even in their singular use in definite descriptions, concepts do not function logically as singular representations of objects because objects are thoroughly determinate, whereas concepts are inherently determinable. The concept *house that Jack built,* for instance, can be made more determinate by conjoining the concept *stone* to yield *stone house that Jack built,* or by conjoining the concept *built with Jane* to yield *house that Jack built with Jane.* The process is, as Kant says, endless: "in regard to the latter [in regard, that is, to concepts], logical determination can never be regarded as completed."[6] One can always add another predicate to yield a more determinate concept. One can approach the limit of a thoroughly determinate cognition through concepts; one cannot achieve it. More exactly, one cannot achieve it if one pursues Kant's strategy of conjoining concepts. The alternative, Frege's strategy, is to appeal to a second-level concept under which fall all and only the first-level concepts through which the object in question can be given. The strategy is a good one because, as Frege says in obvious reference to Kant, "the concept has the power of collecting together far superior to the unifying power of synthetic apperception" (*GL* §48). Although a thinker could not collect together all the requisite concepts to yield a fully determinate concept of an individual, a (second-level) concept can. So, instead of trying to define a number by using a description of the form 'the number of Fs', where *number* is functioning as the governing sortal (which cannot work because we cannot, for the purposes of logicism, take the concept *number* as given), we define a number in terms of the second-level concept *equal (gleichzahlig) to F* under which fall all and only the first-level concepts to which some one number (namely, the number assigned to *F*) is assigned, thereby achieving a kind of all-sided determination of that number, a definition within which is contained all the ways it can be given. Obviously, then, the definition fixes all identities; it solves the Julius Caesar problem. We can furthermore simply identify the number with this second-level concept, Frege seems to have thought at this point, because any sentence that contains a concept word for the second-level concept *Φ is equal (gleichzahlig) to the concept F* can yield an object name, the object name 'the concept *equal (gleichzahlig) to the concept F*', on a different analysis. Because the move might seem to a reader to be paradoxical, given that concepts are not objects, Frege suggests that the same effect can be achieved by appeal to the extension of the concept *equal (gleichzahlig) to the concept F.*

A central task of *Grundlagen* is to show, if only in outline, how through logic alone numbers are given to reason. Frege approaches this goal in stages, each of which is to help us see why the next is needed. At the first, we are given the necessary and sufficient conditions for assigning a number to a concept; but because this does not adequately fix the consequences of assigning a number to a concept, the first definition is rejected. What is needed, we are now to see, is a definition of the number itself. The second stage is set by Hume's principle together with the idea, fundamental to Frege's conception of a properly logical language, that a sentence can be analyzed into function and argument in various ways. The number of *F*s can be defined as the number of *G*s by way of a different analysis of the content expressed by 'the concept *F* is equal (*gleichzahlig*) to the concept *G*'. This strategy, we have argued, requires that there be independent grounds for thinking that the relevant object exists (because the mathematician cannot create things at will but only discover what is there and give it a name). The content of a sentence 'aRb', where R is an equivalence relation, can be differently analyzed to yield the sentence 'the f(a) = the f(b)' only in the case in which there is a third object c and a relation R* such that if aRb then aR*c and bR*c. Yet, Frege thinks, the strategy can be applied even in the case in which, so it would seem, there is no such object, for instance, in the case of two objects that are the same color. He does so, we have seen, because he thinks, for a time, that corresponding to any concept such as ξ-is-red there is an object, the concept *red*. Because, on that view, any equivalence relation is grounded in a relation to some third thing, the strategy can be applied to Hume's principle to yield the second *Grundlagen* definition of number. But this definition too is quickly rejected. Even it does not give the definition that is wanted because it does not fix the truth-values of all identities—though it would if the logicist program were to be abandoned and the concept *number* accepted as a primitive notion in arithmetic. Because the logicist cannot accept the concept *number* as primitive, the proposed definition is not, properly speaking, a definition of a number at all.

The most natural form of a definition of an object through concepts is by way of a definite description of the form 'the K that is F', where K is the governing sortal and F a uniquely identifying mark of the K that is wanted. But as Frege sees, this is not the only form such a definition can take. If one conjoined all the ways an object could be given—thereby achieving something very much like a Leibnizian individual concept, an all-sided determination of the object—then appeal to a sortal could be dispensed with. This, it has been suggested, is Frege's strategy in the third definition. Appealing to a second-level concept under which all the relevant first-level concepts fall, thereby conjoining all the ways the defined object can be given, the third *Grundlagen* definition uniquely identifies the number that is wanted. The number of Fs is the (extension of the) concept *equal (gleichzahlig) to F*.

5.2 A Further Difficulty

Frege claims in *Grundlagen* that he "[attaches] no decisive importance even to bringing in the extensions of concepts at all" in his definition of number (*GL* §107). The number of Fs, he suggests, could be defined simply as the concept *equal to F*. In *Grundgesetze* we are told that "we just cannot get on without them [extensions]" (*GG* 6). Numbers, Frege had come by 1893 to think, can be apprehended only as extensions, more exactly, courses of values, of concepts.[7] The notion of a course of values must, then, be admitted in logic, though, as Frege notes already in the Introduction to *Grundgesetze*, a reasonable person might legitimately question its admission. "A dispute can arise, so far as I can see, only with regard to my Basic Law concerning courses-of-values (V), which logicians perhaps have not yet expressly enunciated, and yet is what people have in mind, for example, where they speak of extensions of concepts. I hold that it is a law of pure logic. In any event the place is pointed out where the decision must be made" (*GG* 3–4).[8] Basic Law V was not immediately evident in the way that a basic law of logic ought to be, and yet, Frege came to think, there was no other way to formulate logically adequate definitions of the numbers. "Only with difficulty," he writes to Jourdain in 1910, "did I resolve to introduce classes (or extents of concepts), because the matter did not appear to me quite secure—and rightly so, as it turned out" (*PMC* 191 n 69). But, as he goes on, there seemed no other way.

> By this I was constrained to overcome my resistance and to admit the passage from concepts to their extents. And, after I had made this resolution, I made a more extended use of classes than was necessary, because by that many simplifications could be reached. I confess that by acting thus, I fell into the error of letting go too easily my initial doubts in reliance on the fact that extents of concepts have for a long time been spoken of in Logic.

In a letter to Hönigswald, written in the last months of his life, Frege writes that he found the expression 'the extension of *F*' "very convenient," that "while I sometimes had slight doubts during the execution of the work, I paid no attention to them" (*PMC* 55). The notion of an extension was logically suspect, and yet it seemed to Frege overwhelmingly likely that arithmetic is merely derived logic. The trouble was that the means by which to show that it is had come to seem to require appeal to extensions. To understand the nature of this difficulty, we need to understand both Frege's reservations about extensions and how those reservations were overcome.

Although every object is some kind of thing or other, whether essentially or not, the notion of an object is not logically dependent on the notion of a function. The two notions are rather correlative, neither fully intelligible without the other. But, Frege suggests in "Function and Concept," the notion of a function is fully intelligible without the notion of an extension, whereas the converse is not the case: "function, in the sense of the word employed here, is the logically prior notion" (*CP* 142 n 5). The reason the notion of an extension is not intelligible except in terms of the logically prior notion of a function is revealed by comparison with the notion of a manifold, that is, an aggregate or collection of objects. First, whereas one can talk of parts and wholes in the case of a manifold—for instance, that one manifold (the collection of books in a certain box, say) is a part of another (the collection of books on the table on which the box sits)—no distinction can be drawn between membership in a manifold and the inclusion of one manifold in another. Parts of parts of wholes that are manifolds are at the same time parts of the wholes themselves. There are, then, no proper elements in a manifold. The collection of books can be "divided" ad infinitum; the books can be regarded as a collection of pages, of parts of pages, of fibers, of molecules, of atoms, and so on. Furthermore, because a manifold just is a collection of objects, there can be no empty manifold: "a class, in the sense in which we have so far used the word, consists of objects; it is an aggregate, a collective unity, of them; if so, it must vanish when these objects vanish" (*CP* 212). Extensions, we will see, are quite different from such manifolds.

Collections of objects (that is, manifolds) are entities whose parts are held together by some relation or interaction. "Such relations may be spatial, temporal, physical, psychical, legal, even intervals of pitch" (*PW* 181); collections of objects can be held together "by customs, institutions and laws" (*PMC* 140). An extension, by contrast, is a logical unity held together by a concept.

A whole, a system [that is, a collection or manifold], is held together by relations, and these are essential to it. An army is destroyed if what holds it together is dissolved, even if the individual soldiers remain alive. On the other hand, it makes no difference to a class [extension] what the relations are in which the objects that are members of it stand to one another. Secondly, if we are given a whole [a manifold or collection], it is not yet determined what we are to envisage as its parts. As parts of a regiment I can regard the battalions, the companies or the individual soldiers, and as parts of a sand pile, the grains of sand or the silicon and oxygen atoms. On the other hand, if we are given a class [extension], it is determined what objects are members of it . . . For wholes or systems [manifolds] we have the proposition that a part of a part is part of the whole. This proposition does not hold for classes [extensions] as regards the objects that are members of them. (*PMC* 140)

The extension of a concept is constituted in being, not by the individuals, but by the concept itself; i.e. by what is said of an object when it is brought under a concept. There is then no objection to our talking about a class of objects that are *b*s even when there are no *b*s. Moreover, all empty concepts now have the same extension. (*CP* 224–225)

An extension cannot be divided ad infinitum, and it can be empty. An extension, then, cannot be identified with a collection of things or manifold. It is "not . . . a physical object but a logical one" (*PMC* 140).

Any object, and any collection of objects, can be arrived at in different ways, can be thought of in different ways, and can be divided into parts in different ways. An extension, though it can, we will see, be arrived at in different ways and can be thought of in different ways, cannot in the same way be divided into parts in different ways. An extension is not, then, merely a collection of objects. It is a logical object grounded in a concept that determines the principle of inclusion in it. That is why there can be an empty extension though there is no collection of zero objects.

What is less clear is why, if an extension has its being in a concept, there is only one extension where two concepts are mutually subordinate rather than two. As Russell puts the worry in a letter to Frege of 24 July 1902:

In general, if one connects ranges of values closely with concepts, as you do, it seems doubtful whether two concepts with the same extension have the same range of values or only equivalent ranges of values. I find it hard to see what a class really is if it does not consist of objects but is nevertheless supposed to be the same for two concepts with the same extension. Yet I admit that the reason you adduce against the extensional view [in "A Critical Elucidation of Some Points in E. Schroeder's *Vorlesungen ueber die Algebra der Logik*"] seems to be irrefutable.

Every day I understand less and less what is really meant by the extension of a concept. (*PMC* 139)

The puzzle is resolved by Frege's mature "extensionalist" conception of concepts according to which mutually subordinate concepts are really one and the same concept thought under different aspects: "concepts differ only in so far as their extensions are different" (*PW* 118). Concepts cannot themselves be identical, strictly speaking, because "the relation of equality, by which I understand complete coincidence, identity, can only be thought of as holding for objects, not concepts"; nevertheless, "the relation we had in mind above [corresponding to identity between objects] holds between the concept Φ and the concept X, if every object that falls under Φ also falls under X, and conversely" (*PW* 120). In such cases it is not the meaning, *Bedeutung,* that is different, but only the sense. That is why extensions can be thought of in different ways, arrived at in different ways, despite the fact that they cannot be divided into parts in different ways. If two concept words express different senses although they designate one and the same concept, then names for the extension of that concept formed from those two concept words will also differ in sense although they designate one and the same extension.

If extensions are objects that have their being in concepts, then they are not properly objects at all. They are not self-subsistent. At the same time, however, Frege was becoming increasingly dissatisfied with the idea that a concept can itself be transformed into a kind of object so "that an object that is connected with it in accordance with a rule [can] be substituted for it" (*PW* 97). By 1893 that idea had been dropped altogether. The thought that a sentence 'Fa' can be analyzed as involving a (first-level) relation, $\zeta(\xi)$, for two objects as arguments, namely, the concept F and a, had been a mistake. The relevant relation is unequal, taking as arguments not two objects but instead an object and a concept: in '——$\Phi(\xi)$' "'ξ' occupies and renders recognizable the place of the object-argument and '$\Phi(\ )$' that of the function-argument" (*GG* §22). There is a relationship of objects in the vicinity, but, Frege now holds, it must involve an explicit transformation of a concept word into a name for a course of values. A sentence such as 'Fa', we are told, means the same as *(Gleichbedeutend sein)* 'a $\cap$ $\acute{e}$F(ϵ)'.

Courses of values are objects; concepts are not. Frege explains the point in a 1906 discussion of Schoenflies's *Die logischen Paradoxien der Mengenlehre:*

> Language brands a concept as an object, since the only way it can fit the designation for a concept into its grammatical structure is as a proper name. But in so doing, strictly speaking it falsifies matters. In the same way, the word 'concept' itself is, taken strictly, already defective, since the phrase 'is a concept' requires a proper name as grammatical subject; and so, strictly speaking, it requires something contradictory, since no proper name can designate a concept; or perhaps better still, something nonsensical. (*PW* 177–178)

The point is made again in the 1906 "Introduction to Logic" (*PW* 193), in 1914 in "Logic in Mathematics" (*PW* 239), in 1919 in the "Notes for Ludwig Darmstaedter" (*PW* 255), and finally in the essay "Sources of Knowledge" written in the last year of Frege's life (*PW* 273). Natural language, in collusion with Frege's insight into the way sentences are variously analyzable into function and argument, had misled Frege into thinking that corresponding to any concept, for instance, that designated by 'Fξ', there is an object F, that is, the concept F. But there is no such object. Concepts are inherently unsaturated.

But if there are no objects that are concepts, a number cannot be defined by appeal to such an object. Numbers must, then, be extensions of concepts. But are extensions really objects? Frege's reflections on the differences between a manifold or collection of objects and an extension suggest that they are not. Extensions have their being in concepts; they are not self-subsistent. Yet, we have seen, the strategy of the second definition requires that the equivalence relation in question be grounded in another relation that the relevant objects bear to some third thing. The strategy cannot create the relevant object but only discover and name it. It requires, then, that we have some independent grounds for thinking that there are such objects as the strategy reveals. What is the logicist to do?

The strategy of the second definition, and of Basic Law V, is to transform a sentence of the form 'aRb', where R is reflexive, symmetric, and transitive, into an identity of the form 'the f(a) = the f(b)'. It is legitimate, we have suggested, only if it is known that there is an object c and a relation R* such that aR*c and bR*c. Frege, then, must show that there is something, that is, some object, to which both concepts are related in the case in which they are mutually subordinate. He must produce the object that is related in common to two concepts that are mutually subordinate because if he does not, his account falls into the error of formalist theories, the error of creating things at will. But Frege has good reason to think that an extension is not, properly speaking, an object at all, that it is not a self-subsistent entity but instead something that has its being in a concept. How, then, does Frege let go his doubts? He does so in essentially the way we let go our doubts about directions, by producing the relevant object in an intuition, by putting it before our eyes. As Frege argues in "Function and Concept," although a function is not merely a set of ordered n-tuples of points but is instead a law of correlation determining that set, a function can nonetheless be intuitively represented as a curve in Cartesian coordinates.

> If we regard the argument as the numerical value of an abscissa, and the corresponding values of the function as the numerical value of the ordinate of a point, we obtain a set of points that presents itself to intuition (in ordinary cases) as a curve. Any point on the curve corresponds to an argument together with the associated value of the function.
>
> Thus, e.g.,
>
> $$y = x^2 - 4x$$
>
> yields a parabola. (*CP* 141–142)

Furthermore, it is clear that where the values of two functions are the same for every argument, they yield the same curve in Cartesian coordinates: "the curve we get from $y = x^2 - 4x$ is the same as the one that arises out of $y = x(x - 4)$" (*CP* 142). Speaking more exactly, it is the same function that is designated in both cases; the expressions '$x(x - 4)$' and '$x^2 - 4x$' designate one and the same function but differ in sense. But that does not affect the essential point: that there is a curve that "arises out of" the function. The curve is not a representation of the function itself; it cannot be because a function is not an object and a curve is a kind of object. Instead, what is intuitively represented in the graph is "the values of a function for different objects" (*CP* 141). Given that such an object can be intuitively represented in this way, we can conclude that there actually is such an object, that is, that it is a self-subsistent entity, like a point at infinity. Because concepts are functions from objects to truth-values, they give rise in the same way to objects that are identical one to another just in case the two concepts are mutually subordinate (that is, actually one and the same).

Frege calls such objects courses of values. Applying the strategy of the second definition, we can, then, transform an equality that holds generally between values of functions into a strict identity of just those objects that are intuitively represented as curves in Cartesian coordinates.

We know that an extension is not merely a collection of objects because, first, collections of objects can be divided into parts in various ways and extensions cannot, and second, there cannot be a collection of zero objects though there can be an empty extension. This was puzzling because it seemed to show that an extension has its being in a concept. If we think instead of the correlation of objects and truth-values that a concept determines, the situation is very different. Just as the numbers correlated by a function constitute an object that can be intuitively represented as a curve in Cartesian coordinates, so the objects (arguments and truth-values) that are correlated by a concept constitute an object. Obviously we should not expect the parts of this latter to divide into parts. It is given what the arguments are that are correlated with the relevant truth-values. Nor should it now seem surprising that there should be something that is an empty extension because that is nothing other than a course of values that has the False correlated with every object as argument. We can, then, let go our initial doubts regarding the self-subsistence of extensions, acknowledge the truth of Law V, and get on with the logicist program. Or so, for a short while, it seemed to Frege.

5.3 Russell's Paradox

Frege needed Basic Law V in order to complete the logicist program outlined in *Grundlagen*. He needed to produce an object as that to which mutually subordinate concepts stand in a relation in order to define the numbers. Given that arithmetically equivalent functions determine one and the same curve in Cartesian coordinates and that concepts just are functions that take objects as arguments to yield truth-values as values, it follows that mutually subordinate concepts determine one and the same value-range. We have produced the object that is wanted. But Russell's concept *class that does not belong to itself* is a logically adequate concept; it has sharp boundaries in Frege's technical sense because it yields either the value True or the value False for every object as argument; *tertium non datur*. Yet Russell's concept does not determine an extension or course of values. It is, as Dummett argues, "a proto-typical example of an indefinitely extensible concept": "For, once we form a definite conception of a totality **W** of such classes, it is evident that **W** cannot, on pain of contradiction, be a member of itself, and thus the totality consisting of all the members of **W**, together with **W** itself, is a more extensive totality than **W** of classes that are not members of themselves."[9] In the case of a concept such as Russell's, a concept that has sharp boundaries in the sense of yielding a value for every object as argument but is indefinitely extensible, there is no course of values by means of which it can be represented in logical space. It is, then, false that having "sharp boundaries" in Frege's technical sense implies that the relevant course of values exists. Law V is not true.

Frege argues in "Function and Concept" that concepts determine courses of values on the grounds that, first, concepts are functions taking objects as arguments to yield truth-values as values, and second, that functions determine curves in Cartesian coordinates. But we know that concepts do not invariably determine courses of values because Russell's concept does not. Does it follow that concepts are not functions from objects to truth-values? Certainly that was not Frege's conclusion. Frege nowhere calls into question his logical notion of a concept as a function that yields either the True or the False for every object as argument. It would seem to follow, then, that it is false that functions (invariably) determine curves in Cartesian coordinates. If it could be shown on independent grounds that this claim is false, that would be enough to establish that the error was indeed to assume that all logically permissible concepts determine courses of values.

The thought that arithmetically equivalent functions determine one and the same curve in Cartesian coordinates is certainly intuitive; and it is well illustrated by Frege's example of the function $y = x^2 - 4x = x(x - 4)$, which determines a parabola. Nevertheless, it is not generally true that functions determine such curves. Some functions do not determine any curves at all in Cartesian coordinates. One such function is the Koch curve, which Friedman has characterized thus:

> We start with a horizontal line segment *AB* which we divide into three equal parts by points *C* and *D*; on the middle segment *CD* we construct an equilateral triangle *CED* and erase the open segment *CD*; we repeat the same construction on each of the segments *AC*, *CE*, *ED*, *DB*; finally, we continue this process indefinitely on each remaining segment (see Figure). The resulting curve is continuous, but at no point is there a well-defined tangent . . . no finite segment of the Koch curve can be drawn by the continuous motion of a pencil: we must think of each point as laid down independently, as it were, yet nevertheless in a continuous order.[10]

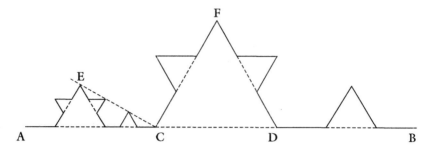

Though the Koch function is continuous, it is nowhere differentiable. It follows that we cannot draw such a curve, cannot represent the function intuitively as a curve in Cartesian coordinates. There is simply no such curve; and we know that there is no such curve because its representation involves continuing indefinitely a process of construction on segments. In just the same way the representation of the class (or course of values) that is the extension of the concept *class that does not belong to itself* involves continuing indefinitely a process of construction on classes. There is no curve that is the Koch curve, and there is no class that is the class of classes that do not belong to themselves.

Mathematicians long assumed that continuity entails differentiability, and they did so, at least in part, because continuity was understood intuitively, in terms of the idea of continuous motion. Functions such as the Koch curve show that this intuitive character is a mere appearance, an irrelevant accretion to the concept of continuity that must be stripped off it if we are to grasp the concept in its pure form. Similarly, we assume that every logically permissible concept, that is, every concept with sharp boundaries in Frege's technical sense, determines a course of values, and we do so, in part, because the idea of sharp boundaries is conceived intuitively as involving the idea of something literally like a bounded space. Russell's concept *class that does not belong to itself* shows that this intuitive character is a mere appearance, an irrelevant accretion to the concept *concept*. It must be stripped off if we are to grasp the concept of a concept in its pure form. Frege's Law V, according to which it can be inferred from the mutual subordination of two concepts that they share something in common (other than the concept itself), namely, an extension or course of values, is not true. Though some concepts do determine courses of values (just as some continuous functions are differentiable), there is nothing in the very idea of a concept that requires that concepts determine courses of values. All that logic requires of a concept is that it yield a truth-value, either the True or the False, for every object as argument.

5.4 A Final Reckoning

Frege always had doubts about the logician's notion of an extension; for, as he saw, an extension is essentially different from a collection or manifold of objects. It is a logical object that has its being in a concept that fixes a principle of inclusion in the extension. Because an extension so conceived is not self-subsistent, it is not an object, properly speaking, at all. Yet, as Frege came to see, his logicist program of deriving the truths of arithmetic from logic alone required that there be some such objects. If Frege's life's work was to be completed, he had somehow to find sufficient reason to let go his initial doubts; he had to articulate a conception of an extension that was manifestly a conception of a self-subsistent object. Frege's notion of a course of values modeled upon that of a curve in Cartesian coordinates was, he thought, just the conception that was needed. Although an extension conceived as the set of objects falling under a concept is not self-subsistent but has its being in that concept, an extension conceived as a correlation of objects and truth-values, that is, as a kind of curve in logical space, is a self-subsistent object. Because any logically permissible concept has sharp boundaries in the sense of yielding a truth-value for every object as argument, it seemed reasonable to conclude that corresponding to every concept there is such a "curve." Frege had discovered, so he thought, a logically permissible conception of an extension on which to found his logicist program.

In the Introduction to *Grundgesetze*, we have seen, Frege claims that "a dispute can arise, so far as I can see, only with regard to my Basic Law concerning courses-of-values" (*GG* 3). It is clear, nonetheless, that he does not think that any substantive objection to it can be made. No one, he confidently claims in the conclusion of the Introduction, will be able to demonstrate that his principles "lead to manifestly false conclusions" (*GG* 25). When Russell demonstrated exactly that, Frege was, he says, "surprised . . . beyond words and, I should almost like to say, left . . . thunderstruck" (*PMC* 132). For a time Frege continued to think that a logically permissible conception of an extension might yet be found. Eventually he came to see that the hope was forlorn: "the paradoxes of set theory . . . have dealt the death blow to set theory itself" (*PW* 269). The notion of an extension is a fiction. No concept is designated thereby. Law V is *bedeutungslos*.

In Russell's original formulation of it in his letter of 16 June 1902, the paradox arises because one allows a function to serve as an argument for a function at the same level as the original function. But, as Frege notes in his reply of 22 June 1902, "a first-level function . . . requires an object as argument and . . . cannot therefore have itself as argument" (*PMC* 132). In Frege's logic the paradox can be formulated only in light of Basic Law V, which enables a concept (function) to be transformed into an object that can then serve as an argument for the original function. In the 1879 logic Frege does not allow functions to serve as arguments for functions at the same level (as Russell does), though he does not explicitly outlaw this either, and he does not have any mechanism for transforming a function into an object. There is no trace of Law V in the early *Begriffsschrift*, and this is to be expected, given Frege's early dissatisfaction with the notion of an extension. Furthermore, Frege has already in the notation of his logic implicitly marked the distinction of first- and second-level functions. Frege's concavity notation with German letters enables him to form concept words for second-level concepts that are manifestly different in form from concept words for first-level concepts. Again, Frege does not explicitly note the distinction between first- and second-level concepts in *Begriffsschrift*, but it is marked already in his notation and is respected in his inferential practice.

By 1893, we have seen, Frege came explicitly to recognize the distinction between lower- and higher-level concepts and began self-consciously to understand the role his concavity notation plays in the formation of concept words for second-level concepts. At the same time, he introduced Law V, but its introduction, we have seen, was wholly driven by the demands of his logicist program. It was also apparently legitimated by the "fact" that any arithmetical function can be represented as a curve in Cartesian coordinates. This "fact," we have seen, is no fact at all; it is not true. Basic Law V is similarly untrue. It does not follow from the concept *concept* that any concept determines a course of values; some concepts, Russell's, for example, do not determine a course of values. Law V, and with it Frege's logicist program, must be jettisoned.[11] Because that leaves untouched both the distinction between first- and second-level concepts and the demand that only a lower-level function can serve as an argument for a higher-level function, Russell's paradox cannot be formulated. Basic Law V, as well as everything that in any way depends on it, must be banished from logic; but, just as Frege claims, logic itself, at least in its principal parts, those dealt with in the 1879 *Begriffsschrift*, remains intact: "in my fashion of regarding concepts as functions, we can treat the principal parts of Logic without speaking of classes, as I have done in my *Begriffsschrift*, and that difficulty [that is, Russell's contradiction] does not then come into consideration" (*PMC* 191 n 69). Basic Law V is needed for Frege's logicism. It is not needed, either explicitly or implicitly, in his logic.

As here understood, Frege's logic is founded on a distinctive conception of a law as a principle that governs inference; laws, on this conception, have the form of rules according to which to reason as they contrast with premises from which to reason. Sentences of *Begriffsschrift* that express such laws take the form of generalized conditionals, or genuine hypotheticals, where such sentences are to be understood as relating concepts one to another. It follows, as Frege comes explicitly to see in the mature logic, that concepts must be something in their own right, something objective, albeit unsaturated or incomplete. Just as objects can, concepts, as Frege regards them, can stand in relations and can serve as arguments for (higher-level) concepts. No recourse to the objects that fall under the relevant concepts is needed to understand logically general sentences of *Begriffsschrift*. As Frege's mature understanding of the quite different roles played by his Latin italic letters and his concavity with German letters makes abundantly clear, though a generality of the form

$$-\!\!\!\overset{\mathfrak{a}}{\smile}\!\!- F(\mathfrak{a})$$

is true just in case the concept $F\xi$ yields the value True for every object as argument, the thought expressed by the sentence does not in any way involve reference to a totality of objects. The thought involves only the senses of concept words. Relative to one analysis, for instance, it ascribes the second-level concept

$$-\!\!\!\overset{\mathfrak{a}}{\smile}\!\!- \phi(\mathfrak{a})$$

to the concept $F\xi$. Relative to another, it ascribes the third-level concept $\mu_\beta(F(\beta))$ to the argument

$$-\!\!\!\overset{\mathfrak{a}}{\smile}\!\!- \phi(\mathfrak{a}),$$

and so on. On no analysis does it yield an expression that designates an object or a collection or totality of objects. Just as Frege says, "the difficulties which are bound up with the use of classes vanish if we only deal with objects, concepts and relations, and this is possible in the fundamental part of Logic" (*PMC* 191 n. 69). More exactly, this is possible in the fundamental part of Frege's logic.

Epilogue

> What pig-headedness! This way academics have of behaving reminds
> me of nothing so much as that of an ox confronted by a new gate: it
> gapes, it bellows, it tries to squeeze by sideways, but going through
> it—that might be dangerous.
> —"INTRODUCTION TO LOGIC," 1906

Frege's logic is distinctive in "giving pride of place to the content of the
word 'true'" (*PW* 253). This does not mean, however, that sentential
meaning is given by truth conditions in his logic. In Frege's logic, at least
as it has been read here, that notion of meaning is to be split into the
thought expressed by a sentence and the truth-value designated. The reason it must be so split goes to the very heart of Frege's logic: thoughts
must be variously analyzable into function and argument. Judgment and
inference, that is, the acknowledgment of the truth of a thought either directly, on its own merits, or on the basis of other judgments, can be adequately understood in no other way. Frege's two-dimensional notation
puts this insight before our eyes. Rather than directly saying something
about something, a sentence of *Begriffsschrift* presents, in a two-dimensional array, a thought that can be variously analyzed into function and argument; and only relative to such an analysis into function and argument
does it ascribe a concept to an object (or to another, lower-level concept).
Even in the simplest cases more than one analysis is possible. As Frege
clearly saw, no linear notation can adequately express thoughts so conceived.

Nor is it only Frege's strange two-dimensional notation that is provided
a properly logical justification on our reading. The judgment stroke,
which has no place in a quantificational logic, is essential to Frege's logic as
it is understood here because conclusions can be drawn in that logic only
from premises that are, and are acknowledged to be, true, where this stipulation is required in turn because in Frege's logic generality is understood
first and foremost in terms of the notion of an inference license, something
according to which to reason rather than something from which to reason.
Generalized conditionals of *Begriffsschrift* count as, or have the status of,

178

laws governing inferences. In this, Frege's logic as here construed is diametrically opposed to a quantificational logic: whereas the quantificational logician begins directly with truth (and, perhaps, satisfaction) and aims to construct truth conditions adequate to capture inference potential, Frege begins instead with inference potential, what follows if a sentence is true (everything necessary for a correct inference), and only relative to an analysis aims to specify truth conditions.

Frege's use of two different sorts of letters with and without the concavity is also logically justified on our reading. It is justified by the fact that the two sorts of letters play logically different roles, German letters together with the concavity to enable the formation of higher-level concept words and Latin italic letters directly to raise everything up a level. From (first-level) consideration of properties and relations of objects, the introduction of the literal notation enables (second-level) consideration of properties and relations of concepts. Then again, given the relevant second-level concept words, the use of the literal notation enables the passage from consideration of properties and relations of first-level concepts to (third-level) consideration of properties and relations of second-level concepts. It is at this third level that the concern of the science of logic as Frege comes to understand it is apparent. The concern of logic, as Frege understands logic, is the properties and relations of those second-level concepts that are definable in strictly logical terms. Already in Part III of *Begriffsschrift* Frege shows this concern; only much later does he come to full, self-conscious awareness of it as the concern of logic. Logic, on this view, is a science, and as in any science, its body of truths is fully realized only in an adequate axiomatization.

Having given up the uncritical assumption that Frege's logic is a quantificational logic, we were also able to render intelligible all the major developments in Frege's views, both those culminating in the distinction between *Sinn* and *Bedeutung* that constitute, on our reading, an extraordinary intellectual achievement, and Frege's misbegotten Law V. On our account, Frege's mature logic (omitting Law V and all the innovations that depend on it) is, just as Frege himself conceives it, the full flowering of the seeds first planted in the 1879 notation. Taken together, Frege's two-dimensional notation, with its Greek, Latin, and German letters, and his mature understanding of the logical functioning of that language in terms of the logical notions of *Sinn* and *Bedeutung* afford us the first glimpse of a world hitherto unimaginable.

As a system of signs, Frege's notation is completely unambiguous. The only question is whether it is, as standardly assumed, a notation of a logic we already have, albeit remarkably ill conceived, or whether, as has been assumed here, it is a remarkably well conceived notation of a logic about which we know nothing. Should we start with quantificational logic and aim to squeeze Frege's work into that mold—much as, on Frege's view, Peano aimed "to squeeze each formula onto one line" (*CP* 236)? Or should we start instead with Frege's writings, letting quantificational logic fall where it may? The former path is well trodden. The latter might teach us something we do not already know.

Notes

Abbreviations

Index

Notes

Introduction

1. Not that these questions have not been asked, or answers proposed. The secondary literature is vast, without, however, revealing any compelling logical motivation for these various features of Frege's logic.
2. W. V. O. Quine, *Philosophy of Logic* (Englewood Cliffs, N.J.: Prentice-Hall, 1970), p. 36.
3. Frege makes the point in *Grundgesetze* §12. It is discussed more fully here in section 2.2.
4. In his discussion of Peano's notation and his own, Frege suggests such a contrast between a notation aimed at tracing truth conditions and a notation aimed at presenting a structure that, for the purposes of judgment and inference, is variously analyzable: "the intention [of Peano's notation] seems oriented towards the storage of knowledge rather than towards proof [as Frege thinks his own notation is], towards brevity and international intelligibility rather than towards logical perfection" (*CP* 237); "the main emphasis [in Frege's conceptual notation] is on inference, which is not stressed so much in the Peano calculus" (*CP* 242).
5. Even Carnap, though he studied with Frege for three semesters at Jena—*Begriffsschrift* in the fall of 1910, *Begriffsschrift* II in the summer of 1913, and *Logik in der Mathematik* in the summer of 1914—was blind to the enormous expressive power and philosophical significance of Frege's logic until after he had read *Principia Mathematica* around 1919. "The beginnings of a symbolic logic of relations were also in Frege's system," Carnap would come to think, "but in *P.M.* the theory was developed in a very comprehensive way and represented in a much more convenient notation" (Rudolf Carnap, "Intellectual Autobiography," in *The Philosophy of Rudolf Carnap*, ed. Paul Schilpp [La Salle, Ill.: Open Court, 1963], p. 11). That even Frege's student Carnap did not learn quantificational logic from Frege is a measure of how odd and unperspicuous Frege's two-dimensional notation is as a notation of that logic.
6. Frege did at first think that inferences can be drawn from false, or merely unacknowledged, premises. We are told in *Begriffsschrift* §2 that one can derive conclusions from a sentence that lacks the judgment stroke and might do so in

order to "test the correctness of the thought." In the "Seventeen Key Sentences on Logic"—which seems also to have been an early work (see Michael Dummett, "Frege's 'Kernsätze zur Logik,'" reprinted in *Frege and Other Philosophers* [Oxford: Clarendon Press, 1991])—Frege says that "the task of logic is to set up laws according to which a judgment is justified by others, irrespective of whether they are themselves true" (*PW* 175). In his later writings Frege again and again emphasizes that "only true thoughts are admissible premises of inferences" (*PW* 180), "only a thought recognized as true can be made the premise of an inference" (*PW* 261), "from false premises nothing at all can be concluded" (*PMC* 182). In a letter to Hugo Dingler dated 31 January 1917, Frege describes an inference from premises whose truth is not acknowledged as a "pseudo-inference" (*PMC* 17).

7. Wittgenstein's objection to the judgment stroke is made already in his "Notes on Logic" (see Ludwig Wittgenstein, *Notebooks, 1914–1916*, ed. G. H. von Wright and G. E. M. Anscombe [Oxford: Blackwell, 1979], p. 103) and is repeated in the *Tractatus*: "Frege's 'judgment stroke' '⊢—' is logically quite meaningless: in the works of Frege (and Russell) it simply indicates that these authors hold the propositions marked with the sign to be true. Thus '⊢—' is no more a component part of a proposition than is, for instance, the proposition's number" (*Tractatus Logico-Philosophicus*, trans. D. F. Pears and B. F. McGuinness [London: Routledge and Kegan Paul, 1961], §4.442). In a letter dated 15 January 1914, Philip Jourdain asks Frege "whether you now regard assertion (⊢—) as merely psychological" (*PMC* 78), indicating thereby that Frege would by then be familiar with Wittgenstein's objection. Since Wittgenstein's "Notes on Logic" was written in the fall of 1913, and in December of that year Wittgenstein visited Frege to discuss his views, presumably Frege was. (This seems to have been Wittgenstein's second visit to Frege; the first was in the summer of 1911.) Frege's answer is as quoted.

8. Depending on just how quantifiers are conceived, one might well argue that different sorts of letters should be used for the two cases in our standard logics. Even so, we will see, Frege's motivation for the use of the two sorts of letters seems to be very different from that of the quantificational logician.

9. Michael Dummett, *Frege: Philosophy of Language* (London: Duckworth, 1973), p. 14; William Kneale and Martha Kneale, *The Development of Logic* (Oxford: Clarendon Press, 1962), p. 516.

10. In the Introduction to *Grundgesetze* Frege describes the new explanations of his symbols in that work as "consequences of a thoroughgoing development of my logical views" (*GG* 6). The development in question is his discovery of the distinction between the *Sinn* and the *Bedeutung* of an expression. The years "since the appearance of my *Begriffsschrift* and *Grundlagen*," that is, the years between 1884 and 1893, "have brought the work to maturity" (*GG* 7).

11. Gareth Evans, *The Varieties of Reference*, ed. John McDowell (Oxford: Clarendon Press, 1982), p. 8.

12. Dummett, *Frege: Philosophy of Language*, p. 83.

13. Frege writes in "On Sense and Meaning" that "to every expression belonging to a complete totality of signs, there should certainly correspond a sense . . . But this is not to say that to the sense there also corresponds a thing meant . . . In grasping a sense one is certainly not assured of meaning anything" (*CP* 159). In a letter to Russell we read that "the sense is independent of whether there is a meaning" (*PMC* 165). In the 1906 "Introduction to Logic" Frege writes that "as far as the mere thought content is concerned it is indeed a matter of indifference whether a proper name has a meaning" (*PW* 192); whether accounts of Odysseus's exploits are fictional or whether they are properly historical narratives, "the thoughts would remain strictly the same" (*PW* 191).

14. Evans, *Varieties of Reference,* p. 24.

15. Ibid., p. 25.

16. Bertrand Russell, *The Autobiography of Bertrand Russell* (London: George Allen and Unwin, 1975), p. 147.

17. Ibid., p. 148.

18. The letter is included in *Dear Russell—Dear Jourdain,* ed. and trans. I. Grattan-Guinness (New York: Columbia University Press, 1977), p. 133. See also *Dear Russell—Dear Jourdain,* p. 144; Russell, *Autobiography,* p. 65; Russell, "My Mental Development," in *The Philosophy of Bertrand Russell,* ed. Paul Schilpp (New York: Tudor, 1944), pp. 12–13; and Russell's note added in 1917 to his 1901 essay "Mathematics and Metaphysics," in *Mysticism and Logic and Other Essays* (New York: Longmans, Green, and Co., 1918), p. 78.

19. In 1870 Peirce published "Description of a Notation for the Logic of Relations, Resulting from an Amplification of the Conceptions of Boole's Calculus of Logic." "The Logic of Relations," which completes the project, was published in 1883. Both essays are reprinted in C. S. Peirce, *Collected Papers of Charles Sanders Peirce,* ed. C. Hartshorne and P. Weiss, vol. 3: *Exact Logic* (Cambridge, Mass.: Harvard University Press, 1933).

20. Bertrand Russell, "The Logic of Relations," reprinted in *Logic and Knowledge: Essays, 1901–1950,* ed. R. C. Marsh (London and New York: Routledge, 1956), p. 3.

21. This insight is, of course, also manifest in Frege's logic.

22. Bertrand Russell, *Our Knowledge of the External World* (London: George Allen and Unwin, 1914), p. 50.

23. See Jourdain's record of a conversation with Russell on 20 April 1909 in Grattan-Guinness, *Dear Russell—Dear Jourdain,* p. 114.

24. Russell, "Logic of Relations," p. 4; Russell, *Autobiography,* p. 148.

25. The review, which appeared in *Rivista di Matematica* 5 (1895): 122–128, would have been one of the papers Peano gave to Russell at the 1900 World Congress. See Bertrand Russell, *My Philosophical Development* (London: George Allen and Unwin, 1959), p. 65.

26. In his discussion of Frege's logic in *The Principles of Mathematics* (London: George Allen and Unwin, 1903), Russell describes Frege's notation as "exceedingly cumbrous and difficult to use" (p. 519).

1. The Starting Point

1. As Frege writes in the Preface to *Begriffsschrift*, "the modeling upon the formula language of arithmetic refers more to the fundamental ideas than to the detailed structure . . . The most immediate point of contact between my formula language and that of arithmetic is in the way the letters are used" (*BGS* 104). In §1 of *Begriffsschrift* we are told that Frege will "*adopt* [from arithmetic] *this fundamental idea of distinguishing two kinds of symbols . . . those which one can take to signify various things* and *those which have a completely fixed sense*. The first are the *letters*, and these are to serve mainly for the expression of *generality*." Later Frege will reject this way of characterizing such letters as signifying various things. As we will see in section 2.3, on Frege's mature view, letters that lend generality of content (in the laws of arithmetic and in *Begriffsschrift*) have neither sense nor meaning.

2. According to Frege, the essentials of his mature conception of *Sinn* and *Bedeutung* are developed already in *Grundlagen*. See, for instance, his 1891/1892 discussion of Biermann's views in "On the Concept of Number" (*PW* 85). Both in "Function and Concept" (*CP* 144–145) and in *Grundgesetze* §2, Frege's conception of the sense and the meaning of a *Begriffsschrift* expression is explained first for the case of arithmetic.

3. Michael Dummett, in *Frege: Philosophy of Language* (London: Duckworth, 1973), declares *Begriffsschrift* an "astonishing work," "astonishing because it has no predecessors: it appears to have been born from Frege's brain unfertilized by external influences" (p. xvii). On the account pursued here, Frege's logic does seem to have been largely unfertilized by external logical influences—"largely" because his reading of George Boole (or more plausibly of Ernst Schröder and Wilhelm Wundt on Boole, as Wolfgang Kienzler has suggested to me), probably after *Begriffsschrift* was completed, did influence how he thought about his logic. In a recent biography of Frege, Lothar Krieser explores the possibility that Frege may have been further influenced, if only indirectly, in the design of his notation by a two-dimensional notation developed by Friedrich Krause. See *Gottlob Frege: Leben—Werk—Zeit* (Hamburg: Felix Meiner Verlag, 2001), section 3.2, "Pasigraphe und Begriffsschrift." (This work was brought to my attention by an anonymous reader.) What is most important for present purposes is that Frege's logic was not born unfertilized by external mathematical influences. As will be shown in detail as we go on, Frege's understanding of logic is heavily influenced by his understanding of mathematics and of the formula language of arithmetic.

4. This familiar point is developed and defended by Lewis Carroll in "What the Tortoise Said to Achilles," *Mind* 4 (1895): 278–280.

5. The two tasks are intimately related. As Frege points out in the 1885 essay "On Formal Theories of Arithmetic," "the first requirement of basing all modes of inference that appear to be peculiar to arithmetic on general laws of

logic" can be fulfilled only if "the requirement that everything arithmetical be reducible to logic by means of definitions" is fulfilled (*CP* 114).

6. See Bertrand Russell, *The Principles of Mathematics* (London: George Allen and Unwin, 1903), §434, "Mathematical reasoning requires no extra-logical element."

7. Immanuel Kant, *Critique of Pure Reason*, trans. Norman Kemp Smith (London: Macmillan, 1933), A234/B287.

8. Michael Friedman, *Kant and the Exact Sciences* (Cambridge, Mass.: Harvard University Press, 1992), p. 65 n. 14.

9. Bynum, whose translation is otherwise followed here, translates *beurtheilbare Inhalt* as "assertible content." This is a mistake insofar as assertion is inherently communicative, whereas judgment (as Frege understands it) is not. For the same reason, Frege's *Urtheilsstrich* is a judgment stroke, not (as it is sometimes translated) an assertion stroke.

10. For reasons that will become clearer later, after the discovery of the distinction between *Sinn* and *Bedeutung* Frege will deny that the conditional stroke relates contents of possible judgment. "Is the relation I designate by the conditional stroke in fact such as can obtain between thoughts? Strictly speaking, no! The most we can say here is that *the sign for this relation* (i.e. the conditional stroke) *connects sentences*" (*PW* 187).

11. Frege immediately goes on to remark that "this difference [between the two examples] is quite inessential." What he means, I take it, is that the difference is logically inessential. That is, the mere fact that 'if 3 > 2, then $3^2 > 2$' sounds odd, whereas 'if $(17^2 \cdot 19)/2^{11} > 2$, then $((17^2 \cdot 19)/2^{11})^2 > 2$' does not, does not show that they should receive different forms of expression in a logically adequate language.

12. Sextus Empiricus, *Outlines of Scepticism*, trans. Julia Annas and Jonathan Barnes (Cambridge: Cambridge University Press, 1994), bk. II, §195.

13. Ibid., bk. II, §165.

14. The formulation is John Stuart Mill's in *A System of Logic Ratiocinative and Inductive*, 8th ed., ed. J. M. Robson (Toronto: University of Toronto Press, 1973), bk. II, chap. iii, §4.

15. See also Gilbert Ryle's discussion in "'If', 'So', and 'Because'," in *Philosophical Analysis*, ed. Max Black (Ithaca, N.Y.: Cornell University Press, 1950), pp. 332–339, of the idea that a generalized conditional should be understood as an inference license.

16. A more adequate account can be given only in Chapter 4 in light of Frege's understanding of the distinction between *Sinn* and *Bedeutung*.

17. As Frege claims in *Begriffsschrift*, "if an italic letter occurs in an expression which is not preceded by a judgment stroke then this expression has no sense {*ist sinnlos*}" (*BGS* §11). In *Grundgesetze* he notes merely that "the use of Latin italic letters is explained only for the case in which there occurs a judgment stroke" (*GG* §17 n. 22).

18. I owe to Michael Kremer this way of putting the difference between my reading of Frege's texts and standard readings.

2. Logical Generality

1. In the Introduction to *Grundgesetze,* Frege stresses "as especially important for comprehension the first half of §8, and also §§12 and 13" (*GG* 9). Because the first half of §8 introduces signs for generality and §12 the conditional stroke, while §13 then explicates standard combinations of the two, Frege himself (at least in the mature logic) emphasizes the central importance of understanding *Begriffsschrift* generalized conditionals for an understanding of *Begriffsschrift* overall. One must start with *Begriffsschrift* generalized conditionals.

2. See Michael Dummett's discussion of this point in *Frege: Philosophy of Language* (London: Duckworth, 1973), chap. 2.

3. In fact, this account is not quite right, either about the language of arithmetic or about Frege's concept-script, though to understand why requires resources that cannot be properly introduced until Chapter 4. What we will find there is that independent of an analysis, a sentence of *Begriffsschrift* expresses a sense and designates a truth-value; individual objects and concepts are designated only relative to an analysis into function and argument. Strictly speaking, then, a sentence such as '——Lrj' of *Begriffsschrift* does not present Romeo, Juliet, and the relation of loving in a relation except relative to an analysis. As the point can also be put, the signs 'r', 'j', and 'L' have no meaning *(Bedeutung)* except in the context of a whole proposition; prior to their involvement in a sentence, such signs express senses but have no designation. That just is Frege's famous context principle, that we are "never to ask for the meaning of a word in isolation, but only in the context of a proposition" (*GL* x). Only in the context of a proposition, and relative to an analysis, does a subsentential sign (whether simple or complex) designate something, either a concept or an object. Since we do not yet have any account of the notion of *Sinn,* it is easier for now to understand a sentence of *Begriffsschrift* as we have outlined, as presenting objects, concepts, and relations in various logical relations.

4. Already in *Begriffsschrift* Frege does also provide some grounds for reading such conditionals differently because, as he says, the conditional in our first example can also be read as 'if the circumstances B and Γ obtain, then A too obtains' (*BGS* §5).

5. We could, of course, dispense with the sign '&', using only signs for negation and the conditional. What is critical is the order of embedding of connectives, the fact that any of the connectives in 'S ⊃ (R ⊃ (Q ⊃ P))' can be made the main connective, given appropriate transformations.

6. It can be variously conceived if one reads it as a notation, albeit remarkably unperspicuous and clumsy, of the sort of logic Frege's is on our reading.

7. The contraposition of the point is made in a letter to Russell: "wherever the

coincidence of meaning is not self-evident, we have a difference in sense" (*PMC* 152). In fact, this criterion seems too strong as Frege formulates it. A series of contrapositions in a complex formula might render two formulations of the same thought apparently different. That they are nonetheless not really different is indicated by the fact that each successive transformation is self-evident, that is, from a thought in one form to that same thought in another.

8. As already pointed out in section 1.3, once Frege had seen that sentences of *Begriffsschrift* express thoughts and designate truth-values, his elucidations of his primitive symbols, which in the early logic provide necessary and sufficient conditions for the correctness of judgments, could be reformulated so as to provide necessary and sufficient conditions for the relevant sentences to designate the True. Judgeability conditions obviously follow.

9. Only in the late 1890s does Frege himself fully appreciate this logical difference. See section 3.3.

10. Bertrand Russell, "Mathematical Logic as Based on the Theory of Types," in *Logic and Knowledge: Essays, 1901–1950,* ed. R. C. Marsh (London and New York: Routledge, 1956), p. 66 and, for the long passage directly to follow, p. 64.

11. Ibid., p. 66.

12. Ibid., p. 65.

13. Ibid., p. 67.

14. See *Grundgesetze* §5 n. 15. The objects designated by uppercase Greek letters need not themselves be truth-values, given the role specified for the horizontal stroke in *Grundgesetze*. Whether or not 'Δ' designates a truth-value, if it designates any object at all, '——Δ' will designate a truth-value, either the True or the False.

15. Richard G. Heck Jr., "*Grundgesetze der Arithmetik* I §§29–32," *Notre Dame Journal of Formal Logic* 38 (1997): 437–474, p. 444.

16. Later Frege will see that the concavity with German letter has a much more important role to play in his logic than merely that of marking distinctions of scope. The expressive role of the concavity is explained in section 3.3.

17. Frege remarks in *Grundgesetze* §17 that "already earlier [in §8] we made an attempt to express generality by the use of a *Roman* [Latin] *letter,* but we left off again, because we observed that the scope of the generality was not well enough demarcated."

18. Russell, "Mathematical Logic," pp. 64–65.

19. The point designated by the name '*B*' in the example varies with the position of the line; it has the logical form 'f(x)'. In "On Sense and Meaning" Frege uses a different example, one that involves no appeal to variable names (see *CP* 158).

20. Frege is generally read (following Dummett) as rejecting only the word 'variable' "as leading to the misunderstanding that . . . a numerical variable stands for a variable number, one whose magnitude varies" (Dummett, *Frege: Philosophy of Language,* p. 525). It is clear that Frege did object to the word (see

PMC 78 and *PW* 159); but once one has called into question the assumption that Frege's logic is a quantificational logic, it is also easy to read him as rejecting the very idea of a variable, at least as it is used to signify some object or other though it is left undetermined which—that is, as it is used in the rule of universal instantiation of quantificational natural deduction.

21. As the point is put in "Function and Concept," at "the next higher level" at which function names are replaced by indicating letters, one is dealing with "particular second-level functions" (*CP* 156). This passage is considered at greater length in section 3.1.

22. Victor Dudman, in "From Boole to Frege," reprinted with original pagination in *The Philosophy of Frege*, vol. 1, ed. Hans Sluga (New York and London: Garland, 1993), denies that in quantificational logic primary propositions are reduced to secondary. By contrast with Boole, who does attempt a reduction, Dudman thinks, "quantification theory does not reduce to the logic of truth functions but is superimposed on it" (p. 134). This, I would say, is a distinction without a difference. On the one hand, Boole has also to superimpose, in his case the account of hypothetical syllogism on his understanding of categorical syllogism; and he must introduce classes of time instants to effect the transition. On the other, as Dudman himself points out, the fundamental insight of quantificational logic is that one can always resort to singular clauses "and hence bring the logic of truth functions to bear" (p. 126). If Boole's is an attempted reduction then so, in the reverse direction, is the quantificational logician's.

23. "The most we can say here is that *the sign for this relation* (i.e. the conditional stroke) *connects sentences*" (*PW* 187).

24. Again, this is not exactly right. As we will see in Chapter 4, independent of an analysis, a *Begriffsschrift* sentence can be said only to express a thought and designate a truth-value. Its subsentential parts designate only relative to an analysis.

3. A More Sophisticated Instrument

1. Frege spoke before the society in 1879, on "Applications of the 'Conceptual Notation'," again in 1882, "On the Aim of the Conceptual Notation," and again in 1885, "On Formal Theories of Arithmetic." Frege is presumably referring to the 1882 paper in "Function and Concept"; the later (1885) paper is not on *Begriffsschrift*.

2. Wilfrid Sellars, "Naming and Saying," reprinted in *Science, Perception and Reality* (London: Routledge and Kegan Paul, 1963).

3. The shift is highlighted by the fact that whereas the 1879 elucidation of Frege's fundamental logical notions begins, in §1, with the distinction between indicating letters and signifying symbols and introduces functions only in §9, the 1893 elucidation of those same notions begins instead with the notion of a function. Section 1 of *Grundgesetze* is titled "The Function is Unsatu-

rated." It is this point, on Frege's mature view, that one first needs to understand in order to understand *Begriffsschrift*.

4. Here again, the mistake is to think that the notation traces the constructional history of the function. We do construct complex function signs in a stepwise fashion, for instance, beginning with '$x + 1$', then "squaring" to yield '$(x + 1)^2$', then adding '$+ 3x$' to give '$(x + 1)^2 + 3x$', and so on. The result is a complex sign that is nonetheless a sign for a function that simply correlates numbers. It is, then, the same function that is designated by '$x^2 + 5x + 1$' as by '$(x + 1)^2 + 3x$' because in these cases the same correlation is set up. What differs in the two cases (as will be explained in detail in Chapter 4) is only the sense, which contains the mode of presentation of the relevant function.

5. Infinitesimals, Leibniz writes to Wallis in 1699, are numbers "such that when their ratio is sought, they may not be considered zero but which are rejected as often as they occur with quantities incomparably greater" (quoted in Morris Kline, *Mathematics: The Loss of Certainty* [New York: Oxford University Press, 1980], p. 137).

6. Quoted in Morris Kline, *Mathematical Thought from Ancient to Modern Times* (New York: Oxford University Press, 1972), p. 428.

7. Frege's early confusion on this point and its later resolution for the case of concept words in particular is taken up again in section 4.1.

8. This difference is intimately related to the distinction Frege draws already in *Grundlagen*, and again in later discussions, between a characteristic mark of a concept, that is, a property of things that fall under the concept (which is a subordination of concepts), and a property of a concept (which has the form of a subsumption of one concept under another, higher-level concept).

9. Obviously, then, it would be sheer perversity to take the "existential quantifier," that is, the concavity flanked by negation strokes, to be logically primitive. The idea is barely coherent, given Frege's conception of logical generality.

10. There is one sense in which they are very different from the laws of other sciences; as Frege at first thinks, laws of logic contrast with laws of the special sciences in being prescriptive rather than descriptive. (See section 1.2.) This difference, however, is not reflected in the *Begriffsschrift* sentences used to express them and can be ignored here.

11. As already noted, in the "Dialogue with Pünjar" Frege claims that the content of what is predicated in an existence claim such as 'men exist' lies "in the form of the particular judgment" (*PW* 63). "The existence expressed by 'there is' is not contained in the word 'exist' but in the form of the particular judgment" (*PW* 66).

12. This is just what Wittgenstein suggests in the *Tractatus*.

13. A quite different difficulty with this discussion of the formation of concepts out of concepts is considered in section 4.3.

14. Later Frege will point out that Leibniz's principle cannot be a definition because definitions presuppose the use of the sign for identity (*PW* 200). None-

theless, sentences containing the identity sign can everywhere be replaced by sentences expressed without it.

4. The Work Brought to Maturity

1. As should by now be evident, Frege often corrects his earlier views without explicitly identifying them as such, for instance, in "Function and Concept," regarding the idea that a concept is an expression, in "On Sense and Meaning," regarding the idea that judging is predicating "is true," and in almost any late discussion of identity, regarding the idea that the sign for identity designates only partial agreement.

2. Wittgenstein draws just this conclusion in *Tractatus Logico-Philosophicus*, trans. D. F. Pears and B. F. McGuinness (London: Routledge and Kegan Paul, 1961): "roughly speaking, to say of *two* things that they are identical is nonsense, and to say of *one* thing that it is identical with itself is to say nothing at all" (§5.5303); "the identity-sign, therefore, is not an essential constituent of a conceptual notation" (§5.533). A fuller account of the relationship between Frege's views and those of the early Wittgenstein on this and other points is developed in my "Frege and Early Wittgenstein on Logic and Language," in *From Frege to Wittgenstein: Perspectives on Early Analytic Philosophy*, ed. Erich Reck (Oxford and New York: Oxford University Press, 2002).

3. This may account, at least in part, for Frege's assuming in *Begriffsschrift* that the traditional square of opposition (which is reproduced at the end of Part I) is valid. Later he explicitly denies that generalized conditionals involve any existence assumptions (*GG* §13 n. 21).

4. This point was developed in section 2.1.

5. Michael Dummett, "Frege on Functions: A Reply," reprinted with original pagination in *The Philosophy of Frege*, vol. 2, ed. Hans Sluga (New York and London: Garland, 1993), p. 98.

6. As will become clear later, Frege recognizes the possibility of a sentence that expresses a sense, a Fregean Thought, but lacks meaning, *Bedeutung*. That there are such cases is critical to an adequate understanding of the striving for truth on our account.

7. The horses that draw the King's carriage form a collection that can be counted under various concepts, under the concept *horse that draws the King's carriage* certainly, but under other concepts as well. The concept relative to which one counts is thus more fine grained than the collection itself. Because the number of horses that draw the King's carriage (in Frege's example) is identical to the number of seasons in the year and to the number of a great many other things, the notion of a number is much less fine grained than that of a collection of objects.

8. These abbreviations, in particular, the notation for four, make even the Roman numeration system slightly more complex than a pure *lingua characterica* of relative magnitude.

9. If it is possible, after invention of the Arabic notation renders tractable the problem of the rigorization of arithmetic, then to go back and develop algorithms for the Roman numeration system, this does not affect the essential point, that the problem of rigorizing arithmetic is untractable in the setting of the Roman numeration system. Ian Stewart, in *The Problems of Mathematics* (Oxford: Oxford University Press, 1992), puts the general point this way: "a new viewpoint [for example, that provided by the Arabic numeration system] can have a profound psychological effect, opening up entirely new lines of attack. Yes, *after* the event the new ideas can be reconstructed in terms of the old ones; but if we'd stuck to the old approach, we'd never have thought of them at all, so there'd be nothing to reconstruct *from*" (p. 17).

10. Frege's criticisms, first formulated in *Grundlagen*, and his alternative conception in terms of the distinction of sense and meaning, are reiterated again and again in his published writings: in 1895 in a criticism of L. E. Ballue in "Whole Numbers," in 1896 in "On Mr. Peano's Conceptual Notation and My Own," in 1899 in "On Mr. Shubert's Numbers," and finally, more than twenty years after the appearance of *Grundlagen*, in "Reply to Mr. Thomae's Holiday *Causerie*" (1906). The difficulties for the standard conception as they appear in lectures given by Weierstrass, as well as Frege's own view, are rehearsed at length in the lecture notes of 1914, "Logic in Mathematics." Even as late as 1919, thirty-five years after Frege's criticisms of the conception of number as a collection of units first appeared in print, Frege is still trying to combat the view that the equal sign in arithmetic means identity in a respect (see *PMC* 96–98).

11. In his own reflections on number, Frege often seems to retain more of the traditional view, emphasizing the application of number over its role in computations. In his reflections on *Begriffsschrift*, by contrast, it is clear that inference and judgment are of equal importance. It is the latter insight that is our guiding thread here.

12. Gottfried Wilhelm Leibniz, "What Is an Idea?" (1687), in *Philosophical Papers and Letters*, ed. L. E. Loemker (Dordrecht: Reidel, 1969), p. 207.

13. Wittgenstein also makes this point in the *Tractatus*, §§4.061–4.0641, but draws a very different conclusion from it. See my "Frege and Early Wittgenstein on Logic and Language."

14. As was suggested already in section 1.3, Frege's elucidations of his primitive symbols can be read in just this way, as elucidations of the judgeability conditions of sentences that contain them.

15. Frege himself occasionally appeals to the language of chemistry to clarify features of his *Begriffsschrift*. See, for instance, *PW* 37.

16. In section 3.3 this point was made for the case of arithmetical functions. The function expression '$(1 + x)^2$' is more complex than the function expression '$1 + x$', but the function designated by the former is not more complex than the function designated by the latter. Both are simply laws of correlation of numbers. As we have also put the point, the function $(1 + x)^2$ is not constructed

out of the functions $1 + x$ and x^2, though the sign for it is constructed out of the signs for those functions.

17. In his "Notes for Ludwig Darmstaedter" Frege himself expresses misgivings along these lines about the name '*Begriffsschrift*' (*PW* 253).

18. As already noted in section 2.1, Frege makes no mention of the compositionality of language before 1890.

19. Fully to explain such discourse would require an account of the relationship between a scientific theory, expressed as an axiomatic system, and the evidence for it. Though I cannot defend the claim here, I would say that in Frege's view, scientific laws (excepting those that are axioms of the theory) are properly described as synthetic a priori in his *Grundlagen* sense because they are grounded in the primitive truths of the theory—in spite of the fact that the theory as a whole is accepted on empirical, that is, a posteriori, grounds. The difference between a law such as that anything less dense than water floats on water and a merely accidental regularity such as that all swans are white (had that happened to be true) lies in the fact that the former follows from the fundamental laws of an established (true) scientific theory, the latter from the fact that this swan is white and that swan is white, and so on for all the swans there are. This difference is connected to the fact that, on Frege's account, there are three different ways to express a judgment such as that all S is P: in a statement of number, that the number of Ss that are not $P = 0$; in a generalization using the concavity notation, that is, on our reading, as an ascription of a second-level property; or, finally, in a generalization using Latin italic letters to exhibit the concepts $S\xi$ and $P\xi$ in a relation of subordination and thereby to express an inference warrant or law. Of course, a generality expressed in any of these forms can be used to derive either of the other two; what is not possible in various cases is to derive any one form directly, that is, not by way of another. In the case of a merely accidental generality, for instance, one might prove the judgment expressed using Latin italic letters by way of the relevant statement of number. In the case of a law, conversely, one might not be able to prove the judgment of number except as a consequence of the proof of the relevant law. In the case of a law, the proof would take one ultimately to fundamental laws of the relevant science.

20. The imagery here was suggested to me by Mark Wilson's wonderful discussion of developments in projective geometry and their significance for Frege's thinking in "Frege: The Royal Road from Geometry," reprinted in *Frege's Philosophy of Mathematics,* ed. William Demopoulos (Cambridge, Mass.: Harvard University Press, 1995).

21. As pointed out in section 4.3, the judgments will themselves be different if the thoughts are different, even if the state of affairs that obtains if the sentence is true is the same in both cases. The judgment that $2^4 = 16$, however it is arrived at, is different from the judgment that $2^4 = 4^2$ because the thoughts from which the advance to the True is made are in that case different.

22. "It must be determinate for every object whether it falls under a concept or

not; a concept word which does not meet this requirement on its meaning is meaningless" (*PW* 122). A concept must have sharp boundaries, because if it did not then the laws of logic could not be formulated: "just as something that is not extensionless cannot be recognized in geometry as a point, because otherwise it would be impossible to set up geometrical axioms," so "if something fails to display a sharp boundary, it cannot be recognized in logic as a concept" because otherwise it would be impossible to set up logical axioms (*CP* 133). The principle of noncontradiction requires "that it shall be determinate, for any object, whether it falls under the concept or not" (*CP* 148).

23. William Frend, *Principles of Algebra* (1796), quoted in Ernest Nagel, "Impossible Numbers: A Chapter in the History of Modern Logic," in *Teleology Revisited* (Cambridge: Cambridge University Press, 1971), pp. 170–171.

24. Leonhard Euler, *Complete Introduction to Algebra,* quoted in Morris Kline, *Mathematical Thought from Ancient to Modern Times* (New York: Oxford University Press, 1972), p. 594.

25. These remarks are of course merely suggestive of the wholly new metaphysics of judgment that would need to be developed on the basis of Frege's logic.

5. Courses of Values and Basic Law V

1. See Mark Wilson's discussion of such "ideal" points as they were understood by projective geometers in the nineteenth century in "Frege: The Royal Road from Geometry," reprinted in *Frege's Philosophy of Mathematics,* ed. William Demopoulos (Cambridge, Mass.: Harvard University Press, 1995), especially pp. 128–129.

2. As Frege says, "we cannot by these methods obtain any concept of direction with sharp limits to its application, nor therefore, for the same reasons, any satisfactory concept of Number either" (*GL* §68).

3. In both the Introduction and the conclusion to *Grundlagen,* Frege provides clear evidence for thinking that this definition is merely a technical fix, that it (by contrast with the second definition) is not *deeply* motivated—though, as we will see, it is motivated. He writes in the Introduction in response to an anticipated criticism that his definitions are unnatural: "the point here is not whether they are natural, but whether they go to the root of the matter and are logically beyond criticism" (*GL* xi). He writes in the concluding sections that "this way of getting over the difficulty cannot be expected to meet with universal approval, and many will prefer other methods of removing the doubt in question" (*GL* §107). It is the second definition that contains the essential insight into the nature of number (that goes to the root of the matter); it is the third, or something like it, that logicism requires (that is logically beyond criticism).

4. Immanuel Kant, "Jäsche Logic," in *Lectures on Logic,* trans. and ed. Michael Young (Cambridge: Cambridge University Press, 1992), p. 595, and for the quotation immediately following, p. 597.

5. Saul Kripke, *Naming and Necessity* (Cambridge, Mass.: Harvard University Press, 1980), pp. 48–49.

6. Kant, "Jäsche Logic," p. 596.

7. Frege writes in his first letter to Russell: "the collapse of my law V seems to undermine not only the foundations of my arithmetic but the only possible foundations of arithmetic as such" (*PMC* 132). In the Appendix to *Grundgesetze* ii we read that "I do not see how arithmetic can be scientifically founded, how numbers can be conceived as logical objects and brought under study, unless we are allowed—at least conditionally—the transition from a concept to its extension" (*GG* 127).

8. Frege refers back to this passage in his Appendix to the second volume discussing Russell's paradox: "I have never concealed from myself its [Basic Law V's] lack of self-evidence which the others possess, and which must properly be demanded of a law of logic, and in fact I pointed out this weakness in the Introduction to the first volume. I should gladly have relinquished this foundation if I had known of any substitute for it" (*GG* 127).

9. Michael Dummett, *Frege: Philosophy of Mathematics* (Cambridge, Mass.: Harvard University Press, 1991), p. 317.

10. Michael Friedman, *Kant and the Exact Sciences* (Cambridge, Mass.: Harvard University Press, 1992), p. 79.

11. This includes all the uses to which courses of values are put in Frege's *Grundgesetze* logic, uses that are not necessary to logic (as the original *Begriffsschrift* makes clear), but that were introduced as simplifications when it seemed that the notion of a course of values was logically sound.

Abbreviations
for Works by Gottlob Frege

BGS   *Begriffsschrift, a Formula Language of Pure Thought Modeled upon the Formula Language of Arithmetic* (1879). In *CN*.

CN   *Conceptual Notation and Related Articles.* Trans. and ed. T. W. Bynum. Oxford: Clarendon Press, 1972.

CP   *Gottlob Frege: Collected Papers on Mathematics, Logic, and Philosophy.* Ed. Brian McGuinness. Trans. Max Black, V. H. Dudman, Peter Geach, Hans Kaal, E.-H. Kluge, Brian McGuinness, R. H. Stoothuff. Oxford: Basil Blackwell, 1984.

GG   *The Basic Laws of Arithmetic: Exposition of the System* [*Grundgesetze*, 1893/1903]. Trans. Montgomery Furth. Berkeley: University of California Press, 1964.

GL   *The Foundations of Arithmetic* [*Grundlagen*, 1884]. Trans. J. L. Austin. Evanston, Ill.: Northwestern University Press, 1980.

PMC   *Philosophical and Mathematical Correspondence.* Ed. Brian McGuinness. Trans. Hans Kaal. Chicago: University of Chicago Press, 1980.

PW   *Posthumous Writings.* Ed. Hans Hermes, Friedrich Kambartel, and Friedrich Kaulbach. Trans. Peter Long and Roger White. Chicago: University of Chicago Press, 1979.

Index